DAWN
&
DECLINE

Max Horkheimer

DAWN & DECLINE

NOTES 1926-1931 AND 1950-1969

Translated by Michael Shaw

with an Afterword by Eike Gebhardt

A Continuum Book

THE SEABURY PRESS : NEW YORK

1978
The Seabury Press
815 Second Avenue
New York, New York 10017

Originally published as *Notizen und Dämmerung*. Copyright © 1974 by S.
Fischer Verlag GmbH, Frankfurt am Main. The text of *Dammerung* follows that
of the first edition published in 1934, under the same title but under the author's
pseudonym of Heinrich Regius, by Verlag Oprecht & Heilbling, Zurich.

Printed in the United States of America

Library of Congress Cataloging in Publication Data
Horkheimer, Max, 1895-1973.
Dawn & decline: notes 1926-1931 and 1950-1969.
(A Continuum book)
Translation of Notizen und Dämmerung.
1.   Germany—Civilization—20th century.   I. Title.
DD239.H6713   943.085   77-13342
ISBN 0-8164-9329-4

Contents

DAWN
Notes 1926–1931

Contents 7

DECLINE
Notes 1950–1969

1950–1955

1956

1957–1958

1959–1960

1961–1962

1966–1969

Translator's Preface

This volume contains selections from two Horkheimer works, *Däm-merung, Notizen in Deutschland* (here translated as *Dawn, Notes 1926–1931*) which was originally published in 1934 under the pseudonym Heinrich Regius, and has never been republished since, and *Notizen, 1950–1969* (here translated as *Decline, Notes 1950–1969*).

Concerning the earlier work, Horkheimer wrote: "This book is outdated. The reflections contained in it are occasional notes formulated between 1926 and 1931, in Germany. They were written down during periods of rest from a demanding piece of work, and the author did not take the time to polish them. This is also the reason they do not constitute an orderly sequence. They contain repetitions and even some contradictions. Yet the themes explored provide a kind of unity. They critically examine and re-examine the meaning concepts such as metaphysics, character, morality, personality and the value of the human being had during that phase of capitalism. Since they predate the final victory of National Socialism, they deal with a world that has become anachronistic since. . . . Yet the thoughts of the author who lived his life as an individualist may not be wholly without significance at a later time."

The second part of this volume may suggest an additional reason for Horkheimer's use of the term "outdated" for his earlier book. This section not only marks the end of the liberal bourgeoisie for Horkheimer but may also define the beginnings of a rethinking of the sanguine Marxism developed in the late twenties. Commenting on Horkheimer's development, his German editor, Werner Brede, writes: "He was no theoretician of decline; but he did recognize that the historical and philosophical climate had changed." Or again: "In the *Notizen, 1950–1969,* Horkheimer's unorthodox sociological perspective defined the contours of a 'society in transition.' Here, the critical pessimism never wholly absent from his philosophy definitively supplants the hopes of Marxism."

Each reader will have to decide for himself whether the pervasive pessimism of the later work is total despair or a more complex, more highly differentiated assessment of a later phase in the development of man and society; whether it is mere "expression," or philosophical insight with a claim to truth.

MICHAEL SHAW

DAWN

Notes
1926-1931

Dusk: The less stable necessary ideologies are, the more cruel the methods by which they are protected. The degree of zeal and terror with which tottering idols are defended shows how far dusk has already advanced. With the development of large-scale industry, the intelligence of the European masses has grown so greatly that the most sacred possessions must be protected from it. To do this well means to be embarked on a career. Woe to the man who tells the truth in simple terms. There is not only the general, systematicaly engineered brainwashing but the threat of economic ruin, social ostracism, the penitentiary and death to deter reason from attacking the key conceptual techniques of domination. The imperialism of the great European states need not envy the Middle Ages for its stakes. Its symbols are protected by more sophisticated instruments and more fear-inspiring guards than the saints of the medieval church. The enemies of the Inquisition turned that dusk into the dawning of a new day. Nor does the dusk of capitalism have to usher in the night of mankind although today it certainly seems to be threatening it.

Monadology: A philosopher once compared the soul to a window-less house. Men relate to each other, talk to each other, deal with each other, persecute each other, yet they do not see each other. But because people have ideas about each other, the philosopher explained them by saying that God had placed an image of the others into the soul of each individual. During the course of life and in the absence of impressions coming from the outside, this image would develop into a full consciousness of man and the world. But this theory is questionable. It is not my impression that man's knowledge of others comes from God. Instead, I would say that those houses do have windows but that they let in only a small and distorted segment of events in the outside world.

17

But this distorting effect is not so much a consequence of the peculiarities of the sense organs as of the worried or joyful, anxious or aggressive, slavish or superior, sated or yearning, dull or alert psychic attitudes which constitute that ground of our life against which all other experiences stand out, and which gives them their specific quality. Here are two images that might serve as symbols for the degree to which people communicate with each other in capitalist society: annoyed because it was interrupted while playing with its friends, the child pays a visit to its sick uncle; at the steering wheel of his new convertible, the Prince of Wales drives past an old woman.

I know of only one kind of gust that can open the windows of the house wider: shared suffering.

Roulette: Systems are for the little people. The big ones have intuition. They place their bets on the numbers that occur to them. The larger the capital, the better the chances for making up for wrong intuitions. The wealthy will never stop betting because they run out of money, nor hear as they leave that their number is winning now, where they no longer have any money to place on the table. Their intuitions are more dependable than the laborious calculations of the poor which always fail because they cannot be thoroughly tested.

Debased Concepts: A scholar of repute who sympathized with socialism heard an unbiased participant in a scientific table conversation speak of humanity. He flushed with noble wrath and took the unsuspecting man to task. Through the worst sort of capitalist practice which had been used as a cloak for centuries, the concept of humanity had become disreputable and meaningless, he said. Decent people could no longer take it seriously and had stopped using it. "A radical scholar," I thought to myself. "But in that case, what terms can still be used for what is good? Because they have been used to camouflage a bad practice, haven't they been just as thoroughly debased as "humanity?"

Some weeks later, a book by this scholar on the reality of Christianity came out. At first, I was surprised but then I discovered that he had not meant the word but the thing.

Unlimited Possibilities: The twentieth century is the age of unlimited possibilities. Technological advances occur every day. Abilities which were admired as exceptional just a short time ago are now below average. And human productivity keeps increasing. During the last hundred years, the skills of the worker have developed beyond all expectations, and the average energy, promptness and endurance of the individual has risen enormously, not only in industry but everywhere. A degree of virtuosity on the cello which in earlier days could be achieved only by the greatest artists and which borders on the miraculous today has become the stock-in-trade of the conservatory graduate. Not only in sports, but probably also in the writing of verse, the great periods of the past are being outdone. The composer plays ironically with melodies that would have been the highlights of old symphonies. Ford Motor Co. turns out nine thousand cars per day and children navigate them through the traffic of New York. The extra-ordinary has become commonplace. For centuries, men spoke with horror of St. Bartholomew's Eve, and the martyrdom of a single individual became a religion. Today, the massacres of St. Bartholomew that imperialism stages, or the heroic courage of the person that resists them, have become daily events which are reported as miscellaneous items in the press. There are so many Socrates', Thomas Münzers and Giordano Brunos that their names get lost in the local papers. Today, a single Jesus of Nazareth would barely cause a ripple of annoyance. "Jerusalem, on such and such a date: The leader of the revolt we reported on a short time ago was sentenced to death today, and executed on the spot." Of course, there are people that shed tears over "Sunny Boy" at the movies. And they do that at the very moment that, in the service of their own interests, real persons are slowly being tortured to death, simply because they were suspected of fighting for the liberation of mankind. Photography, telegraphy and the radio have shrunk the world. The populations of the cities witness the misery of the entire earth. One would think that this might prompt them to demand its abolition. But simultaneously, what is close has become the far-away. Now, the horror of one's own city is submerged in the general suffering, and people turn their attention to the marital problems of movie stars. In every respect, the past is being excelled by the present.

Philosophical Conversations in the Salons: Fields of inquiry are unlimited. People who concern themselves with truth for its own sake easily dismiss our astonishment at their odd and far-fetched subjects. Can't anything at all become important in some way or another? But more than the problem under discussion, what really interests me about the talk in high society is the reason behind its pompousness. That's how I found out that a good deal of this talk can be explained chiefly by the personal competition and the desire for self-advertisement among the academic participants. They want to show how well they are suited for the job of distracting attention from real problems by training others in obscurantist methods of thinking, by bringing up remote problems. For that reason, mere skill, the "level" of these discussions is much more important than their content. Not infrequently, the mere confusion and obfuscation of reality by fuzzy modes of expressions already seems meritorious.

Ordinarily, the reason for the interest in a given problem is not stated. As was pointed out, anything and everything may become important in some way. There is another consideration. Notwithstanding the special importance of the topic or the names and concepts that may come up, it appears that the participants do not really address each other. It suffices that every one cuts a good figure and emerges as especially clever and useful from this bloodless contest. Sometimes, especially when wealthy laymen are present, such clever talk reminds one of the medieval tournaments, except that one engages in it not in the service and for the greater glory of beautiful women but because it is an aptitude test for a career.

The Partiality of Logic: A person that drily notes some evil, some injustice, some cruelty which are part and parcel of this social order is often told that one must not generalize. Counterexamples are brought up.

But it is precisely here that the method of argument by counterexample becomes inadmissible. The statement that justice obtains somewhere can be confuted by the proven existence of a single counterexample. But the reverse is not the case. The protest against a prison which a tyrannical director turns into an inferno loses none of its force because a few instances of decency can be named. Conversely, a single instance of cruelty suffices to invalidate the administration of a good director.

Logic is not independent of content. In real life, the privileged among men find cheap what remains out of reach for the rest. In view of this fact, an impartial logic would be as partial as a legal code which is the same for everyone.

Character and Getting ahead: Many will recognize that those on top in this society are horrible. The existence of that ilk regularly produces hecatombs of human material that has been stunted and choked in misery, yet they can barely even be coaxed into a superficial lie, a hypocritical justification concerning the "necessity" for this unending scourge. One wonders what human qualities are decisive in a competition where that is what the successful are like.

But the eye that can still discern conditions at the highest levels of the social hierarchy usually loses its acuity when it turns to its own sphere. It is tacitly assumed that with decreasing wealth, the moral worth of those that fight for it increases or that their viciousness becomes more moderate, at least. But the capitalist economy is organized in such a way that greater affinity with the psychological makeup of the men at the top actually insures better chances on all levels. More correct than the smaller capitalists' belief in their superior morality would be the opposite point of view. While up above, the relationship between the exploiting individual and the exploitative activity may be quite mediate, inhuman qualities cannot but express themselves directly in those on the lower levels. A millionaire, and especially his wife, can afford to be very honest, noble people. They can develop all sorts of admirable qualities. The greater the enterprise, the more it permits a certain latitude in the adoption of measures that will "benefit" the worker and be humane when compared to those of their colleagues without becoming unprofitable. Here also, the smaller manufacturer is at a disadvantage. He has to be exploitative as a person if he wants to survive. This "moral" disadvantage becomes more pronounced as responsibility in the process of production decreases. In the competitive struggle among foremen, the one least inhibited morally, and sometimes simply the most brutal, will ultimately be the winner, i.e., *he* can get ahead. The carefully manicured hand of a cabinet minister who issues a minor order affecting the execution of a sentence can still be that of a "bel esprit," but just look at the prison flunkies that carry it out.

No. The smaller quantity of mischief one can bring about does not become the better quality of the character. A person that does well on the lower echelons shows his competence in the same moral order in which the more fortunate magnates operate. Nor can it be said of the incompetent, or the man that loses out that his failure results from greater sensitivity although in his case that question can at least be raised. Generally speaking, one may say that although there are some social spheres above the true proletariat where a certain decency can survive for a time, there can be no doubt that getting ahead is a poor index of moral scruples.

Violence and Harmony: The refusal to use violence is purer than the attempt to do away with it by using it. The pacifist is more certain of himself and when he becomes the victim of violence, that violence which he despised will not refute him. His life is more harmonious than that of the revolutionary, and there are wretched situations in which he may seem a light in hell to the latter. What a sight: the man of violence, overpowered by his enemy and lying on the ground like those he led, a pathetic object of others' power, and the angel for whom violence was always an evil and who can now give help because his principle protected him.

But what if mankind were to be still more barbarous, had it not been for those who always acted violently because they wanted to liberate it? What if violence should be necessary? What if we purchased our "harmony" by renouncing effective help? This question destroys all peace and quiet.

Time Is Money: As if it were a matter of indifference whom we are talking about! Whether my time or yours, the time of Mr. Krupp or of an unemployed, it is money. Nor are we told whose money it is, or how much of it, although it is clear, for example, that when Mr. Krupp wastes time, it costs him his own money. And when the worker wastes it, the same is true. In that case also, Krupp loses. It may be objected that when a Krupp worker wastes time, it does not cost Krupp money. Instead, the worker is fired and will now discover the general truth of the proverb that "Time is money." But *in the first place*, this objection is valid only when one contrasts this one worker with all others (a general slowdown by all workers would necessarily reduce Krupp's profit). In *the second place*, the earlier, slower pace for which the individual worker is fired is first of all a loss to the factory, and it is precisely the infinite smallness, the insignificance of this loss for Krupp (in contrast to the consequences for the worker) which would be a fertile theme for a philosophical treatise. In *the third place*, the objection perverts the meaning of the proverb; originally, it meant: any and every minute may become productive for you, and therefore it would be foolish to waste a single one. Now it is interpreted to mean: unless you work hard, you'll starve to death. The two statements apply to two different classes, but under the wings of the proverb both, the curse that weighs on the life of the worker, and the encouragement for the capitalist, can be accomodated.

"Time is Money." There seems to be a need to find a criterion by which to judge how much money a certain span of time is worth. The following observation may be useful in the search for it: A worker who leases a car to get to his place of work in time in the morning is stupid (one only has to compare the cost of transportation with his daily wage). An unemployed person with a few dollars in his pocket who uses a car to save time is crazy. But a middle level administrator who does not use a car to transact his business may already be called untalented. A minute in the life of an unemployed person does not have the same value as the administrator's minute. One should figure out how many hundreds of lives of workers would have to be added up to equal the value of a moderately well-off banker's day. Time is money—but what is the value of the lifetime of most people? If one feels free to talk as loosely as a proverb, one might say that time is not money, but that money is time, just as it is health, happiness, love, intelligence, honor, peace and quiet. For it is a lie that a person who has time also has money. Mere time is not enough to make money. But the reverse is a fact.

Contradiction: The earth is big, too big for a hungry Chinese to get where there is something to eat, too big for a German agricultural laborer to pay the fare to a place where he can find better work.

The earth is small. The man out of favor with the powerful finds no home, he is not given a passport that is respected by their officials. When they catch the vagrant, they deport him. But even on the other side of the border, he finds no home. When the right kind of people pass a border at night, they turn their tickets and passports over to the sleeping car conductor the evening before, and express the justified wish not to be awakened at the checkpoint. God is fond of them.

Education and Morality: Morally undesirable qualities are frequently simply due to the fact that a person did not learn to satisfy his desires in a socially acceptable manner. The obduracy and stubbornness of the bad character that persist in spite of the loving efforts of others then seem a consequence of his also not having learned to learn, i.e., he derives no pleasure from learning. This pedagogic error also is more common among the lower than the upper classes, of course. Here also, the former are disadvantaged. Insight into this nexus destroys the desire to take revenge on bad human beings.

The Pitfalls of Terminology: As one walks through an insane asylum, the horrible impression the sight of the raving mad makes on the layman is allayed by the matter-of-fact statement of the physician that the patient is in a state of excitation. Being subsumed under a scientific category, the terror at the phenomenon is presented as somehow out of place. "It's just a state of excitation." There are people who will not be disturbed about the existence of evil because they have a theory that accounts for it. Here, I am also thinking of some Marxists who, in the face of wretchedness, quickly proceed to show why it exists. Even comprehension can be too quick.

Categories of Burial: When the theory of a genius becomes so influential that it is widely discussed, the work of assimilating it to what already exists begins. Among others, numbers of experts start squaring the new thought with their scientific intentions by weaving the concepts of the revolutionary theory into the texture of their writings as if they belonged there. They put them into the service of their ideological endeavors. This creates the impression that these progressive thinkers have already made their own what is positive and useful in the new theory, that they are better custodians of it than the author or his actual disciples. But in the opinions of the so-called "orthodox," who repeat it as though they were wearing blinders, the teaching of the master loses its original meaning because the rest of the intellectual landscape keeps changing. As reality and therefore the general state of knowledge are restructured, doctrines that are rigidly clung to may become twisted, false, or at least irrelevant. But the most popular way of making a theory innocuous these days is not really orthodoxy but the brisk transplantation of its categories into a nexus which is totally at odds with the author's. Especially after his death, the latter will always enjoy a formal respect. But though they strive at least to carefully preserve his ideas, the orthodox will be despised as pitiful, barren intellects.

The person of the creator is thus shown greater respect than the substance of his thought. The attitude toward the revolutionary pioneers of the bourgeois spirit is a particularly striking instance. The names of those who became known as forerunners of the bourgeois order because they fought the Middle Ages and continued trying to promote intellectual liberation and to serve truth even after the victory of that order, and who disregarded the new wishes of the bourgeoisie once it had acquired economic power, have become too glorious to be passed over in silence. From Voltaire, Rousseau, Lessing, Kant on down to their successors in modern literature and science, all are acknowledged as great men, profound thinkers and fiery spirits. But wherever they are actually encountered, their beliefs, drives and motives, the meaning of their teaching, their uncompromising rejection of the prevailing injustice, are spurned and mocked, called pathetic, superficial and onesided, and even persecuted and exterminated when conditions warrant. The Middle Ages banished the dead authors of heretical views to hell. In its heyday, capitalism is more tolerant. It divinizes greatness, productivity, personality, potency itself, but rejects what they bring forth. It idealizes mere qualities. The portraits of the philosophers and writers whose real adherents the bourgeoisie ridicules and harasses find their places in its hall of honor.

The visitor to the Pantheon in Paris will be surprised to see tribute being paid both to the fighters for freedom and to reactionary leaders. To revere the manes of the man that denounced the mendacious worship of Jeanne d'Arc in a room whose walls depict her hagiography seems mockery. Superstition and the person who wanted to rid us of it are celebrated at one and the same time. If we were to protest, the representatives of the prevailing intellectual climate would explain that there is no incompatibility between Voltaire and the canonization of Jeanne d'Arc, Robespierre and Chateaubriand. The formalism of contemporary thought, its relativism and historicism, the assimilation to the prevailing consciousness which begins the moment a great thought appears, the reification of all of life as chapters in history and sociology, have so accustomed us to merely take note of contents and substance instead of taking them seriously that all of them can live in peace with present conditions, i.e., with capitalist ideology.

There lives today a scribbler who is totally incapable of historical insight. With humorous zeal, he writes books of handy format about Bismarck and Napoleon Bonapart, Wilhelm II and Jesus of Nazareth, and imagines he understands all of them better than they understood themselves. He retains the upper hand over them, as gravediggers retain it over people in the end. What happens to most from the moment they have died in their bed and until they lie in their grave has little to do with differences in their existence. Forms of burial are few in number. In death, people with the most widely varying character and goals, and who have led the most diverse lives, become the objects of a primitive procedure. In the books of the above writer, the different meaning of the lives of the persons he writes about is not given much importance. The facts, i.e., the events whose connection with the lives of his heroes he just barely notices are pleasingly described, but here also, the categories of burial are not numerous. For this writer, Napoleon and Bismarck are *great* men, just as Karl Marx and Mister Miller are dead men for the grave digger. They become objects of burial procedures. The present triumphs.

Just Fate: That everyone deserves his fate is a view which appears under the most widely differing philosophical and unphilosophical guises. It implies not only the clearsightedness of blind nature but also the justice of the present economic system.

Bridge: A game of bridge among members of the upper middle class astonishes the layman. He rightly admires the qualities of class in evidence: the seriousness, the assurance, the freedom, the technical superiority, the speed with which decisions are made. He also rightly admires the marvellously functioning mechanism by virtue of which these same intelligent, trained, self-assured persons utter the most pathetic drivel the moment discussion turns to socially significant topics. Their cleverness is such that it can become stupidity, should the protection of their good conscience require it. They know how to live harmoniously.

Limits of Freedom: Just as the structure of capitalist society forever transforms itself while the basis of that society, economic relationships, are left untouched, so the cultural superstructure also constantly changes, yet certain principal elements persist without significant modification. For that reason, a fairly radical criticism of changing views concerning nature, the law, man and society is permitted. Should it be out of season, the critic will merely be blamed for his ignorance or eccentricity. But those ideas which are an important component in the apparatus of domination of the ruling class because they play a role in the psychic economy of the individual for which it is difficult to find a substitute, are taboo. A superficial comparison between the seriousness with which belief in a super natural power and love of country are taken in public education, and the development of other intellectual capacities such as a strict sense for truth and justice, for example, immediately makes this difference clear. The nation and religion are not to be treated lightly. As a citizen of a presently liberal country, you may approvingly discuss the economic theories of Marxism without serious risk. You may speak deprecatingly of the most famous scholars, or even politicians and important industrialists. But the moment you make a contemptuous remark about God, let alone the German fatherland or the field of honor where the masses are to stand ready to die, it won't be long before you become personally acquainted with the very direct interest

capitalism takes in the inviolability of these concepts. Provided it
stayed within certain limits, atheism was almost permitted in nineteenth century Germany. This had something to do with the struggle
against feudalism and the self-confidence of the rising bourgeoisie.
But that freedom was never wholly general, and quickly withdrawn.
Today, the indignation provoked by all serious criticism of religion
already contains a hint of the beating or the violent death the enemy
of the religious and nationalist lie may expect, should the occasion
arise. In between, there exists a finely gradated scale of legal and
extralegal punishments for the man who sins against these most
sacred possessions. One might have thought that because of the lost
war where millions of men were sacrificed to naked economic interests and none of the promises made the heroes and their families were
kept, the masses would have caught on. But that did not happen after
that time of lies and murder. Only the masters, it seems, have become
smarter. Today, they put down with fire and sword whatever may
even remotely jeopardize the readiness of the masses for a new war,
a new bloodletting. In this persecution, in this remorseless suppression of all decisive insights, capitalists of all varieties see truly eye to
eye. This understanding constitutes a class solidarity, the great cultural bond. In the factories, the mines, the offices, the proletarian is
already spurred by hunger. So that millions of them will let themselves be maimed, killed, poisoned on the battlefields, a latent enthusiasm is needed, and that cannot be maintained without the fetishized and interconnected concepts of nation and church. They are
part and parcel of the system, and anyone who transgresses against
them lays hands on its very foundations.

A Premium Placed on Vileness: The capitalist system in its present phase is organized exploitation on a world-wide scale. Its preservation creates boundless suffering. This society certainly has available
the human and technical means to abolish the most blatant forms of
physical wretchedness. We know of no era where this possibility
existed to such a degree. Only property arrangements stand in the
way of its realization, i.e., the fact that the huge productive apparatus
of mankind must function in the service of a small stratum of exploiters. All of official economics, the humane sciences and philosophy,

schools, the church, the arts and the press consider it their principal task to obscure, minimize, distort or deny this incredible fact. When surprise about the considerable social recognition accorded some obviously false theory or the perpetuation of such nonsense as current historiography leads to a thorough examination of such matters, it usually turns out that the intent to distract from the truth lies behind these minor reactionary phenomena.

But ideology reflects the material base. Because the latter is characterized by an exploitation that is no longer justifiable, only the person that cooperates in maintaining it can expect rewards. Conditions are very complex, however. For although it brings unnecessary suffering, an outdated social order that has gone bad also fulfills functions which maintain and renew the life of mankind at a certain level. Its existence is an evil because a better one would be technically possible. It is good because it represents the present form of human activity and also includes elements of a better future. It follows from this dialectical relationship that during such a period, the struggle against things as they are also appears as the struggle against what is necessary and useful. On the other hand, positive effort within the existing framework is also positive cooperation which helps assure the continued existence of an unjust order. Because a bad society transacts mankind's business although it does it badly, the person that endangers its survival also acts directly against mankind; its friend appears as its enemy. In reality, the bad cannot be disentangled from the good, and therefore the fight against what is outdated also appears as the fight against the necessary. The insistence that work have dignity must manifest itself in strikes, obstruction, resistance to "positive" effort. Conversely, the reward for socially important activity also becomes the payment for cooperating in this bad order. Things are so oblique that English textile workers profit from the hunger of the Indian pariah and the drudgery of Chinese coolies, and that work in Bacon's and Galileo's science serves the interests of today's armaments industry.

Of course, sensitive mechanisms to indicate what kind of work has specific usefulness in the act of exploitation have developed. In this perverse state of things, the scale of rewards corresponds less to the real value an achievement may have for the existence of mankind, more to its importance for the survival of the old system. That work in the service of the ruling class is, in the main, useful does not preclude activities which are of little or no benefit to society as a whole but which primarily or exclusively prop up the bad society. To the extent to which it is endangered in its present form, it is precisely such activities which are highly rated. This applies not only to leading positions in the actual apparatus of suppression and the large-scale ideological institutions such as the military, the police, the church, philosophy and economics, but even to mere attitudes and beliefs. Their market value lies in the delicate social mechanisms which have developed for the selection of candidates for positions, whether it be that of a proletarian or a minister. The play of "good connections" comes in here. Their mere possession constitutes a certain guarantee of the reliability of the individual. The system has organs by which it can take account of every "good" tendency where that becomes necessary. Of course, the price of someone's will is also measured by its usefulness and the cost of reproduction. The good will of a servant girl is worth less than that of a professor. Real dependability of the highest order means an unalterable, mulish determination in the defense of an order which exists to insure the profits of a small number of persons, even if that entails new seas of blood or misdeeds of whatever description. It also involves the conviction that this is doing one's duty. Real dependability is the absolute readiness to loyally adopt all significant values of the ruling class, to hate and libel the person who commits his life to the improvement of conditions, to believe and spread every lie that vilifies him, and to greet his death as a salvation. One might think that such a well developed attitude is rare, but actually it is fairly widespread.

Every thought, every show of sympathy, every relationship, every minor or major act *against* the ruling class involves the risk of personal disadvantage. Every thought, every show of sympathy, every relationship and every act *on its behalf* i.e., on behalf of the worldwide apparatus of exploitation, means an opportunity. People who want to get somewhere must early acquire beliefs which enable them to have a good conscience as they do what reality demands, for if they do it *contre coeur*, it will be noticed by others, and they will perform badly. The system affects everything, down to the most delicate tendrils of the individual's soul. It has placed a premium on vileness.

The Undiscovered Land: When contrasted with all less conscious beings, man's position seems enormously privileged. The more inner and outer freedom a person has compared to those less fortunate, the greater this privilege becomes. In decisive respects, we are the same as animals, indeed the same as everything living, and may feel that we are their natural advocates in much the same way the fortunate, released prisoner may be the advocate of his fellow sufferers who are still locked up. But our privileged position, our capacity for experiencing the suffering of all living beings within ourselves does not mean that we can truly become one with them and certainly not that we can free anyone by that act of identification. We can make the life of individuals easier, we can deduce some practical consequences from empirical insight. But we are still surrounded by a sea of darkness which cannot be illuminated by any language. Language has the choice of being a finite tool, or an illusion.

This understanding is a better weapon against fideism than the inflated claim that our fragmentary insight is total knowledge. This claim is empty even when it preaches a crusade against metaphysics. The proof that those regions of which we have no experience cannot be discovered, that no consequences can therefore result from alleged news about the Beyond replaces the optimistic denial that we are surrounded by darkness.

Concerning Resentment: A neat trick: the criticism of the system is to be the prerogative of those that have an interest in it. The others, who have the opportunity of getting to know its underside, are disarmed by the contemptuous remark that they are annoyed, vengeful, envious. They harbor 'resentment.'

It should never be forgotten, however, that there is no possible way of getting to know a penitentiary unless one is really locked up in it for five years and knows that the golden freedom one longs for during that time will be a life of starvation.

To restrict testimony about this society which is largely a penitentiary to those who do not experience it as such almost seems like a tacit agreement among the fortunate ones.

Absolute Justice: Earthly justice, or the fate one deserves, are certainly things that can be improved upon, and the historical struggle is being waged to that end. But they can never be set absolutely right. Who will have justice done him, who will deserve his fate? Human beings? But aren't the outside and the inside, the nose, the head, the talents, excitability, jealousy, an empty or a well-stocked mind part of every human being? Surely there is no doubt that poverty, sickness, early death are no greater blows of fate and therefore to be made up for by justice than an ugly face, bad character qualities or intellectual impotence. Since even "personality" merely "belongs" to it, what then is that self that needs help? Vauvenargue contradicted Rousseau when he said that the equality of means could not be derived from natural equality since men were in fact unequal. Instead of arguing for the improvement of nature, Vauvenargue thus rose to the defense of social inequality. Social change must also change "nature." But what becomes increasingly problematical are the subjects to whom justice is to be done. They finally appear as utterly abstract, "pure" selves that are bare of any real qualities. As everywhere else, the "radical" philosophical question leads nowhere, for these selves are insubstantial appearance or, rather, the appearance of being. The foundation of the changes to be effected by perfect justice is undiscoverable. When the term justice is used in the real world, very precise, specifiable changes are demanded. Absolute justice is as unthinkable as absolute truth. The revolution need not bother with it.

Nietzsche and the Proletariat: Nietzsche derides Christianity because its ideals derived from impotence. By calling them virtues, the weak deliberately misinterpret love of mankind, justice, mildness because they cannot avenge themselves or, more precisely, because they were too cowardly to do so.

He despises the mass, yet wants to preserve it as such. He wants to preserve weakness, cowardice, obedience, so that he may have room for the breeding of his utopian aristocrats. There must be those who sew togas for these men so that they don't walk about like beggars, for if they could not live off the sweat of the mass, they themselves would have to operate the machines, and there no one intones Dionysian dithyrambs. Actually, Nietzsche is extremely pleased that the mass should exist. Nowhere does he appear as the real enemy of a system based on exploitation and misery. According to him, it is therefore both just and useful that men's gifts atrophy under wretched conditions, however strongly he may advocate their development in the 'superman.' Nietzsche's aims are not those of the proletariat. But the proletariat might note that the morality which recommends that it be conciliatory is mere deception, according to this philosopher of the ruling class. He himself inculcates in the masses that it is only fear that keeps them from destroying the system. If the masses understand this, even Nietzsche can contribute to the process which turns the slave rebellion in morals into proletarian practice.

Rules of the Game: If the man who merely makes a living is to associate with members of the upper classes, it is essential that what is most important, the class difference between the two, not be mentioned. Good manners require not only that nothing be said about this but that the difference be skillfully masked by expression and behavior. The pretense that both move on the same social plane must be maintained.

The millionaire does his part. When he goes to Trouville for his summer vacation and his impecunious acquaintance into some wretched Black Forest hamlet, the millionaire is not going to say: "That's all you can afford," but "We'd like to go back to that beautiful Black Forest some time," or "I don't really enjoy going to Trouville, I dislike everything about it, but what can you do?" Now his poor acquaintance must answer, "It's true, I am really looking forward to the Black Forest." Should he say, "I'd also rather go to Trouville but I can't afford it," the first thing he will be told is, "You must be joking." Should he insist, not only as regards his summer vacation but whenever this answer is relevant, he would appear vulgar, and the association would terminate.

But should he actually go to Trouville although he cannot really afford it, he will notice that his upper-class friends consider the distribution of income in the capitalist order the absolutely equitable yardstick for the sensual gratification people are permitted. How can this man go to Trouville! In his circumstances, how "dare he?" Why doesn't he go to the Black Forest?

The association rests on both the ideational smokescreen and the very real observation and recognition of the class structure. Because the less well-off individual usually derives some practical benefit from it or, more precisely, because he expects such benefit, he ordinarily suppresses the clear recognition of the difference, first within the relationship, and then more generally. His consciousness adapts itself to his acts. Because people like to act according to their beliefs, they usually wind up believing what they would like to act in accordance with. The petit bourgeois who cultivate such relationships, particularly intellectuals, usually do in fact have a consciousness that is ideologically abnormally confused. They not only suffer from the illusion of their class that all is harmony but from a personal thick-headedness as well, however gifted they may otherwise be. In the end, the results of repression also affect the rest of their thinking. They begin by exaggerating the good qualities of their upper class friends. Have you ever run into a person with good connections who did not tell you "how nice" and "how intelligent" those ladies and gentlemen are? "How exploitative" they are is something he does not recognize. Associations have their effect on consciousness. The more intimate and sincere they are, the weightier those effects become.

Archimedes and Modern Metaphysics: Because he was interested in his science, Archimedes forgot that people were being slaughtered all around him, and so he perished. Because they are interested in their science, today's philosophers forget that people are being murdered all around them. They call reports of such occurrences horror stories. But they run no risk, for it is not the enemy troops but their own which have the upper hand.

Like Archimedes' figures, their systems are machines devised for the defense of their fellow citizens. But in contrast to the Greek scientist, they sail under false colors. He did not claim that his catapults would benefit friend and enemy alike. But modern metaphysics believes that its cause is that of mankind.

Change of Thought: Among Marxist thinkers, the avowal of moral motives, particularly compassion which is the secret mainspring of their thought and action, is looked down upon, not only because they are ashamed of it but also because it has been their experience that such a confession usually becomes a substitute for practice. Consciously or not, they assume that the moral impulse either manifests itself in actions or in words. That is the reason they mistrust the latter.

But that exposes them to the same sort of danger as their observation that what the real world is all about is material things. When it is emphasized that there are needs and qualities other than hunger and power, they point to sober reality where everything turns on the satisfaction of the most primitive needs. In so doing, they tend to transform the bitterness in that comment into an apology. Under such circumstances, the assertion that in today's reality the ideal merely serves as ideological camouflage for a bad materialistic practice easily turns into the realism of certain journalists and reporters: "Don't bother us with culture. We know that that's a hoax." They are perfectly at home with and reconciled to that state of affairs.

All or Nothing: Be mistrustful of the person who says that unless everyone is helped, it's no use. That is the fundamental lie of those who actually do not want to help and hide behind a theory to excuse their failure to do their duty in a concrete case. They rationalize their inhumanity. There is a resemblance between them and the devout: both preserve their good conscience by pleading "higher" considerations when they abandon you to your helplessness.

Skepsis and Morality: Socialism does not "follow" from the economic laws discovered by Marx. It is true that there are many scientific predictions which have a high degree of probability. That the sun will rise tomorrow would be one example. They are the result of an enormous amount of experience. But who is going to believe that this applies to the prediction that socialism will come?

Socialism is a better, more effective form of society whose elements are present in capitalism in a certain sense. In capitalism, there are "tendencies" that make for change in the system. But the empirical knowledge which would support our belief that these tendencies will really prevail is quite limited. If a bridge spanning an abyss had been constructed according to principles deriving from data no more precise than those that lead us to expect the advent of socialism, people using it would court extreme danger.

Although it is correct, this consideration can not only count on the approval of all the well-meaning bourgeois friends of socialism but will also be countenanced by its enemies. One may be an adherent of Marx, provided one has the necessary degree of skepticism. But approval and tolerance stop the moment we amplify the bridge image and say that taking the risk of crossing that bridge might determine whether the overwhelmingly larger measure of injustice, the withering of human capacities, the lies, the senseless degradation, in short the unnecessary material and spiritual suffering is to disappear, or not. One has to fight for socialism, in other words. The hedged approbation of Marxist theory, its respectful integration in the history of philosophy, is something the bourgeoisie likes to see. The correlate of this contemplative treatment of Marxism in real life is the accomodation to things as they are. To say that socialism does not "follow" from Marxist theory even though socialism is desirable, and to add nothing further, is to scientifically and morally justify capitalism. It is an expression of social skepticism.

But when it is said that Marx and Engels did not "prove" socialism, not pessimism but the commitment to practice which theory needs, will follow. Marx unveiled the law of the dominant inhuman order, and pointed to the levers that must be used to create a more human one.

What the transition from one part of a system to another is for the bourgeois scholar, a "problem" like so many others, something to which "justice can be done" on a few sympathetic pages in a textbook, i.e., the resolution of the question whether class society continues or is successfully replaced by socialism, is something that will decide if mankind progresses or perishes in barbarism. The position a person takes here not only determines the relationship of his life to that of mankind but also the degree of his morality. A philosophical system, an ethic, a moral teaching which merely treats our outdated, progress-inhibiting property relations, the existence of a class society and the need to transcend it as "part of a larger picture" rather than identifying itself with that need is the opposite of morality, for the form morality has taken in our time is the implementation of socialism. By their skeptical treatment of it, the scholars serve the prevailing social order. Those professors and literati who find encouragement, recognition and honors in the world as it is certainly would concur in the "moral" condemnation of robbery. But they calmly look on the legal rape of countless children, women and men in capitalist societies and even more in their colonies, and ingest their share of the loot. They support the system in their civilized books and journals where they use "scientific" language to discuss all sorts of problems—the teachings concerning a socialist society among others —and then pass on with a skeptical comment to the business at hand.

It is well known that the bourgeoisie can "discuss" anything. That is part of its strength. Generally speaking, it grants freedom of thought. Only where thought takes on a form which directly leads to practice, where it becomes "unscientific" in the academic sphere, things stop being cozy. Mere skepticism essentially means that theory remains just that. The opposite of such skepticism is neither optimism nor dogma but proletarian practice. Should socialism be improbable, it will require an all the more desperate determination to make it come true. What stands in its way is not the technical difficulty of its implementation but the apparatus of domination of the ruling class.

But if skepticism is bad, certainty is no better. The illusion that the advent of the socialist order is of the same order of necessity as natural events is hardly less of a danger to correct action than is skeptical disbelief. If Marx did not prove socialism, he did show that capitalism harbors developmental tendencies which make it possible. Those interested in it know at what points they must attack. The socialist order of society is not prevented by world history; it is historically possible. But it will not be realized by a logic that is immanent in history but by men trained in theory and determined to make things better. Otherwise, it will not be realized at all.

Heroic World View: There is no world view which more ingeniously accomodates the objectives of the ruling class than the "heroic." The young members of the petite bourgeoisie have little to gain for themselves but must defend everything on behalf of the trusts. The fight against individualism, the belief that the individual must sacrifice himself so that the totality may live fits in perfectly with the current situation. In contrast to the real hero, this generation is not filled with enthusiasm for a clear goal, but it is enthusiastic in its determination to attain it. The ruling class in Germany could hardly have wished for anything better than that the strata it ruined would constitute its own vanguard and aspire not even to the sparse pay but to sacrifice, or at least to devotion and discipline.

True heroism is unmindful of its own interests but passionately concerned with a socially significant value. The heroic world view, on the other hand, is ready to sacrifice its own life, but takes that life as its most important theme. The economic interests on whose behalf its adherents are to give up their lives must not enter their consciousness, of course. Instead, their passionate consciousness must fasten directly on sacrifice, which means on blood and murder. The imagination ignores the fact that the person doing the imagining is himself at stake. It wallows in cruelty without regard to persons. In actual practice, the devotees of the religion of sacrifice usually think more of killing than of being killed. They seem to wish to purchase their right to the former by their readiness for the latter, and certainly place no great value on such subtle distinctions. Future research that enjoys a greater freedom from prejudice than is current today may discover that there were times when the power Christianity had over the souls of men also derived from its connection with martyrdom and wounds, and that the stakes of the Inquisition were as closely tied to the worship of the cross as are the pistols of the rightists to their idealist doctrine.

Everyone Must Die: Everyone must die, of course, but not everyone dies in the same way. I won't even mention the fact that the rich can prolong their life in countless ways which are not available to the poor, or that the skill of eminent surgeons is a function of their fee. I shall simply talk about dying itself.

I admit that the more or less painful causes of death are distributed relatively evenly. But it is also true that varying degrees of attention in treatment and care make a difference even where the disease is the same. But that is the least of it. Just one observation suffices to cast doubt on the whole ideology of the impartiality of death. Let it be published everywhere that the survivors of those who die of whatever cause within the next fourteen days will be decently clothed and fed for the rest of their life. If that were done, global suicide rates would not only leap upward but a respectable number of individuals, men and women, would commit these suicides with a calm that would honor any stoic. And now consider whether the death of a millionaire is the same as that of a proletarian. Dying is the final part of life. During that time, the poor man knows that his family will be chastised when he dies. A female worker has both her feet smashed. A minute after this calamity, she wails, "Now I can no longer work, my poor husband, my poor children, now I am useless." She does not think of herself. A lady who has fallen off her horse or been in an automobile accident faces different perspectives on her sick bed, and the large number of her friends need not worry about the loss of her usefulness but only that of her personality.

I don't know what comes *after* death, but what happens before it takes place in capitalist class society.

A Discussion About Revolution: The real bourgeois has the capacity to look at all things objectively, and in post-war Germany, that even extends to revolution. Once he begins to reflect objectively about it or, rather, its political preparation, it seems like any other activity within the context of social reality and is judged accordingly. Because in capitalist production the entrepreneur thinks less about the use value of his products than about ingenious manufacturing and selling techniques, he is less interested in the content than the execution when he makes an objective judgment about any social activity whatever. In present-day Germany, people therefore blame the revolutionary party more for its inadequate performance than for its goal which has been felt to have some chance since the end of the war. What is stigmatized is the incompetence of its leaders. Of course, it is not only these formal elements of bourgeois thought but much more concrete causes that are responsible for this. Not just among those with leftist leanings, but in the psyche of large counter-revolutionary segments which condemn its leadership when proletarian action has failed, the psychologist will recognize a secret guilt feeling because they did not participate, and the unconscious fury that it all came to nothing. What also plays a part is the infamous belief in success as a divine judgment, which has deep roots in European life. As long as it is not victorious, the revolution is no good.

The inadequacies of revolutionary leadership can indeed be a misfortune. But however incompetently the political struggle against the inhumanity of present conditions may be led, the fact remains that that is the form which the will to a better order can take at this historical juncture, and that is how many millions of the suppressed and tormented all over the world understand it. Any inadequacy of the leadership therefore does not negate the fact that it is the head of the struggle. Someone closely associated with a revolutionary party, a person whose theoretical and active involvement with it is beyond all doubt, may perhaps also fruitfully criticize the leadership from the outside for a time.

But a proletarian party cannot be made the object of contemplative criticism, for every one of its mistakes is due to the fact that the effective participation of more qualified people did not prevent it from committing them. Whether or not the contemplative critic would have strengthened such elements in the party by his own activity cannot be determined by his later statements about its actions, for it can never be decided whether his view would have seemed plausible to the masses in the situation at hand, or whether his theoretical superiority was matched by the required organizational talents, whether his policy, in other words, was possible at all, or not. It will be objected that the leaders monopolize power in the party, that the party apparatus makes it impossible for the single individual to prevail, and that consequently any attempt by reasonable people is doomed from the very start. As if any political will throughout history had not always encountered similar obstacles when it tried to assert itself! Today, it may be the intellectual before whom they pile up. But who other than those who overcome practically whatever defects there are can prove that, all things considered, such problems are really the least significant? Bourgeois criticism of the proletarian struggle is a logical impossibility.

Bourgeois modes of thought are adapted to the economic system that gave rise to them. But prevailing patterns of thought do not apply to the political movement which attempts to put a better society in the place of the present one, for the power of the economic laws of capitalism affects it only through multiple mediations, and indirectly. Under capitalism, automatic adjustments occur when an enterprise is badly managed. The judgment that management is incompetent is confirmed when the business goes bankrupt, and its economic function is then taken over by others that perform better. There is thus an objective criterion which is independent of any critic, and which evaluates how social activities are being carried out. For wherever in the capitalist system a certain kind of work can be utilized, there will also be people who do it in a way that corresponds to the state of the productive forces. Any gap caused by failure is closed immediately. But this kind of replaceability does not apply in the case of proletarian leaders. Somehow or other, those that are killed or put out of action are replaced from the rank and file, but usually such replacements aren't up to par, for the enemy knows how to eliminate whom it considers dangerous. The world in which the proletarian élite grows up is not academies but struggles in factories and unions, punishments, dirty dispute within and outside the parties, prison sentences and illegality. Students don't rush in here with the eagerness with which they crowd into the lecture halls and laboratories of the bourgeoisie. The revolutionary career is not a series of banquets and a string of honorific titles, nor does it hold the promise of interesting research or professors' salaries. It is a passage toward the unknown, with misery, disgrace, ungratefulness and prison as its way stations. Only an almost superhuman belief illumines it, and merely talented people therefore choose it only rarely.

NOTE: At times such as the present, revolutionary belief may not really be compatible with great clearsightedness about the realities. Perhaps those qualities indispensable for leading a proletarian party are now to be found precisely among those whose character is not the best. Does the "higher level" of the bourgeois critics, their more acute moral sensibility, not in part result from the fact that they keep away from the real political fight? If keeping away became the general maxim, would this not spell the death sentence of liberty? Do the better educated have any good reason to damn those who are actually involved in this struggle?

Animism: Man discovers that he produces his movements by autonomous impulses. Already at the very beginning of his history, he transfers this experience not just to the movements of other living beings but to events generally. More precisely, what is involved here is not so much a transfer but the direct experience of all events as acts of will similar to his own.

Our philosophers have long since understood this. But here also, a change has been taking place during the last few decades. While during the past century this insight led to the doctrine of the animism of the primitives and the tendency to criticize present-day religion as the last trace of that original psychic mechanism, it is used today to discredit the concept of causality. The life of the mind, it is said, is not subject to it. Religious acts are regarded as unconditioned and science is not qualified to judge them. It might be added that it is doubtful that animist theory accurately describes the primitives. Perhaps the ethnologists are telling us something different although the religion of the deluded masses under capitalism certainly is a form of animism. Faced with death in a horrible reality, men wish that there might be someone with good intentions known only to himself that is responsible for it all. Although a clearer understanding is possible, suffering keeps the psychic mechanism of animism going, and those responsible for that suffering see to it that nothing interferes with the mechanism. The doctrine of the animism of the primitives can therefore be more adequately explained by the wretchedness of the present than can the present by recourse to the primitives.

On the Formalization of Christianity: That Christ used a rod to drive the merchants from the temple has served as theological justification for many acts of violence. It is curious how rarely the purpose of the biblical act is discussed. The French Revolution tried to put a bloody end to the misuse of Christianity by absolutism. During the World War, our priests misused Christianity to help in the extermination of millions of Christians. To justify their acts, both can refer to that biblical episode, but those theologians who only concern themselves with the problem of the legitimacy of violence create the impression that what was important for Christ was the blows of the rod, not the temple. What fine Christians they are!

Belief and Profit: Jewish capitalists become terribly excited about anti-Semitism. They say that what they hold most sacred is under attack. But I believe that their unspeakable annoyance merely comes from the fact that something about them is being threatened which yields no profit, yet cannot possibly be changed. If present-day anti-Semitism were directed against religious belief and not "the blood," a great many of those who now show the most profound indignation about it would renounce this thing they "hold most sacred" "with a heavy heart." As the material base of ghetto life was left behind, the willingness to sacrifice life and property to one's religious belief also became a thing of the past. Among bourgeois Jews, the hierarchy of goods is neither Jewish nor Christian but bourgeois. The Jewish capitalist brings sacrifices to power, just like his Aryan class colleague. He first sacrifices his own superstition, then the lives of others, and finally his capital. The Jewish revolutionary in Germany is not different from his "Aryan" comrade. He commits his life to the liberation of man.

Either–Or: Without money, without financial security, we are defenseless, and that means a terrible punishment: degrading drudgery, enslavement by petty dealings, unending, mean worries, dependence on the most vicious people. Not only we but those we love and are responsible for are crushed by the wheel of the everyday. We become the targets of stupidity and sadism. Forces whose existence we were ignorant of in happier days acquire power over us and not only drag our lives but our thoughts into wretchedness and filth. People who, though not sincerely but from a grovelling respect for our social position, allowed us to think as we pleased now triumphantly maintain the opposite. They are like the director of a penitentiary who will put up with a well-connected visitor's way of thinking but would deny an inmate the most insignificant alleviation, were he to express an identical attitude. Total impotence, a withering of all good qualities and the development of all bad ones will mark our own and our family's existence, should we lose our financial security in this society.

All this is undoubtedly true and would amply justify the irrevocable decision to use any means whatever to prevent the loss of that security. But does not the conscious or unconscious determination, the tenacious boldness and the unbreakable will of the person of means to maintain it give all his acts, even the least calculated and most generous ones, the stamp of deadness? Doesn't this safety, this resolve to retain one's place in society and never to be pushed to its edge turn people into machines, predictable in everything that counts? Doesn't their entire life become a formula? In everything of fundamental importance, they think, feel and act as mere functions of their property interests. The meaning of their life is defined not by their humanity but on the thing that is their property and its immanent laws. They only become real, autonomous human beings when at play or engaged in activities that do not matter. But even here it becomes apparent that everything else in their lives is ancillary. The way these ladies and gentlemen travel, make love, discuss politics, engage in sports, bring up their children, discuss a book always seems to contain the proviso, "However that may be, I have no intention of jeopardizing my money and my income." This is the reason that anyone who knows them senses the atmosphere of infinite boredom in which they live. It does not matter what happens in one's social intercourse with such people for fundamentally everything is already determined. They have autonomous impulses, are human beings only in the "private" sphere; however that is merely derivative in their view. Where reality sets in for them, they are not human beings but functions of their wealth and their income. What is true of the very rich applies equally to the small fry. The employee's determination not to be fired will gradually come to have the same deadening effect on his life. This resoluteness will finally make him lose the capacity for autonomous decisions and even the freedom of his thought.

We thus face an alternative: either we sink into the social hell, or we lead a futile life. One might think a proper middle course existed, a *juste milieu,* but even the slightest weakening of the will to stay on top means that the downward slide is left to the vagaries of chance. Just as merely remaining at a given level does not assure the survival but the decline of a business, just as being passed over does not permit the employee to settle into his position but brings the threat of dismissal, so the hardening of the spirit today will not preserve freedom but make ruin a sure thing.

Political Maxim: For the peaceful citizen, there is a good political maxim which will help him survive all the dangers of the
class struggle: Avoid antagonizing the reactionaries. Should the
workers ever come to power, there will be time enough to per-
suade them that you are on their side. If you did not become
prominent as a political leader of the right, if you simply stayed
on good terms with them, you need not be afraid when the revolution comes. But if you sympathized with the proletariat during
times of internal peace or just failed to express your hostility to it
among your friends, you might be murdered, should civil war
break out. For the smart citizen who cares about his and his family's life, and especially for the intellectual, this rule is a dependable guide in turbulent times. Of course, the man of means does
not have to worry about this problem. He can permit himself leftist leanings, provided he goes abroad in time.

Metaphysics: The number of things people mean by the term
metaphysics is truly enormous. It is difficult to come up with a
formulation which will appeal to all learned gentlemen and their
views about ultimate things. If you are reasonably successful in your
attacks on some such pompous "metaphysics," you may expect all the
rest to say that they always had something altogether different in
mind.

And yet it seems to me that there is some sense in which metaphysics means insight into the true nature of things. Judging by the
example of all important and unimportant philosophical and unphilosophical professors, the nature of things is such that it can be
explored and that one can live with it without becoming indignant
about the prevailing social system. The wise man who sees the core
of things may deduce all sorts of philosophical, scientific and ethical
consequences from his contemplation, he may even sketch the image
of an ideal "community," but his understanding of class relationships
will not noticeably improve. Indeed, the fact that the flight toward
the eternal is possible under existing class relationships will constitute
a certain vindication of them, particularly when the metaphysician
imputes absolute value to this flight. A society in which the person
may fulfill his high destiny in such important respects cannot be

altogether bad. At least its improvement does not seem a particularly pressing matter.

I don't know to what extent metaphysicians are right. Perhaps there is an especially apposite metaphysical system or fragment somewhere. But I do know that ordinarily metaphysicians are not terribly impressed by what torments men.

Character and the Structure of Society: It is violently disputed that material conditions shape man, but in extreme cases this becomes too apparent to be denied. When a magnanimous and intelligent individual is justly or unjustly put into prison and spends ten years of his life in the cells and corridors of these frightening buildings, his needs and anxieties, his interests and joys will also shrink further and further as they adjust to the tiny measure of this pathetic existence. Of course, thoughts about his earlier life persist tormentingly in the background, but that does not change the fact that the most petty chicanery or a pleasurable change can trigger emotions whose vehemence can hardly be grasped by the outsider. In contrast to the penitentiary inmate, the life of the great capitalist is lived at such a level that pleasures and afflictions which would make for considerable ups and downs in the lives of others become irrelevant. For those without insight into social nexuses, philosophical and moral ideas play the role of fetishes. But for the powerful who have the chance to grasp the changing courses of such ideas in the play of social forces, and who participate in maintaining or modifying them, their fetishistic character gradually dissolves. In the case of these extremes, the magnate and the prison inmate, the poles of society, it will be largely admitted that psychic reactions and the formation of character depend on material conditions. But the differences in character between a minor union official and a factory director, a big landowner and a letter-carrier, are just as tied to their situation as are those between the inmate and the powerful. We certainly cannot maintain that men are born equal, and who can say how many behavioral nuances we inherit. But the horizon defined for each of us by his function in society, the structure of those fundamental interests which fate inculcates in us from childhood on, is such that a relatively smooth development of those individual dispositions is probably extremely rare. The higher the social stratum in which a person is born, however, the better the chance for such a development becomes. In spite of the isolation inside the cells, the psychological typology of the inmate is easily sketched: all are reduced to the same level. And that is generally true of poverty and wretchedness. Most people are born into a prison, which is precisely why the present form of society, so-called individualism, is actually a society of standardization and mass culture. So called collectivism, i.e., socialism, on the other hand, is the development of individual talents and differences.

NOTE: In society as presently constituted, the following law applies to individual development: the more elevated the social position, the more easily intelligence and every other kind of talent will grow. On the higher social levels, the objective conditions for the development of socially necessary qualities are more favorable than on the lower ones. This is obvious as regards education in family and school. But the same law applies to adults. What a fairly big capitalist can accomplish in a given day, for example, is multiplied by the technical and human apparatus at his disposal for all of his activites, from complicated dealings to the dictation of an unimportant letter. The success due to this superiority affects his personal skills, his routine. At first, he only wrote ten letters during the time the petit bourgeois wrote one. In the end, he will dictate fifteen or twenty, and take no longer. His skill in the performance of his more important tasks grows, for the inconsequential has been turned over to his subordinates. He can thus become a master where it counts. But the little man labors away at trifles, his day is a succession of unpleasant chores, and in the background misery lurks. This applies not just to social achievements but also to the individual's other qualities. The pleasure taken in cheap amusements, the thickheaded attachment to petty property, the vapid talk about one's private affairs, the comical vanity and sensitivity, in short the whole paltriness of a straitened existence need not exist where power gives man substance and develops it.

Platitudes: The objection that a rational sentence is onesided, crude, platitudinous or banal may well shame the person that formulates it even if no discussion occurs. For it is not maintained that the sentence is incorrect or inadequately demonstrated. The person thus attacked cannot therefore debate with his opponent. It is merely pointed out that every child already knows what he is saying, and that there are also other sides to the question. What answer is there to such an objection? No one disputes that there are also other aspects, that what was said is common knowledge. He has been beaten.

Of course, if such a brief rejoinder refers to a statement which notes the universal dependence of present conditions on the technically unnecessary preservation of relations of exploitation, or some aspect of this relationship of dependency, it is simple insolence. Whatever other aspects contemporary events may have, none is as decisive as this one, of none is it as important that all understand it. If it were really generally recognized that the continuation of exploitation which benefits only a small number of men is the source of present day social wretchedness; if every newspaper reader grasped that the preservation of the present order is the cause of all the wars, crimes, poverty, misery and murder he reads about; if these platitudes which not even people with an average knowledge of the world, let alone our learned men understand because we have a marvellously functioning brainwashing apparatus, if these platitudes, I say, were even to penetrate the understanding of the lowest guardian of this order, mankind could be spared a terrible future.

Of course, the assessment of any contemporary historical event can always stress aspects other than its nexus with class rule. But what counts today is precisely an insight into this nexus. The suspicion cannot be rejected out of hand that the antipathy to onesidedness, crudeness, platitudes, banality, and ultimately to all explanation, derivation, investigation of causes and systematic theory is based on the fear that the social cause of our present regression might enter public consciousness. This assumption is also platitudinous and onesided.

Health and Society: If by health one means the absence of impediments or constraint which have their cause in the personality—and this would not be an altogether useless definition of this difficult concept—then a curious connection between it and society becomes immediately apparent. Impediments or constraint show up primarily when someone either cannot perform the tasks his existence requires, or when he can do so only at the price of inordinate suffering. The worker, for example, will perform less well than his colleagues and therefore be fired. Or he gets his hand into a machine, and is maimed. In this sphere, where reality, i.e., foremen and dangerous machines, confine man within narrow boundaries, one easily becomes useless, inferior, psychologically ill. The entrepreneur of the older type with a speculative bent not only has more space and therefore doesn't run up against difficulties so quickly, there is also the additional circumstance that it is hard to decide whether his initiatives in a given case are stupid or brilliant. Similarly, the modern entrepreneur, the trust director, is not nearly as likely to be considered crazy as one of his workers, particularly when he owns stock. He has much more room to maneuver—I am not considering attacks of raving mania or similar "commonplace" varieties here—before his madness will be seen for what it is.

In the case of a commanding general or the German Kaiser while he was at the helm, there is no way of deciding whether their leadership is insanity or wisdom, and this applies a fortiori to world government.

The Ones Who Are Not Marked: Forty years ago, God's or nature's justice under capitalism at least revealed itself by "marking" the exploiters. Those who had a good time while mankind starved had a big belly, and this was something of a stigma. But this esthetic justice God once showed has long since come to an end. Not only the sons and daughters of the big capitalists but they themselves are about to become muscular, slender people, models of harmonious proportions and self-restraint. The big belly has become the mark of small folk who have no chance to take up sports or massage. Usually, they are condemned to a sedentary life and pay for their small measure of well-being not only with the fear of a stroke but the justified contempt of the proletariat. Rockefeller is ninety years old, and plays golf.

Rule of the Church: The reader of a historical work on the late Middle Ages or the Counter Reformation who skips ahead and picks up the word "tongue" and the name of a person further down the page without having grasped the connection, will involuntarily supply the missing words and conclude that the Holy Inquisition cut off the man's tongue. When, as he reads on, it turns out that the sentence merely states that that person spoke the German tongue, the reader may feel temporarily reassured. But his anticipatory instinct will prove correct in other cases, on a later page.

Buddhism: From a certain point of view, the earliest form of Buddhism appears as a particularly virile position. It directs that possessions which cannot be preserved through one's own efforts be scorned. Everything falls into this category: life, health, wealth, even the self.

The Little Man and the Philosophy of Freedom: In socialism, freedom is to become a reality. But because the present system is called "free" and considered liberal, it is not terribly clear what this may mean. Yet anyone who keeps his eyes open and has a little money in his pocket actually has ample occasion to familiarize himself with this concept. He may, for example, ask an acquaintance for a job in his firm. That has nothing to do with philosophy. But his acquaintance knits his brow and says that that is objectively impossible. Business is bad, he says, and he's even been obliged to let many employees go. The man should not be angry with him, for it is not within his power, his freedom doesn't extend that far.

The businessman is subject to laws which neither he nor anyone else nor any power with such a mandate created with purpose and deliberation. They are laws which the big capitalists and perhaps he himself skillfully make use of but whose existence must be accepted as a fact. Boom, bust, inflation, wars and even the qualities of things and human beings the present society demands are a function of such laws, of the anonymous social reality, just as the rotation of the earth expresses the laws of dead nature. No single individual can do anything about them.

Bourgeois thought views this reality as superhuman. It fetishizes the social process. It speaks of fate and either calls it blind, or attempts a mystical interpretation. It deplores the meaninglessness of the whole, or submits to the inscrutability of God's ways. But in actuality, all those phenomena which are either experienced as accidental or given a mystical interpretation depend on men and the way they arrange their social existence. They can therefore also be changed. If men consciously took their life in society in hand and replaced the struggle of capitalist enterprises by a classless and planned economy, the effects the process of production has on human beings and their relationships could also be understood and regulated. What today appears as a fact of nature in the private and business dealings of individuals are the effects of social life as a whole. They are human, not divine products.

Because these effects of life in society are present but not conscious, willed or controlled, and are the results of an equal number of individual wills that grasp neither their dependence nor their power, the limitation on individual freedom in our time is immeasurably greater than would be necessary, given the available means. When the businessman whom his acquaintance asks for a job refuses because conditions don't permit it, he thinks he is referring to something purely objective and totally autonomous—reality itself. Since everyone else, including the petitioner, feels the same because the reality they themselves created through their social activity appears as something alien by which they must abide, it follows that there are many agents but no conscious and therefore free subjects of social conditions. Men must submit to conditions they themselves constantly create as to something alien and overwhelmingly powerful.

Insight is not enough, of course, to change this state of affairs. For the error is not that people do not recognize the subject but that the subject does not exist. Everything therefore depends on creating the free subject that consciously shapes social life. And this subject is nothing other than the rationally organized socialist society which regulates its own existence. In the society as it now is, there are many individual subjects whose freedom is severely limited because they are unconscious of what they do, but there is no being that creates reality, no coherent ground. Religion and metaphysics claim that such a ground exists. In so doing, they try to keep men from creating it through their own efforts. Of course, the present lack of freedom does not apply equally to all. An element of freedom exists when the product is consonant with the interest of the producer. All those who work and even those who don't, have a share in the creation of contemporary reality, but the degree of that consonance varies considerably. Those for whom it is high seem responsible for reality in a sense. They speak of "our" reality, as if they were royalty, and rightly so. For although they did not themselves create the world, one cannot but suspect that they would have made it exactly as it is. It suits them perfectly that the production and preservation of reality in our society proceed blindly. They have every reason to approve of the product of this blind process and therefore support all legends concerning its origin. But for the little man who is turned down when he asks for a job because objective conditions make it impossible, it is most important that their origin be brought to the light of day so that they do not continue being unfavorable to him. Not only his own lack of freedom but that of others as well spells his doom. His interest lies in the Marxist clarification of the concept of freedom.

An Old Story: There once was a rich young man. He was so charming and captivating that everyone liked him. And he was charming not only with his equals but especially with subordinates. When he came to his father's place of business, he chatted delightfully with the employees, and whenever he went shopping, his witty talk put the sales people in good spirits for the rest of the day. His moral sensibility was evident in everything he did. He got engaged to a poor girl, and sympathized with poor artists and intellectuals.

Then his father went bankrupt. There was no change whatever in the exquisite qualities of our prince. When he made his small purchases, he chatted as charmingly as he always had, he kept up his connections with artists, and adored his fiancée. But lo and behold, the sales people became annoyed with him because he took up their time, the artists discovered his lack of any sort of productivity, and even the poor girl found him incompetent and insipid, and finally ran off.

This is an old story and would not be worth repeating if it weren't always misunderstood. For it isn't the prince that remained the same, it isn't the others that changed—that would be the customary and superficial interpretation. It is the others that remained the same while the father's bankruptcy gave the character of our prince an entirely different meaning. A person may suddenly seem stupid, and nothing more need have changed than his bank account.

Our story would become even more pointed and disquieting if the rest of the world had known for some time that the father's business wasn't doing well and only the young man had no inkling of it. In that case, our talented prince would have become a dodo, yet nothing in his consciousness would have altered. That's how dependent we really are.

The Disinterested Striving for Truth: If we wish to test the statement that there is such a thing as pure, disinterested striving for truth, that we have a drive to knowledge which is independent of all other instincts, the following thought experiment should be made: one should abstract from one's love for others, one's thirst for recognition up to and including its most sublime manifestations, one should radically destroy in thought the possibility of any and every kind of desire and thus of any pain or joy, one should imagine a total lack of interest in the fate of society and all its members so that not only no love or hatred, fear or vanity, but not even the tiniest spark of compassion, let alone solidarity, remain. One should, in other words, play the role of the dead that appears as a ghost (although with the difference that one is not only impotent like a ghost but also without any tie to past or present so that one would not even have reason to haunt anyone or anything, and one will discover that under the conditions of the thought experiment, there sets in a disquieting indifference to any sort of knowledge whatever. The world looks as the female body does to the old man whose drives are dead. The claim that there is a disinterested striving for truth and its complement, the lie that there are personalities that are somehow above and beyond society, is a philosophical delusion which has been made ideologically effective. Originally, the bourgeois doctrine of the pure striving for truth may have been proclaimed as the opposite of thought in the service of religious ends. Nowadays, capitalist professors deny that any emotion enters their work. They don't want anyone to find out that they pursue wisdom for the sake of their career.

Although there is no disinterested striving for truth, there is such a thing as thinking for thinking's sake, a ritualized thinking which has lost its purpose, namely as a means to improve people's lives. It should not be confused with the pleasure that lies in the activity of thinking and which enlightening and intensely interested minds feel when historical trends are progressive. The other is the ape of real thinking and cannot claim to be a striving for truth, if only because it has to replace truth by a phantom—absolute, i.e., supernatural truth.

Bourgeois Morality: This bourgeois morality functions extremely well. That a man spends thousands of dollars every day but refuses an employee an increase of twenty is not immoral. But when a revolutionary writer earns a few hundred dollars somewhere and uses the money to have a good time or even derives a regular income from his radical scribbling which at least has a respectable content, and earns more than a craftsman—what a shame, what lack of principles! After war and inflation, German industry is more powerful than ever and the number of its leaders who were killed in action is no greater than that of princes and generals. They kept none of their promises. The horrible decline of the middle-class which we are witnessing even now is a further chapter in the suffering imposed by the ruling clique. The glamor of the people at the top is not immoral, they can lead decent, civilized, religious, ethical lives. But if the few proletarian leaders and functionaries who risk their skin day after day don't die of hunger or at least get themselves killed the next time workers are shot, they are called scoundrels, people who look only to their own advantage. This bourgeois morality works admirably well. Anyone who fights for the liberation of his fellow men may be certain that at the end of his life, he will be judged an exceptionally vain, ambitious, selfish individual, a person with more than his share of human weaknesses. The *chronique scandaleuse* of revolutionaries is the other side of the legends about princes. Bourgeois morality and religion are nowhere as tolerant as when they judge the life of the rich, and nowhere as strict as toward those that want to eliminate poverty.

Revolutionary Theater or "Art Reconciles": As long as for a variety of reasons, the German bourgeoisie still permits oppositional theater after the war, it cannot have a revolutionary effect. It is true, of course, that it reflects the struggles in the real world, and it is not impossible that it may one day help create the atmosphere of action. But that is something the theater has in common with many institutions of bourgeois society.

The reason the theater cannot have a lasting revolutionary effect today is that it turns the problems of the class struggle into objects of shared contemplation and discussion. It thus creates harmony in the esthetic sphere. But proletarian consciousness must break through that harmony; that is one of the principal tasks of political activity. People who wish to liberate themselves from the domination of others and engage in theoretical discussion about this liberation with their rulers have not yet come of age. In theaters or universities, the bourgeoisie is given the chance to consider itself a competent judge of the interests of the proletariat. When it can join the exploited in their indignation at their fate, it affirms its ideological superiority with every burst of applause. Every instance of individual or collective indignation which makes an object of that indignation in confrontation or concert with the authority that is being attacked is still a slavish indignation. The history of contemporary theater and of pseudo-revolutionary plays provide a grotesque confirmation of this state of affairs. Long before conditions in the real world become such that oppositional plays might really pose a danger, the bourgeois theaters stop putting them on. They know why.

Contribution to Characterology: To a very considerable degree, the capacity for work, one's fate or sucess, depend upon the extent to which a person can identify with the powers that be. When he feels at one with existing society and accepts its norms, his career will not be the same as when he merely succeeds in identifying with oppositional groups or, even worse, remains totally isolated spiritually. Because the bases of differences in character lie primarily in childhood, because the decisive events occur within the family, the most important psychic reasons why someone "has his feet on the ground," largely adapts or rebels, will resemble each other as closely in the various epochs of history as do family relationships in class society. In a given case, psychoanalysis can therefore deduce reasoned conclusions about the development of the "character" in question.

But its judgments only deal with the subjective aspects of actions and "character." From its point of view, similar causes may prompt individuals in wholly dissimilar historical periods to identify or not to identify with the social stratum from which they come. This means that similar causes may have made them "social" or "asocial." Psychology cannot differentiate here. But the objective meaning of a life varies with the condition of the collectivity with which someone learns to identify, and this condition does not reveal itself in psychology but through an analysis of the social situation at a given historical moment. The assessment of a person by psychological categories thus deals with only one aspect of his existence and, where history is involved, that aspect is usually irrelevant. The current deplorable custom of dealing with historical personalities merely with the aid of concepts derived from psychology, biology or pathology proves the deliberate indifference to what the historical personality means to the development of mankind. Of course, it is only very provisionally that these two perspectives can be pursued in isolation from each other. Precise knowledge of the historical situation will modify and deepen the psychological insight into individuals that lived in it. Conversely, a historical event cannot be made clear if the psychology of the actors is disregarded. What is decisive in Robespierre's psychology is not only the general question concerning the social role of the Jacobins, but also the special problem of the extent to which his acts benefitted the most progressive stratum of the bourgeoisie. But it is also true that his influence on historical events can only be understood through his instincts and the desires of the masses he led. If someone identified with the society of imperialist tycoons around 1928, or the German capitalism of 1880, or the pre-revolutionary French bourgeoisie of the eighteenth century, if someone today feels at one with the petite bourgeoisie, the hereditary nobility or the proletariat, this may be traceable to quite similar childhood experiences and express similar psychic tendencies. A concept of character which pays no attention to the variety of historical roles of those collectivities and therefore does not differentiate between the characters of those that identify with them because all of them affirm the milieu in which they grew up, would be as empty as a pacifism which condemns both a colonial war and a prison uprising because both are violent.

Of course, in accounts of historical life, the materialist theory of history and psychology do not need each other in the same way. A materialist historiography without adequate psychology lacks something. But psychological historiography is false.

Those Who Have Foundered: Among the varieties of resentment, the impotent bitterness of those that have foundered deserves discussion. A single line connects the senile or merely feeble, moderately well-off pater familias who can no longer adequately perform his many tasks and is therefore treated *en canaille* by his family, the poor old malcontent who once began as a fiery spirit, and the loud-mouthed inmate of a home for the down-and-out. They all began with the idea of world conquest and ended up as pathetic figures. They all rant against the world and society in general, and against their immediate surroundings in particular, and they all make the discovery that their indignation is not taken seriously by others.

But is it really of no consequence? These people whose youthful plans went awry, was it really that they could not match early expectations as closely to experience as did the more competent who not only managed to adapt their plans but their sentiments to reality, a reality to which they are now deeply committed? A serene old age is vitiated by this incapcity to adapt, but doesn't that failure actually provide a certain guarantee of an unclouded judgment? To object that life proved them wrong would be no brighter than the observation that judicial murder refutes the victim's affirmation of his innocence. It would be a foolish application of the maxim that theory must be confirmed by practice, were one to say that individual success in society as it is should serve as the criterion for the correctness of the views of the person that fails. Today, the impotence of those that foundered is not the slightest argument against the objectivity of their judgment, for this society is badly ordered. The person who is wrecked by it has not been judged.

NOTE: The deathbed confession of the heretic does not refute a single sentence of his atheistic beliefs. While still of sound body, many men of reason set down that nothing pain and illness might make them say should be given weight. That the truth of a sentence must be sealed by martyrdom is an age-old and infamous invention of the ruling classes. It turned the fear of methods of repression into an argument against the truth of freer spirits. But only the element of bourgeois slave economy in Socrates which was historically tied to his teaching, only what was ideological in his doctrine may have been responsible for his failure to escape from prison and to ask: What does my life have to do with the correctness of a criticism of conditions in Athens?

NOTE 2: It is a perversion to measure the success of a life by what someone is and has at its end. The relationship between the final condition of a life and the quantity of correct reflection and even of successful acts is totally accidental. It is impossible to infer the whole from the end product. If someone saved a thousand people from drowning and drowned as he saved the thousand and first, one must not conclude: "He couldn't swim for he drowned." For this same reason, death during the very first attempt is no proof either. In our times, it is less his qualities than blind chance that decides what happens to him.

A Different Kind of Criticism: In its symbols, religion places an apparatus at the disposal of tortured men through which they express their suffering and their hope. This is one of its most important functions. A respectable psychology of religion would have to distinguish between its positive and negative aspects, it would have to separate proper human feelings and ideas from an ideological form which falsifies them but which is also partly their product.

Historically, the religious machinery did not always serve to distract from earthly practice; in part, it itself developed the energies which today unmask these distractions. The idea of a justice which is absolutely impartial toward the things of this world is contained in the belief in the resurrection of the dead and the last judgment. If those ideas were to be discarded along with the myth, mankind would be deprived of a propulsive concept which, though certainly not as a belief, might today be applied as a criterion to judge the powers that be, and the church in particular.

The criticism of religion as mere ideology is justified if it reveals that what were previously impulses in religious disguise, such as dissatisfaction with the order on earth, may become effective today in a different form. The life of the revolutionary is such a revelation. But criticism of religion by a bourgeois usually contains none. Instead, it is disquietingly and intimately connected with the blindness to any value except his profit. Bourgeois materialism and positivism were no less the servants of profit interests than conservative idealism which followed in their wake. To the extent that the materialist bourgeois endeavored to talk the masses out of their belief in a Beyond, his age unleashed the economic motive in its place. It could find gratification in this world and he, and sometimes even the masses, benefited from this. That kind of atheism was the world view of a relative prosperity. Now, conservative idealism is inculcating the masses with a belief in the Beyond once again because the economic drive can no longer be satisfied in this world. This is no simple regression to pre-bourgeois religiosity, however, for the Beyond is only one among many, frequently contradictory ideologies within conservative idealism. These days, Christianity is not primarily used as a religion but as a crude transfiguration of existing conditions. The genius of political, military and industry leaders, and especially the nation, compete with God for first place.

The idea of the nation also contains a productive core in perverted form. Since the Enlightenment, the love of nation and country has been the way in which supraindividual, common interests became conscious. It set itself not merely against the narrow egoism of backward members of the bourgeoisie, but especially against the class interests of the aristocracy. Napoleon, not the Bourbons, could put it to good use. In the hands of industrial barons, their allies, the factory owners, the Junkers and their following, the concept of the nation which originally included a sense for the life of the community as a whole has been degraded and become an ideological tool of domination. Just as they use the religious machinery which has been emptied of all meaning and become the embodiment of capitalist morality, so they manipulate the masses with the fetishized name of the nation behind which they hide their own interests. What is true in the case of religion therefore also applies here. Criticism of the nation as a disintegrating symbol is justified if it becomes apparent that impulses previously disguised as nationalist, specifically the feeling of solidarity with the community at large, now become effective in other forms. Bourgeois criticism of nationalism is usually narrow and reactionary. The bourgeois will not uncover the positive core nationalism admittedly lost. The form in which this core is alive today is principally the international solidarity of the exploited.

The criticism of God and country does not become comprehensible unless one looks at its social and historical index. But this is not to be taken too literally. Although such criticism is only imperfectly comprehensible without a historical analysis, it always has a meaning that can be examined. Whether noted by a bourgeois or a proletarian revolutionary, the alliance between the church and the ruling clique, for example, is a fact, and that fact is all the more revolting because it is directed against the one element which might serve the church as an excuse: suffering men.

On the Psychology of Conversations: If a person of modest provenance can for once take part in a conversation between men of rank and prestige, he will have more of a tendency than others to express himself subjectively. Just as father and mother appear as the principal persons in the world when a child talks, so the inferior partner in the conversation also frequently refers to his own private circle. He does not give his view as if it were a statement of fact but introduces his observations by personal comments such as, "It is my opinion . . . I have always felt . . . Just a few days ago, I told my wife . . . My cousin who has such and such a job, told me . . . When I was in the theater the other day. . . ." There is an obvious connection between his remarks and events in his own life.

Whether the more fortunate participants in the conversation know about the social position of their partner or not, they get an embarrassing impression whenever he talks. The personal prelude attenuates the interest in what he has to say. They feel disappointed, his long-windedness is tiresome, something of the odor of cramped quarters attaches to his words. If they were to do likewise, it would not be nearly as awkward, for with growing financial power, the quarters of the rich and cultivated become increasingly the world itself. Their knowledge of the living greats in politics, science and the arts is not third hand. They can discuss them objectively, as parents discuss children, housewives servants, machinists their machines. They know what they are and what they can do. Even their subjective experiences are objectively interesting. Their "I think" and "I have heard" have greater value than the confessions of the less fortunate, merely private person. He would be well advised to remain silent.

The Impotence of the German Working Class: Marx showed that there is a tendency in the capitalist economic process for the number of workers to decrease as more machinery is introduced. An increasingly smaller percentage of the proletariat is really employed. This decrease also modifies the reciprocal relations of the various strata of the proletariat. The more the temporary not to mention the permanent and rewarding employment of an individual becomes the rare exception, the more the life and consciousness of the respectable employed worker will come to differ from those of the regularly unemployed strata. As a consequence, the solidarity of the proletariat, the community of shared interests shrinks more and more. It is certainly true that the working class consisted of multiple layers during earlier phases of capitalism as well, and that there were various forms of the "reserve army." But only the very bottom of these layers, the *lumpenproletariat* properly so called, a relatively insignificant segment from which the criminal element is recruited, was characterized by an obvious qualitative contrast vis-à-vis the proletariat as a whole. Otherwise, there was a steady transition between those who worked and those who didn't. Someone out of work might be hired the next day, and the man who had work was much like his unemployed colleague when he lost it. All the differences affecting the capacity for work, those between skilled and unskilled workers, the sick, the old, children and the healthy did not change the fact that the unity of the working class also expressed itself in the fate of its members. For that reason, they shared not only the interest in the elimination of the rule of capital but also had in common the commitment to this struggle.

Today, the term proletariat for a class which experiences the negative side of the present order, the wretchedness, in its own existence, applies to its components so unevenly that revolution may easily seem an individual concern. For the employed workers whose wages and long-term membership in unions and associations assure a certain, albeit small, security for the future, all political acts involve the danger of a tremendous loss. They, the regularly employed, do not have the same interests as those who even today have nothing to lose but their chains. In our time, the gulf between the employed and those who only work sporadically or not at all is as wide as that between the entire working class and the *lumpenproletariat* at an earlier period. Today, wretchedness weighs even more exclusively on a social stratum whose members society has condemned to utter hopelessness. Work and misery no longer come together, people no longer experience both. This does not mean that the workers are well off, that economic relations change their brutal character toward them, or that the existence of the reserve army no longer depresses wages. Not at all! The misery of the employed continues to be the condition for and basis of this form of society. But the employed worker is no longer typical of those who most urgently need change. Instead, the misery and the restlessness of the existing order bears ever more exclusively on a certain lower segment of the working class, one part of the proletariat. But unlike the pre-war proletariat, these unemployed who are most directly interested in revolution lack the capacities for education and organization, the class consciousness and the dependability of those who are more or less integrated into the capitalist enterprise. This mass wavers, there isn't much to be done with it from an organizational point of view. The younger men who were never part of the work process have faith but no understanding of theory.

The capitalist process of production has thus driven a wedge between the interest in socialism and the human qualities necessary to its implementation. That is the new element. From our present perspective, its development can of course be traced back to the inception of capitalism. Even today, the realization of a socialist order would be better for all proletarians than is capitalism but the difference between the present circumstances of the regularly employed and their personal life under socialism seems less certain, hazier, than the danger of dismissal, misery, penitentiary and death which he can look forward to, were he to participate in a revolutionary uprising or possibly just a strike. The life of the unemployed, on the other hand, is torment. The two revolutionary elements, the direct interest in socialism and a clear theoretical consciousness, are no longer the common property of the proletariat but are now found among different, important segments of it. This is a result of the economic process. In contemporary Germany, it expresses itself through the existence of two workers' parties and the wavering of sizable segments of the unemployed between the Communist and the National-Social-ist parties. It dooms the workers to practical impotence.

The impatience of the unemployed finds theoretical expression in the mere repetition of the slogans of the Communist Party. The quantity of material worked through does not give principles a rele-vant form but leads to their being undialectically preserved. Political practice therefore fails to exploit all available possibilities for strengthening political positions and often exhausts itself in pointless commands or moral reprimands to the disobedient or faithless. The certainty of sinking into the misery of unemployment keeps nearly all who still work from obeying communist strike calls. Even the unemployed become hopeless and resigned as they face the fearful power apparatus which, though no longer a danger for an external enemy, is merely waiting to be used within, anxious to test all weap-ons from truncheon and machine gun to the most effective poison gas in a brisk, certainly riskless civil war. For these reasons, party orders often become meaningless and this cannot fail to have a markedly negative influence on the make-up and condition of its leadership. The disinclination to merely restate fundamentals may therefore have a significance conditions justify, even where that re-fusal extends to remote intellectual spheres, such as sociology and philosophy; it rebels against its own futility.

In contrast to communism, the reformist wing of the workers' movement no longer knows that human conditions cannot be effec-tively improved under capitalism. It has lost its grasp of all theoretical elements, and its leadership is a precise image of the most secure members. Many try with all available means, even the renunciation of ordinary loyalty, to keep their jobs. The fear of losing them gradu-ally becomes the only explanation of their acts. The necessity to suppress what remains of their better consciousness explains the constant readiness of these reformist German politicians to angrily dismiss Marxism as an outdated error. Their hatred of any precise theoretical point of view is greater than that of the bourgeoisie. In contrast to what is of course also an ideological but often truly profound and trenchant bourgeois metaphysics, the cultural trends that reflect their mentality seem to have the single goal of confusing, disintegrating, questioning, discrediting all clear-cut concepts and

views, and painting everything in the same grey of relativism, historicism and sociologism. These ideologues of reformist practical politics
turn out to be the successors of the bourgeois positivism they themselves combatted: they oppose theory and plead for an acceptance of
facts. But because they even relativize our understanding of those
facts and know no absolutes other than this activity of relativizing and
questioning, they strike the outsider as people who merely run everything down. The life of the unemployed is hell, their apathy is the
night, while the present existence of the working population is the
grey everyday. The philosophy that reflects its life therefore seems
impartial and free of illusions. As a way of reconciling itself to the
bad state of affairs, it tends to combine resignation here on earth with
a vague belief in an entirely hazy, transcendental or religious principle. It replaces causal explanation by the search for analogies. To the
extent that it does not wholly reject Marxist concepts, it formalizes
them or makes them academically respectable. The principles of this
late democratic philosophy are as rigid as those of its precursors, yet
so abstract and fragile that their authors have conceived an unre-
quited love for the "concrete," but the concrete discloses itself only
to an interest anchored in practice. To them, the concrete is the
substance they pour into their schematisms. They do not organize
that material by consciously taking sides in the historical struggle, for
they believe they can float above it.

Just as both the positive capacities the worker acquires through his
integration in the capitalist production process, and the entire inhumanity of that process are presently the experiences of different
social groups, so the two elements of the dialectical method—factual
knowledge and clarity concerning fundamentals—do not coexist
among intellectuals of the left, from political functionaries all the way
to the theoreticians of the workers' movement. Loyalty to materialist
doctrine threatens to become a mindless and contentless cult of
literalism and personality unless a radical turn soon occurs. At the
same time, the materialist content, which means knowledge of the
real world, is the possession of those who have become disloyal to
Marxism. It is therefore also about to lose its only distinguishing
characteristic, its existence as knowledge. Without the materialist
principle, facts become blind signs or enter the domain of the ideo-

logical forces that control intellectual life. There are those who recognize existing society as bad, but they lack the knowledge to practically and theoretically prepare the revolution. The others might be able to produce that knowledge but lack the fundamental experience of the urgent need for change. The social democrats therefore have altogether too many reasons for quarreling among themselves. They painstakingly take all circumstances into account, thus pay their respect to truth and objectivity, and shame their ignorant opponents by the multiplicity of possible points of view. The communists don't have enough reasons, in fact they frequently don't advance reasons but refer to authority. Convinced as they are of being the sole possessors of the truth, they are not sticklers for particular truths and use moral and, if necessary, physical force to make their better informed opponents see reason.

To overcome this state of affairs in theoretical questions, good will can do as little as it can toward the elimination of the fragmentation of the working class which underlies it. The economic process which denies employment to a large part of the population from birth on, and dooms it to a hopeless existence, necessarily produces and reproduces it. There is no point in becoming condescending when one notes these intellectual symptoms and to pretend that the person who becomes aware of this condition could escape its consequences. In both parties, there exist some of the forces on which the future of mankind depends.

Atheism and Religion: The complete emancipation from any and every belief in the existence of a power which is independent of history, yet governs it, is a lack that is part of the most primitive intellectual clear-sightedness and truthfulness of modern man. And yet it is enormously difficult to avoid making a new religion of this very absence. As long as the horrors of life and death which prepare the soil of the soul for positive religions have not been reduced by the efforts of a just society, even the spirit free of superstition will seek refuge from its distress in a mood which has something of the reassuring quiet of the temple, though that temple be built in defiance of the gods. In an era where human society is no further advanced than at present, even the most progressive are philistines somewhere in their souls. To the extent that men cannot help themselves, they need fetishes, even if they are those of their wretchedness and desolation.

NOTE: In opposition to the philosophical servants of religion, it should be said that the necessity for creating a religion out of irreligion is a factual, not a logical one. There is no logically compelling reason for replacing the toppled absolute by some other absolute, the toppled gods by others, devotion by denial. Even today, men could forget irreligion. But they are too weak for that.

The Skyscraper: A cross section of today's social structure would have to show the following: At the top, the feuding tycoons of the various capitalist power constellations. Below them, the lesser magnates, the large landowners and the entire staff of important co-workers. Below that, and in various layers, the large numbers of professionals, smaller employees, political stooges, the military and the professors, the engineers and heads of office down to the typists. And even further down what is left of the independent, small existences, craftsmen, grocers, farmers e tutti quanti, then the proletarian, from the most highly paid, skilled workers down to the unskilled and the permanently unemployed, the poor, the aged and the sick. It is only below these that we encounter the actual foundation of misery on which this structure rises, for up to now we have been talking only of the highly developed capitalist countries whose entire existence is based on the horrible exploitation apparatus at work in the partly or wholly colonial territories, i.e., in the far larger part of the world. Extended regions in the Balkans are torture chambers; the mass misery in India, China, Africa boggles the mind. Below the spaces where the coolies of the earth perish by the millions, the indescribable, unimaginable suffering of the animals, the animal hell in human society, would have to be depicted, the sweat, blood, despair of the animals.

We hear a great deal these days about the 'intuition of essence.' Anyone who once "intuited" the "essence" of the skyscraper on whose highest floor our philosophers are allowed to pursue their discussion will no longer be surprised that they know so little about the real height at which they find themselves, and that they always talk only about an imaginary one. Such a person knows, and they may suspect, that otherwise they might become dizzy. He is no longer surprised that they would rather set up a system of values than one of disvalues, that they rather talk about "man in general" than about the concrete individual, about being generally rather than their own. For if they did, they might be punished by being sent to a lower floor. The observer will no longer be surprised that they prattle about the "eternal" for as does the mortar, that prattle holds together this house of present-day mankind. The basement of that house is a slaughterhouse, its roof a cathedral, but from the windows of the upper floors, it affords a really beautiful view of the starry heavens.

The Asceticism of the Rich: The modesty of the rich prompts the following comparison: A dying man who can no longer walk wants to take a final stroll in the garden. Within earshot of the sick man, the uncle explains to the aunt that he himself must work and do without a stroll. The modesty of the rich is infamous, even more infamous than the asceticism of the uncle in our example, for he cannot give the sick his health as a present.

Symbol: A beggar dreamt of a millionaire. When he woke up, he ran into a psychoanalyst who explained to him that the millionaire was a father symbol. "How odd," the beggar answered.

Cain and Abel: The story of Cain and Abel is the mythologized recollection of a revolution, an uprising of the slaves against their masters. The ideologues interpreted it immediately as a product of resentment: "and Cain was very wroth, and his countenance fell."

But if this biblical story were to be taken literally, Cain might have invented that concept when Abel's blood cried to heaven: "Don't listen to that crying, it's just resentment."

The Struggle Against the Bourgeois: In the class struggles of the nineteenth century, the term bourgeois took on the quality of a deadly declaration of war. Bourgeois meant exploiter, bloodsucker, and it was meant to characterize all those who were interested in maintaining the bad social order. Marx has clarified and defined this meaning in all its detail. But following a tradition stemming from romanticism, the profoundly reactionary feudal enemies of capitalism gave the term bourgeois a contemptuous meaning. What has survived of this ideology was absorbed by the nationalist movements in all countries. Much like the pre-war "bohème," they paint the bourgeois as a bugaboo, they contrast the bad bourgeois as a human type of the past epoch, particularly the nineteenth century, with the new man of the future and point out how the biological core, the race, the mode of thought of the one is the diametric opposite of the other.

Big capital has no objection to this second, depreciative meaning of the term where abstraction is made from the economic factor. It uses the aristocratic ideology as readily as aristocratic officers do. Because the modern struggle is directed against the "bourgeois" mentality, it is precisely big capital that is left undiscussed. Those who dispose over it have long since abandoned the life-style at stake in this struggle. Hardly one of the characteristics which defined the small, pedantic, avaricious bourgeois as he struggled for his living during certain periods of the past century applies to the tycoon and his sophisticated, "cosmopolitan" surroundings. Those embarrassing qualities are now found on a lower stratum among dispossessed segments of the middle class that are trying to defend the small enjoyments left them. Good society lives on such an elevated level these days, and its sources of income have so little effect on personality that the forms of consciousness characteristic of petty competition are no longer required. The great bourgeoisie therefore likes to see its ideologues launch this charge against the bourgeois whom it actually destroys through the concentration of capital.

Proletarians have nothing to do with this struggle against the "bourgeois." When the economic type which today is being exterminated by capital was in control, they necessarily saw him as their principal enemy. Except where they become nationalist guards today, these lower classes must be neutralized or pulled along. In proletarian parlance, the bourgeois continues to be the exploiter, the ruling class. In the realm of theory, the struggle is also primarily directed against this class with which there can be no solidarity. When modern metaphysicians attempt a sociological critique of the history of philosophy as the development of "bourgeois" thought, they are not concerned with those aspects of that class which the proletariat has to overcome. These ideologues only want to stigmatize and eradicate the theoretical vestiges of the revolutionary epoch of the bourgeoisie. Nor does the proletariat have the same reasons as capital to approve of the decline of the middle class. Capital is concerned with profit, the proletariat with the liberation of mankind. We have no use for a terminology for which bourgeois life expresses itself in the petite bourgeoisie who is bored and jealous of her husband, but not in the ownership of a Rolls-Royce.

Education to Truthfulness: The Catholic clergy has always tended not to take people too seriously to task for the heretical ideas they might have, provided they kept them to themselves or revealed them only to their father confessor. Our bourgeois morality is stricter: if someone harbors revolutionary ideas, he must at least express them even when or precisely when it is pointless, so that he can then be persecuted on their account. Not his friends but his enemies have the right instincts when they pose as the prophets of revolutionary courage.

It is not that they are concerned with those ideas, for they think they are wrong. But they insist that a person "show the courage of his convictions," as they put it. This sadistic pedantry has two causes: the desire of its declared enemy that the revolution be exterminated root and branch, and the envy the person who seemingly sympathizes with it feels for someone who has the courage to continue thinking as he always did while he himself represses such thoughts for the sake of his career. Bourgeois morality is like a schoolmaster who not only thrashes bad boys when they misbehave but also demands that they raise their hand when the mere thought that they might shoots through their heads. Education to truthfulness indeed! The thoughts that are locked up in the heads are themselves a forbidden pleasure the good child denies himself. They may also mature in those heads and break out at a moment where the schoolmaster would find it difficult to control them with his cane.

Value of the Human Being: In the capitalist economy, it is only in the market place that a person discovers the value of the goods he produced. It is not his own estimate but the anonymous exchange mechanism of the society that decides. Goods that do not find a taker are junk. The same is true of one's relations to others. What someone is worth is determined through the anonymous machinery of society. It must be added, of course, that birth is an important factor. It is an analogy to patent and monopoly. But as in the case of goods, one's way with others is not decided by private fiat but their market value, i.e., the social success due to birth or abilities. Besides that success, there are a person's prospects. Society, not the individual, places values on things. Or rather, the individual's valuations are determined by society. This goes so far that in small enterprises, the boss respects his own employees less than those of his competitor. Or at least he becomes unsure of himself where the control mechanism by which society evaluates individuals no longer clearly finds in his employee's favor. For merchandise may lose value from one moment to the next.

This does not mean that I, as a poor employee or a physician without patients, may not enjoy a modest measure of respect within a small circle. This respect is largely a result of the conviction that I have socially valuable qualities and that it is merely certain fortuitous events which impaired their effectiveness and development. In the background, the secret orientation by the productive process of capitalist society enters into the estimate. That a person failed can only be excused by the belief that he might have succeeded. There is a secret, fixed, frequently unconscious but deeply rooted concept of justice and authority in capitalist society. It governs the most intimate relationship and constitutes a common mentality that extends from the right wing to the socialist bureaucracy.

Strindberg's Women: In Strindberg's theater, the woman appears as an evil, domineering and vengeful creature. This image clearly derives from the experience of a man who was impotent in normal sexual intercourse, for it is in such a context that the women Strindberg portrays develop. His view is an example of bourgeois superficiality. Instead of getting to the bottom of things, it prefers to ascribe everything to nature or, rather, to an unchanging character.

To cite man's impotence as the underlying cause of woman's viciousness as Strindberg understands it would of course be committing the same kind of mistake as Strindberg himself, for both impotence and the judgment that normal intercourse is the proper form sexual desire should take are social products. The man's inability to perform the sexual act the woman desires, and which he himself acknowledges as the measure of his value as a male, results from the fact that he was either already worn out before marriage or requires other forms of satisfaction. Like any derogatory judgment about it, that inability can be explained by the history of society and his fate within it. Strindberg furnished an accurate portrayal of the bad woman, the impotent man, the hell they live through at a particular historical moment, but he interpreted conditions as biological and therefore unchanging, which means he did not understand them. The more "superficial" Ibsen is superior to him because he consciously established a connection between marital problems and a transitory family form, and thereby with history.

Power, Right, Justice: "Might before right" is a misleading proverb, for power need not compete with the law; the law is its attribute. Power has the law on its side, whereas powerlessness needs it. To the extent that power is unable to grant or refuse a right, it is itself limited though certainly not by the law but by other powers which restrict its scope. This constellation is obscured because as a convention between powers in the bourgeois state, the law seems to live a life of its own, especially when a bureaucracy that is relatively neutral vis-à-vis the various bourgeois parties administers it. But how things really are becomes apparent the moment the ruling elements, or rather the groups within the ruling class, are of one mind, i.e., when the proletariat is the enemy. Quite independently of its formulations, the effect of the law then becomes the precise expression of the extent of their power. If the anecdote about the miller of Sans Souci were not a lie, he would ultimately have owed his success to the king's grace or the power of the bourgeoisie, not to the law itself.*

The story of the miller of Sans Souci, though apocryphal, is well known to every German schoolboy. It tells of a miller who refused to turn his property over to Frederick the Great for the building of his castle, Sans Souci. He cited the law in his defense, and won. The moral of the story is that there is one law for commoner and king alike.—*Transl.*

This is true of positive law. But the concept of justice epitomizes the demands of the suppressed at any given moment, and it is therefore as changeable as those demands themselves. Its essence today ultimately calls for the elimination of classes and therefore also the abolition of the law as set forth above. With the advent of justice, the law disappears.

Love and Stupidity: The pleasure the animal trainer takes in the affection of a lion may sometimes be attenuated by the realization that the stupidity of the beast has a good deal to do with it. Because a heightened consciousness of its power would destroy the tie, the animal's present tenderness isn't worth much. The more reason the trainer has to think highly of his art, the less he need feel flattered by the affection of the lion. We don't like it when we are loved from a lack of intelligence. The pride many fine ladies and gentlemen take in the loyalty of their servants, or the Junker in their workers', caricatures the confidence we feel because we know we are genuinely loved.

Indications: The moral character of a person can be infallibly inferred from his answers to certain questions. Such questions vary with each era and usually with each social class, and do not always concern matters of the same moment. What an official in certain parts of the Roman Empire during the first few centuries of our era said when asked if he was a Christian was certainly such a key. In the Germany of 1917, the mere question about the quality of the potato bread was equally revelatory. In 1930, the attitude toward Russia casts light on people's thinking. It is extremely difficult to say what conditions are like there. I do not claim to know where the country is going; there is undoubtedly much misery. But those among the educated who don't even perceive a hint of the effort being made there, adopt a cavalier attitude and dismiss the need to reflect, are pathetic comrades. Their company is unprofitable. The senseless injustice of the imperialist world can certainly not be explained by technological inadequacy. Anyone who has the eyes to see will view events in Russia as the continuing painful attempt to overcome this terrible social injustice. At the very least, he will ask with a throbbing heart whether it is still under way. If appearances were to be against it, he would cling to his hope like the cancer patient to the questionable report that a cure for his illness may have been found.

When Kant received the first news about the French Revolution, he is said to have changed the direction of his customary stroll from then on. The philosophers of our time also scent the dawn of a new day, though it is not for mankind but for the horrible spirit realm of their metaphysics.

On the Question of Birth: Who has not at some time considered the moral question whether or not it may be a good thing to have children, and who did not answer: "It all depends." "It all depends" means that a wealthy woman's child will some day employ others. In the case of the poor woman, it will be someone who can't even get work. So poor people should be careful, the Malthusian philosopher concludes. But this thought goes astray. Instead of keeping millions of unwanted out of the world, they should be permitted to fit it out. Of course, as long as the work the rich won't give may also not be performed by the poor, they have to stay away. The world is the house of the ruling class. They don't let in the carpenters who want to make it bigger and brighter. It follows that their property rights are outdated.

Note: It might appear contradictory that during the last hundred years, it was usually precisely those who claimed that mankind could not be more justly and more adequately provided for that urged the poor to restrict sexual intercourse, that recommended *moral* prevention, i.e., ascesis, but bitterly fought birth prevention techniques and abortion. But there is only a contradiction here if it is man's well-being that really counts. Those loyal servants of capital see only the need to preserve existing conditions, however, and recognize instinctively that pleasure for its own sake, pleasure without justification and excuse and without a moral or religious rationalization is a still greater danger to this obstructive society than even an increase in the army of the unemployed.

Socialism and Resentment: Those who look down on the motives that tend toward the realization of freedom and justice, and confuse and discourage the persons inspired by them, have remarkable success.

In discussions concerning the possibility of socialism, the well-

informed opponent often tells his partner, an enthusiastic supporter
of socialism, that he should first examine how things really are. He
would then come to the conclusion that under socialism, the worker
would be no better off than he is today. Certainly the civilized worker
in this generation would probably be much worse off than he is, he
would never get anything but beans to eat. Perhaps the superior
opponent will illustrate his opinion by telling the infamous joke about
the Baron Rothschild who gave the socialist a coin and told him: "Be
satisfied with this, that's much more than you would get if everything
were divided up."

If the younger partner to the discussion has some Marxist training,
he will point out that socialists aren't interested in distribution but
in the socialization and restructuring of the process of production.
Perhaps he will also give a theoretical exposition. But he may say that
distribution would at least bring justice, and if he does, he is lost. For
now he has revealed the vulgarity of his views, a thinking laden with
resentment. So what he really wants, he will be told, is not material
improvement! He only wants those who are reasonably well off today
not to have *more* than he does. His arguments merely serve to mask
his hatred. It's all right to eat nothing but beans all one's life, provided the others don't have steak! The young socialist will be embarrassed by this reproach and accept it silently; perhaps he will defend
himself. He is confused. He cannot deal with the general contempt
of the will to freedom and justice when it is called resentment.

But the harmless steak which this forbidden attitude begrudges
others is a symbol of the power over men, of independence riding on
misery's back. The danger, the suffering, the constraint, the narrowness, the insecurity, the convergence of these negative elements of
life on the exploited class is today a result of the convergence of the
positive elements on the absurdly small number of the free. In school-
books, the bourgeoisie tells of the idealism of heroes who prefer death
to slavery, but vis-à-vis socialism, it is materialistic enough to counter
the impulse to shake off the yoke, to eliminate inequality, by pointing
out that material improvement is improbable. Love of freedom is
cultivated only in the mendacious form of nationalist chauvinism. It
is true that the Versailles Treaty causes unnecessary suffering, but in
Germany it is most vociferously indicted by those who remorselessly

preserve the capitalist property relations that make it possible. This order where the children of the proletariat are condemned to die of starvation, and members of the board to banquets, does indeed arouse resentment.

The Urbanity of Language: The very nature of language is to create ties, to establish community, to be urbane. To give verbal expression to an animosity is the first step toward surmounting it. It becomes possible to discuss causes, to consider mitigating factors. Through its universality, language seems to make the motive for the animosity a problem for all. It questions its justification.

In post-war Germany, the translation of Marxism into the academic idiom was a step toward breaking the will of the workers to fight capitalism. As the qualified intellectual representatives of mankind, the professors took up the problem. Of course, this translation was only one step, for since there are much more realistic causes for the fatigue and impotence of the worker, this mediating literature is no longer needed, and those translators will be rejected just as the mediators in the political arena are. The concept of ideology illustrates the function of translation with particular clarity. One can hardly say that Marx discussed it in great detail. He used it as a kind of subterrenean explosive device against the mendacious structures of official science. It was the distilled expression of his contempt for the deliberate or half-deliberate, instinctive or considered, paid or unpaid obfuscation of the exploitation on which the capitalist system rests. Now they have given it a pretty formulation. It has become the relativity of knowledge, the historicity of theories in the humanities, and other things. It has lost its dangerousness.

But the light of language is indispensable in the struggle of the oppressed themselves. They have reasons for bringing the secrets of this society to the light of day, to give them the most comprehensible, the most banal formulation possible. They must not stop expressing the contradictions of this order in public language. The spreading of darkness has always been a technique of the right. Language must therefore be prevented from creating the illusion of a community that does not exist in class society. It has to be used as a means in the struggle for a united world. Already today, the words of the fighters and martyrs of that struggle seem to be coming from that world.

The Personal Element: Even in the future, personal qualities will of course make a difference in the careers of people. But I can imagine a society where a young man's voice or a girl's nose do not have a decisive influence on the happiness of their lives.

Social Space: To recognize the space in which one finds oneself, one must discover its limits. At night, when we cannot scan the walls of the room we enter, we have to walk along them and touch them with our hands. That's how we learn whether it is a salon with silken tapestry and large windows or a prison with stone walls and an iron door.

As long as someone stays at the center of society, i.e., as long as he occupies a respected position and does not come into conflict with society, he does not discover what it really is. The further he moves away from that secure center because his means, his knowledge, his relations either dwindle or are lost—and it is largely irrelevant whether that happens through his own fault or not—he finds that this society is based on the total negation of all human values. The way the police occasionally treat the workers during an uprising or beat the imprisoned unemployed with the butts of their rifles, the tone the factory porter uses with the man looking for work, the workhouse and the penitentiary, all these function as the limits that disclose the space in which we live. The more central positions can be understood through the more peripheral ones. The offices of a prosperous factory can only be understood when one looks at the workplace of the temporary employees during times of rationalization and crisis, and this workroom where it is a grace to be allowed to work oneself to the bone can only be explained by recourse to armed might. Whether he becomes aware of it or not, all these elements are part of the vague worry of the employee and set the tone of his life. The order which makes it possible that he may slip from his position into misery is ultimately held together by grenades and poison gas. Between the furrowed brow of his superior and the machine guns, there exists a series of continuous transitions each of which derives its weight from the latter.

Not only the nature of society but also that of the individuals within it is usually only seen from the outside. What underlies the life of an intelligent woman is nothing one discovers during a visit to her drawing room but only when one looks in on the unemployed. The being of the former lies not only in the depths of her soul but also in those of mankind, and in the fragrance of her most charming thoughts, in the discreet perfume of her interior, there is still a whiff of the stench of the daily garbage collection at the penitentiary which helps preserve this order that has gone bad. Even this lady is not protected from those powers which today stand guard at the borders of the whole even though those powers, of which she may be quite ignorant, serve her today. All that has to happen is that her husband buys the wrong stocks.

A Fairy Tale About Consistency: There once were two poor poets. They had already starved during good times but now, when times were bad and a wild tyrant was sacking town and country because he needed money for his court, and cruelly suppressed all resistance, they were about to go to wreck and ruin. Then the tyrant heard something about their talent, invited them to his table and promised both a considerable pension because their witty talk had amused him.

On the way back, one of them reflected on the injustice of the tyrant and repeated the well-known complaints of the people. "You are inconsistent," the other answered. "If that's the way you think, you are obliged to go on starving. If someone feels at one with the poor, he must live like them." His comrade became thoughtful, agreed and turned down the king's pension. He finally perished. The other was named court poet after a few weeks. Both had drawn their conclusions, and both conclusions benefited the tyrant. There is something special about the general moral precept that one be consistent: it favors the tyrant, not the poor poet.

Confession: Nowadays, man becomes the object of the churches when he is totally helpless: in poorhouses, in hospital wards, in prisons. In the sunnier spheres of society, people hardly suspect what figures of the past still live down there, how busy they are and what power they have. Once out of school, only poor devils are asked about their "religious affiliation." They have to know where they belong. In cemeteries also, the dead are grouped according to religious belief. It is a classification of passive masses: human material. In a newspaper report, the term 'parity' was printed in bold type. I did not know what had been distributed evenly and thought it was dividends. Then I read "home for the physically disabled" in the next line and realized immediately that the reference was to distribution according to religious affiliation—the distribution of poor cripples. What a decline since the times of the Thirty Years' War! In those days, people were crippled in the name of two religions. Today, both of them are pleased when they may participate in the medical effort.

The "Unfortunately" Stabilized Capitalism: Though bourgeois intellectuals may be knowledgeable in all aspects of revolutionary theory, they lack expertise in questions relating to the time revolution will break out. This time depends upon the will of men. But that will is not the same in one who leads the life of the intellect in the present society, and one to whom everything is denied and who finally perishes because of it. Whenever during these years 1927 and 1928 "literary radicals" told me that capitalism had once again stabilized for the foreseeable future, they were never as downcast as when they related some personal misfortune. I believe I have discovered that the consciousness of showing a praiseworthy equanimity and an admirable farsightedness as he takes note of this stability functions as a rather important compensation for the speaker. There are so many compensations available to us—and their number increases with the seize of our income.

In the Service of Business: There is a theory that as board chairmen pile up profits these days, they are actually benefiting mankind. This hoax shows up in even the most insignificant details in the lives of these fine people. Just look at their weightiness as they go to a "meeting," or listen to the tone they use to assure someone that there are still matters "to be attended to." How profoundly justified they feel as they stride into the first-class sleeping car when they make business trips. The importance of their deals even confers a touch of equitableness, of just reward on the "little distractions," the holidays, these hardworking fellows permit themselves once a year. They are necessary breathing spells and actually serve the public interest. But the truth of the matter is that every one of these people can only make a good life for himself, keep an elegant wife and handsome children, and satisfy his every desire because others are miserable and wretched and do gruelling and stupefying work. What a lie, the claim that these private aspects of the lives of entrepreneurs are of no moment! It is mere invention to maintain that beyond a certain degree of wealth, the capitalist no longer piles up money for his own consumption. It does, of course, make a difference whether he has ten or twenty million, for the increasing size of the fortune means an ever greater availability of pleasures on all levels. Wealth as the prerequisite of power, independence, gratification is the reason the giant machinery for the preservation of injustice and misery, colonial horrors and penitentiaries functions. So the personal satisfaction of these gentlemen is an inconsequential matter? If so, the existence of imperialist society for the sake of these trivia becomes all the more revolting.

The "importance," the "public interest", "the service in a cause," the indispensability of their "activity" with which they dress up every step they take, this whole obtrusive set of circumstances, is somewhat reminiscent of the naive image of the primitive medicine man who makes solemn gestures as he devours the lion's share of the loot, except that this modern magic is infinitely more of a sham.

Humanity: The great Bacon made it the physician's duty to fight the tortures of illness not only when alleviation restores health, but also "to make it possible for the sick person to die a gentle and peaceful death if there is no more hope." But up to now, that duty only went as far as the belief that its neglect might have to be dearly paid for. From the poor man who is unprotected by any power, the duty of the powerful withdraws into the dark spaces where he settles things only with his Maker, and on his deathbed, the rich will resemble the poor in many respects if his death is certain. With death, he loses his connections, and becomes nothing. The proudest kings of France were not spared that experience. To the extent that the enlightened physician does not act from economic or technical interests but from compassion, and tries to help the man that dies in solitude during the hours of his final need, he is the citizen of a future society. This situation is the present image of a real humanity.

Difficulties in Reading Goethe: "Who never ate his bread in tears,/who never sat crying on his bed throughout grievous nights, does not know you, you heavenly powers." Of the poem in which this stanza occurs, Goethe himself said that its effect would be eternal because "a most perfect, adored queen . . . derived a painful consolation" from it. The implicit premise for this consolation and for the truth of the stanza is that these individuals also spend nights and days which are not grievous. The premise is a sunny life on the heights of human existence where grief is so rare that it takes on a noble glow. It is that which makes it difficult to appreciate Goethe today.

Money Excites: (A Berlin aphorism): For a married man, the love of his wife is a beautiful thing. But nothing slackens a woman's love like the impotence of her husband. Perhaps there have been times when this lack was an irremediable evil, fate. That's no longer true today: sexual potency has its equivalent. If a woman suffers from her husband's fatigue, let him travel to the most beautiful place on earth, take a suite in the best hotel and prove his potency by the amount of money he spends. Money excites; it also makes exciting. Just as the consequences of sexual impotence at home are the same as those of a poor income, petty, wearing quarrels, it is equally true that economic power can take the place of sexual potency. Of course, our present society distributes this equivalent as blindly as nature does those inborn capacities which that equivalent can largely replace.

The Abandoned Girl: Vulgar common sense readily points to the "eternally" recurring situations of the human condition. Birth, love, suffering and death, for example, are allegedly not affected by the course of history. But the moment concrete instances of these situations are discussed, this ideologically useful assertion reduces itself to its abstract and vapid content. No image is more relevant here than that of the abandoned girl, for this seems to be a motif which has been present throughout time and in all kinds of languages and costumes, from the primitive tribes via Faust's Gretchen to the tragedy of the small employee. But that isn't the case. Quite apart from the fact that due to conditions in a number of cultures, the "abandoned girl" is really out of place there, its image in our time is generally confined to the declining class of the petite bourgeoisie. Among its necessary conditions are the chance of achieving economic security through marriage, the contempt for children born out of wedlock, and the parochical education of girls. When these conditions no longer exist, all that remains of that "eternal situation" is an impaired female narcissism that can also be found in many other circumstances, but nothing of Gretchen's tragedy. Nowadays, the counterpart to that situation, the fate of the young unemployed whose salaried girlfriend leaves him, is beginning to become typical, and the vanishing figure of the "abandoned girl" no longer has a place except in socially backward strata.

Among the upper bourgeoisie, it can hardly be found any longer. If we assume relatively informed parents, the abandonment of the millionaire's daughter seems a *quantité negligeable.* The ladies of that bourgoisie have a taste for great and risky erotic situations from which their social position protects them, but in French novels of the nineteenth century, in Balzac and Stendhal, their less fortunate sisters from the petite bourgeoisie still experienced their reality.

Once they are gone, of course, the remembrance of figures such as the "abandoned girl" may abruptly illuminate the entire social space, or rather the social inferno whose symbols they are.

NOTE: The disappearance of many other such "eternal" situations from society as a whole is foreshadowed in the life of the grande bourgeoisie. Their comical complaints about the "impoverishment" and "disenchantment" of life have their grotesque justification here. One need only think of the "poor" rich youth: while the young proletarian and petit bourgeois have abundant opportunities to get to know the "eternal" feeling, the "universal human" feeling of longing for the distant beloved, the former not only has car and airplane but can take his inamorata wherever he goes. He thus has to make do without fully savoring that human experience.

Right of Asylum: Sooner or later, the right of asylum for political refugees will be eliminated in practice. It does not fit into the present. When bourgeois ideology still took liberty and equality seriously, and the unhampered development of all individuals still seemed to be the purpose of politics, the political refugee was also inviolate. The modern right of asylum was part of the struggle of the third estate against absolutism, it rested on the solidarity of the western European bourgeoisie and its counterpart in less developed states. Today, capital is concentrated in a few hands, and although internally at odds, it faces the proletariat as the solidary and reactionary world power. The right of asylum therefore becomes increasingly bothersome. It is outdated. Where Europe's political boundaries do not define the conflicting spheres of interest of hostile, multinational economic groups, they function almost exclusively as a general ideological means of domination and a propaganda device of the armaments industry. Except for refugees from Russia or right wing terrorists, the right of asylum will disappear before the common interests of the international capitalist class. But should someone raise his hand against the monster of cartel capitalism, he will no longer find a place to hide from the claws of power.

Bad Superiors: For someone to conduct himself freely and matter-of-factly as a superior or boss vis-à-vis employees and workers, to act as he should, he must feel that the relationship between himself and those that depend on him is natural. If it becomes problematical for him, he will be hampered and the subordinates will quickly notice that he is not really fit to be in charge. His implicit belief that there is no good reason why the others should be less well off than he will indicate to them that something is amiss in this superior-subordinate relationship. Work suffers as a result. For people to function as good workers, the person in charge of them must express instinctively and by his entire manner that this relationship is both immutable and appropriate. But the superior who is conscious of the irrationality of this relation of dependence in today's world, and aware of its origin in an outdated class society, the man who understands his own role as a partner in exploitation, will justifiably be seen as unsure and constrained. The psychoanalyst would say that he shows guilt feelings and resultant aggressive tendencies. And he does in fact differ from his healthier colleague in the sense that he is aware of the aggressive element in his existence.

There are wives and daughters of great entrepreneurs who visit their husbands or fathers in their offices and even inspect the factory, yet suffer no loss of their poise whatever. For those among them who fear the merest hint of an inhibition, an excellent remedy has now been found: they also have taken jobs. With perfect assurance, the lady can now shake hands with the typist whose father is unemployed and who may herself be fired tomorrow. She can even be "friendly" with her. "I also type half-days now. I am in my uncle's office. I have nothing but contempt for people who don't work."

Freedom in personal relations is a beautiful thing. Capitalism is absolutely right when it proscribes inhibition and lack of assurance. Not only the relations of superior and subordinate but also those of the worker to his boss, the servant to his master and, conversely, the lady to her maid, the poor writer to the banker, the laundry woman to the golf hero, the public health official to the inmate of a poorhouse—all these relationships should bear the stamp of good cheer and matter-of-factness. If people of different classes talk to each other and shake hands, how can one not have the distinct impression that everything is as it should be.

Whoever Doesn't Want to Work Shouldn't Eat: This biblical pronouncement is a popular maxim. It should say: Everyone should eat, and work as little as possible. But even that is much too general. To make work the most important human activity is an ascetic ideology. How harmonious society looks when everyone "works," irrespective of differences in rank and wealth. Because the socialists retain this general concept, they become the instruments of capitalist propaganda. Actually, the "work" of a cartel director, the small entrepreneur and the unskilled worker are just as different from each other as power differs from worry and hunger.

The proletarians demand that work be reduced. This does not mean that in a future, better society, a person should be prevented from being as active as he pleases. Instead, the goal is to rationalize the activities life in society requires, and to distribute them evenly.

Compulsion, not freedom, suffering, not pleasure, are to be curbed. In a rational society, the concept of work changes.

But today, "those that don't want to work shouldn't eat" is secretly no longer meant to define the future but the present. The sentence transfigures the existing order: it justifies the capitalist. He works. But it damns the poorest, for they don't. Everywhere, the bourgeois manages to reconcile an originally revolutionary thought of his own making, and which the socialists retain as a general maxim, with the reactionary morality of the ruling class. But the phrase envisages a future society, and what should be infered from it now is not the sanctification of work but the struggle against its present form.

The Impotence of Renunciation: If you are no good at political activity, it would be foolish to believe that it might mean something if you turn your back on the general machinery of exploitation. Your refusal to continue to profit from the large-scale torture inflicted on man and beast, your resolve to renounce comfort and security, will spare no human being, no animal, any suffering. Nor should you hope that enough people will imitate you. In recent history, the propaganda of personal renunciation, of individual purity, has always been used by the powerful to keep their victims from doing something more dangerous. It has degenerated into sectarianism. The progressive reduction of misery is the result of long, world-historical struggles whose phases are defined by successful and unsuccessful revolutions. Every success involves the danger of terrible reversals, of new barbarism, of heightened suffering. It is not compassion but intelligence, courage, organizational skill that enable one to participate here. If you lack those qualities, you can do nothing for society.

But insight into the ineffectiveness of personal renunciation does not justify the opposite: participation in suppression. It merely means that your personal purity is irrelevant to real change: the ruling class will not join you. It is possible, however, that though there are no rational grounds, you may no longer enjoy being in league with the henchmen. You may turn down some harmless old man's invitation to a springtime excursion because in the penitentiaries of his class, an old man of the same age is refused a pardon after thirty years of hard labor because he cannot find work on the outside and would merely become a public burden. Perhaps the day will come when you simply no longer derive pleasure from taking a walk on the roof garden of the company building, although it is of little moment that you come down from there.

The Good Old Times: The attack on capitalism is always subject to the misunderstanding that it implicitly defends by-gone ages. But this need not be the case. To determine the happiness and misery of various epochs is a matter of historical research. It is likely that periods of a relatively peaceful and productive collaboration of all parts of society have been rare and of short duration, for with few exceptions, the pressure the ruling class brough to bear on the community was extremely cruel throughout the known course of history. Whoever had the courage to attack power at a sensitive spot always had to expect the loss of freedom, honor and life. And he probably also brought ruin on those close to him: his wife, his children, his friends. A veil always covered the viciousness by which power sustained itself. Those who attempted to tear it were doomed.

Present-day capitalism has this oppression in common with earlier forms of society. Although periods of decline when culture became a chain were always preceded by an epoch of upward movement and bloom, the history of the masses is largely one of suffering. The bad aspects of capitalism connect it to the past. Its art may be inferior, but it competes with it in lying and cruelty. Its significant civilizing achievements, on the other hand, point to the future. The theory of relativity and pneumothorax were discovered in our days, the hell of Guiana is the legacy of our fathers.

Transformation of Morality: Some radical writers get along without theory. They think that if they portray reality in its horror by simply enumerating the *faits divers* they cull from magazines, by the listing of crude details or by directing aunts at the low cultural standards of the rich, they have done all that is necessary. Their accounts always seems to carry the caption: "comment superfluous." They know little of the process of transformation ideology is subject to, and think that even today, injustice constitutes an argument *against* something. They tacitly accept the hoax of past decades that everything is harmony, that conflicting material interests notwith-

standing, a common consciousness unites mankind. Instead of being
in the forefront of the fight for a new reality, they become the apes
of an old ideology. An imperialist bourgeoisie has long since divested
itself of the morality to which they make their appeal. Except where
it has already been possible to imbue them with the new moral ideas,
that morality may today be that of the exploited. But those moral
ideas transfigure brutality.

Responsibility: People always say: look at the enormous responsibility weighing on this or that powerful man, look at all the things
that depend on him, at all the things he must keep in mind! Compassion with and admiration for the poor rich goes so far that people are
almost pleased not to be in their shoes. "Enjoy what God gave you,
do gladly without the things you don't have. Every class has its peace;
every class carries its burden." Don't the powerful have even less
peace, don't they carry even greater burdens than the little fellow
who can at least enjoy a relatively carefree time with wife and child
when his work is done?

Cum grano salis, this may once have been true, but I don't believe
it, and it is certainly a hoax today. If a person's responsibility means
that not merely others depend on him but that he may experience
the results of his acts in his own life, then the little people bear an
infinitely greater burden than the powerful. An act of negligence
which will quickly lead to the dismissal of an employee will also ruin
his family. Every day, he has countless opportunities for making
mistakes which may have a catastrophic effect on his and his family's
fate. But how insignificant are such chances in the case of the magnate. Even if he should make a wrong decision, it will only rarely
appear as a clear-cut instance of stupidity or carelessness, and frequently will benefit from the "blessing of revocability." It will hardly
have an effect on the persons he loves. There are a thousand ways of
making up for it. Besides, when things don't go right, i.e., when the
likelihood of further errors increases, he can stop temporarily. Others
will take his place, and their quality will increase with the size of his
capital. Even if he should withdraw from business altogether, this
need not be a disadvantage to him. With increasing wealth, it is not
worry and responsibility but the power over others that grows. In

capitalist society, the former increase in direct proportion to power-lessness and dependence on capital.

During the days of mobilization and the declaration of war, masses of people gathered at night before the palaces of princes and minis-ters. Respectfully, they looked up at the lit-up windows. "What burdens of thought these representatives of the world spirit must be carrying." Even in those days, I was thinking of the more concrete worries in the apartments of the proletariat from which the 'heroes' were to come. And what happened after the war which those repre-sentatives had unleashed? The heroes were dead but the great around whose interests the war had really revolved gained immeasurably, even in Germany. Where is there any evidence of their "responsibil-ity?" Before God, the Lord. But the crippled little volunteer discovers day after day that his parents had reason to fear to let him go, for he might have preserved them from their present wretchedness and humiliation. He carries his responsibility in the real world.

Religion maintains that the capitalist masters are responsible for their acts in war and peace—the responsibility of the exploited shows up in life here on earth.

The Freedom of Moral Choice: In Richard Wagner's work, the characters that profess Schopenhauerian morality, renunciation through compassion, are strong and powerful before their conversion. Wagner wants to preclude the misunderstanding that his heroes convert from weakness, for what is the value of an individual's com-passion if he is incapable of pugnacity. As is well known, the God of the Christians also takes greater pleasure in a repentant sinner than in a thousand just. Buddha was the son of a king—there would have been nothing remarkable in a pariah's leading an ascetic life. He has nothing to eat. Buddha was quite consistent when he kept the lower castes away from the community of monks at first. Translated into the terms of bourgeois society, all of this means that the chance for being moral is a variable that depends on social position. The person that belongs to the wretched is excluded from the problem of moral-ity in a two-fold way. To begin with, there can be no question of his identifying with suffering. For him, the "tat twam asi" as he faces the suffering creature is no "insight," it is a fact. But confronted with

the wealthy, the reverse maxim holds for the poor: that isn't you! In
addition, he has nothing he could do without. Morality and character
are thus largely monopolies of the ruling class. Its members have a
wider freedom of moral choice than the poor.

The Pleasures Taken in Work: If I know that someone likes or
dislikes working, I don't know anything about him. A stenographer
who enthusiastically spends ten hours taking down business letters
that are of no concern to her, a bookkeeper or an assembly line
worker, is not a congenial individual if he does his work because he
enjoys it and not for less obvious reasons. An intellectual or someone
who is independent and can change around belongs to the elect.
There are times when entrepreneurs spend longer hours in their
offices than the greater number of their employees. This happens
during particularly taxing periods, as when profits are calculated, for
example. Then the boss will say: "the employees don't enjoy their
work. I can't understand it. I could work all night long without
getting tired." As regards the entrepreneur, this attitude holds not
only during exceptional periods but really all year long. The employees know what their bosses are talking about.
   NOTE: In a socialist society, pleasure will not derive from the nature
of the work to be done. That is a reactionary aim. Rather, work will
be done with enjoyment because it serves a solidary society.

Europe and Christianity: The gulf between the moral criteria
Europeans have acknowledged since the advent of Christianity, and
their real conduct, is immeasurable.
   It goes without saying that, provided it profits it, there is no infamy
which will not be presented as moral by the ruling class. From the
killing of millions of young men in war to the most infamous murder
of the political opponent, there is no villany which could not be
reconciled with the public conscience. Apart from the most progressive groups, the oppressed classes imitate the mendacity of their
models. This may be difficult to understand but is a fairly well-known
fact nonetheless. For their dependence stems not just from not being
given enough to eat, but that they are also kept in a wretched

intellectual and psychological state. They are the apes of their wardens, worship the symbols of their prison and, far from attacking their guardians, stand ready to tear to pieces the person that undertakes to free them from their tutelage.

All this is known, so well known, in fact, that one might almost give in to the pervasive suggestion that repeated mention of this state of affairs seems even more tasteless than its endless duration. The critical rule that what is known should not be restated too often has today become one more factor that keeps literature from expressing what really counts. Antiquated truths are certainly droned out monotonously, but the criticism that something is already known only smacks of the salt of genuine contempt where the portrayal rebels against things as they are, and where they are at their most vicious.

It is less well known that not just the small literary and scientific luminaries of class society but even the very great will, if necessary, throw all scientific and esthetic precision or even the merest decency to the wind, provided they are of one mind with that society. They will avoid conflict with it no matter what the cost, and that precisely where the application of their views to reality would be called for. Their conscience presumably remained clear, but what if it did? The masters of an exquisite methodology, of the most highly nuanced linguistic and logical apparatus, the kings of poetry, philosophy and science, just happen to have been inattentive where their principles would have benefited the wretched. The author of *Faust* favored the retention of the death penalty for mothers that murdered their children. More in consonance with his principles than the facts, Hegel felt sorry for liberal England because the power of the king vis-à-vis parliament was not great enough. But he held up that country as both a theoretical and practical model for "leaving the poor to their fate and having them content themselves with begging in public." Schopenhauer, the philosopher of compassion, speaks contemptuously of attempts to make the existence of the working class bearable, but would even count "large merchants" among the "leading class." In his view, they are men who "must be exempt from common want or discomfort." From these great men of the past, there extends a long line to those creatures who in their books consciously write the opposite of what they really believe. When embarrassed, they will exclaim: "autre chose la littérature, autre chose la vie," and even boast of making that distinction when cornered. But it should be noted that what is decisive here is not the difference between the teaching and the life of the poet or thinker—an interesting question but too complicated to be discussed in this context—but the inconsistency on their own ground. Perhaps logical contradictions do not demolish a work but are part of its philosophical depth. But that is rarely the case. More importantly, the contradiction here referred to is not part of the literary but of the moral depth of authors; it is a blemish on their work even if it otherwise deserves to be admired.

The daily, perfectly commonplace lie which characterizes private life in our time is even less well known than these literary facts. That Christians remain unruffled when confronted with the misery of others; that they do nothing to help where injustice is done to the powerless but themselves torture children and animals; that they calmly pass by the walls behind which misery and despair take their course because their interests must be furthered; that it is always a misfortune to fall into their hands; that in view of all this, they daily worship someone as their divine model who, they believe, sacrificed himself for humanity, this lie marks every step of European life.

I once saw some very rich and therefore also especially devout persons at one of the most beautiful spots of Europe, on a radiant day, within sight of blossom-covered mountains and a sea of the deepest blue, amuse themselves by having doves startled from their dark boxes in which they had been kept up to this moment. Blinded by the light and fluttering and swaying for the first few seconds of their freedom, these birds were then shot down. When one of the wounded animals fell on the surrounding grass, a trained dog picked it up. If it escaped to a nearby rock, boys followed it there. If it was lucky enough to make its way out to sea uninjured—and this happened rarely—it was trusting enough to soon return to its point of departure, for it had understood nothing of what went on. It thus could serve the amusement again the following morning. This went on day after day. The best shot was solemnly given a prize by the ruler of the country. I asked a spectator whether the dove was a symbol of the Holy Spirit. "No, only the white one," he answered. That same

evening, a jungle expedition which had been organized for no other
purpose than to be filmed was shown at the cinema. A humoristic text
accompanied the scenes. A living lamb was tied down in a trap to lure
the leopard. It came, tore the lamb to pieces, and was shot. Particularly the last caption: "now Mr. Leopard will no longer be going for
walks," aroused laughter. But the lamb is a religious symbol. Usually,
primitives do not devour their sacred or totem animals. The Christians make symbols of them. They don't worship the animals but in
or through them they revere the deity, and this is the reason the
animals are not spared in reality. They have not profited from the
sublimation of our ideas about the godhead.

It is not part of life in this civilization to take religion seriously.
Non-religious values such as justice, freedom or truth are not taken
seriously either. Acknowledging them is no more than a *façon de
parler*. Only the powerful have to be respected; the poor and powerless are worshipped in religion, i.e., in spirit, but mistreated in reality.
The lamb must be embroidered on the white and yellow banner but
for the movie audience, one lets it await its death in the dusk of the
jungle. One must worship the Lord on His cross and drag Him to the
scaffold alive. If someone attacks Christianity in his speeches, he
must be persecuted, but he must also be prevented from making it
a reality. The discovery of the gulf between the moral criteria of
Christians, and their actual conduct therefore impresses one as an
unrealistic, odd, sentimental, superfluous observation. You may call
it a lie or say that it is old hat, just as you please, but you should not
trouble a reasonable European with it. In this regard, Jews and
Christians are of one mind. The compromise between the implementation of religion and its inexpedient abolition is the reconciliation
with God via the all-encompassing lie.

Conversations About the Wealthy: *A:* When money is of no
consequence, private agreements and legal formalities do not amount
to much in a divorce. One cheats a little and takes the affair to a judge
who does not make a big fuss. There's no excitement, no repeated
summons, no endless delays. Financial questions have been settled
beforehand and in the meantime, one simply lives with one's male
or female friend. But for the poor, divorce is a torture, for money is

at stake. Because the guilty party suffers financially, both partners have to look for proofs against each other, relatives and acquaintances are dragged in or involve themselves, all kinds of ugliness are brought out into the open, it's hell. What's more, the two may have to go on living under one roof until they are divorced, the children are there, scenes become a daily occurrence. Not infrequently, they can't go to court because poverty makes an acceptable solution impossible. Then life has simply been ruined.

B: How loosely you talk. You know yourself what sort of marital tragedies occur in rich families. Frequently, they end in suicide. And it isn't true that their dirty linen is not washed in public. Sometimes, the whole town, but always their circle discusses such affairs. The rich suffer exactly like the poor. It is precisely in such cases that it becomes apparent how little economic factors have to do with the inner life. You obviously don't have any idea how much psychological misery there is among those envied people. Because their quarrels take place behind locked doors, or are less noisy, you assume they don't occur. You see things much too simply.

A: Of course the rich have to suffer (they certainly have more antidotes). That's a general truth, and I didn't contest it. I simply wanted to point out that in the majority of cases, it is poverty that makes marital conflict a torture while the wealthy can settle it in ways not open to the poor. Because you can't deny that, you generalize. The moment one points to one of the untold blessings money brings, you and your like try to obscure it though it is as clear as day. In this particular case, you don't want to admit that economics affect even the most sacrosanct psychic regions but that's how it is. Your millionaires may moan because of their marital difficulties but while it might not be possible to free nine-tenth of my indigents from theirs, it would certainly be a consolation to them if they could trade places with the rich. Besides, there is one thing you should have noticed long ago: I do not accuse pleasure. The shamefulness of this order is not that some are better off but that many are poor although everyone could have all he needs. What judges it is not that there are wealthy people but that in spite of what could now be done, the poor continue to be with us. The public consciousness must therefore be poisoned by lies; this order cannot last.

Progress: The munitions manufacturer, his politician and his general say: "There will be wars as long as the world exists. There is no such thing as progress." To begin with, this is a case where the wish is father to the thought. Besides, this belief must also be maintained among the masses. This is quite understandable—it's perfectly straightforward brainwashing. But the literary servants of these people have the additional insolence of looking impartial, like men aware of all the theoretical difficulties, when they raise this question: "What does progress really mean? Progress can only be measured by how close we come to the realization of some particular and relatively accidental value. To look at history from such a point of view would mean to turn something relative into an absolute, to hypostatize something subjective, in short to carry narrowness and onesidedness into science." Because they are furious with the socialist struggle for a better world which derives its hope from the results of earlier struggles, particularly from the revolutions of recent centuries, they go about fabricating their so-called philosophy of history. As if it weren't perfectly obvious what progress the socialists mean, what progress the reactionaries resist, both theoretically and in practice. It is the improvement of material existence through a more purposeful restructuring of human conditions. It can be said emphatically that this improvement means more for most people than the implementation of a relatively accidental value, whether they know it or not. To them, it is the most important thing on earth. It may be true that history stagnates or regresses for long periods in this regard and during the last hundred years, the obfuscation of that fact may often have served to mislead the masses ideologically, but talk about progress is clear and justified nonetheless. For those in control to maintain that progress is being made under their rule has long been a lie, and even their *littérateurs* are dissociating themselves from that claim. It is obvious that they would really prefer to abandon the concept to preserve their rule. For like other bourgeois illusions such as freedom and equality, it no longer functions as an ideological defense but as a criticism of existing conditions, as the encouragement to change them, and that is the result of the dialectics of history.

It should also be said that today, not only the more immediate goal of providing mankind with basic necessities, but also the realization of all so-called cultural and ideal values depends on this progress in a materialist sense, i.e., on a socialist reorganization of society. That social progress *need* not *necessarily* occur is true; that it cannot take place is a crude lie; that it would be onesided to judge the history of mankind by its ability to offer its members a tolerable level of existence is just philosophical chatter.

NOTE: Social progress is always a historical task but no mystic necessity. It is quite understandable that Marxism should explain the theory of society as the theory of reality. The masses suffer from the outdated form of society and expect everything from its rational organization. They do not really appreciate that from the perspective of eternity, their misery is just one fact among many, and that to view the world from that perspective is no more than that, a perspective. Just as the individual assumes that the world revolves around him, that his death and its end coincide, so the exploitation and the misery of the masses is, for them, misery as such, and history revolves around the improvement of their lot. But history does not have to go along unless it is compelled to.

The Idealism of the Revolutionary: The view that Marxism merely advocates the stilling of hunger and thirst and the satisfaction of the sexual drive cannot be refuted by the statement that it is surely much finer, nobler, more profound and inward than that. For rebellion, solidarity, self-denial are just as "materialistic" as hunger. The struggle for the improvement of the fate of mankind includes egoism and altruism, hunger and love as natural links in causal chains. Of course, materialist theory can offer no logical proof that life should be surrendered. It inculcates heroism neither with the Bible nor the cane, it does not replace solidarity or the insight into the necessity of revolution by a "practical philosophy" or a reasoned argument in favor of sacrifice. It is the opposite of every such "idealist" morality. It frees of illusions, unmasks reality and explains what happens. It offers no logical reasons for "higher" values, but it certainly advances none against someone's risking his life to help implement the "lower" ones, that is, a materially bearable existence for all. "Idealism" begins at precisely the point where such conduct is not satisfied with a natural explanation for itself but looks to the crutch of "objective" values, "absolute" duties and other idealistic reassurance and "sanctification," i.e., where the restructuring of society is made dependent on metaphysics rather than on human beings.

Horror Stories: When a good citizen hears these days (around 1930) that a person motivated by pure intentions is seized, tortured and killed by a barbarous soldiery in his own country or anywhere else in the world, he usually does not become indignant but will express the suspicion that this piece of news is probably exaggerated. If the information that such events occur all the time and with terrible regularity is irrefutably precise, that they are an integral part of the system in its present phase, and if he knows that there is a connection between imperialist global policy and the penitentiaries in Hungary, Rumania, Bulgaria, Poland or the terror in the colonies, he will burst into passionate fury. But that fury will not be directed against the originators and perpetrators of these inhuman acts but against those that bring them out into the open. Where, for the sake of naked profit, all those that stand for humanity and spirit in a country are murdered, entire social classes are kept in fear and despair, nations are ignominiously enslaved and even wiped out, the bourgeois layman turns into a critical historian of painstaking precision. The modern antipathy to determining the precise facts notwithstanding, he demands scrupulous accuracy in problems of knowledge; in contrast to the pervasive divinization of intuition, he proclaims that the precise determination of details is the very essence of research. Confronted with bloodshed, he suspects a one-sided history or reports that are partial to the persecuted and hostile to the perpetrators. But it is not the perpetrators of the horrors he has in mind but the comrades, the party, the ideas of the victims of those horrors, and ultimately those victims themselves. For this simple, harmless, normal, sober, well-turned-out and charming man with whom you are talking is only frightened by the bloodshed of civil wars when it is not part of the organized terror of his own class; he is credulous only when anger against the proletariat has to be inflamed; he becomes a human being only when tears are to be shed for a Czar or a Russian upper class for which the World War was a bad speculation. The guileless individual in this world is necessarily in league with the henchmen. And the general consciousness—school, newspapers, the sciences—in short, the objective spirit through its functions and functionaries reacts in the same way, not from hypocritical reflection of course—there is no need to lie—but from honest instincts.

On Goethe's Maxims and Reflections: "One only knows those who make one suffer." Had his reflection been applied to social classes, Goethe would probably have objected, and yet it is relevant to the distribution of income. As the proletarian suffers under the capitalist class, he comes to understand the human nature of these gentlemen much better than do their personal friends. The proletarians have only a rough and one-sided knowledge of the entrepreneurs but that side is the more important, the really serious one. That's the reason the primitive view the worker develops of his boss, the point of view of the workplace, is usually more accurate than the insights of philosophical anthropology.

But Goethe would have rejected this interpretation. "Envy and hatred restrict the observer to the surface," it says in those same maxims where the earlier reflection can also be found. But if the continued existence of a society and of the human type that rules in it is a misfortune for the development of mankind, what conclusions are to be drawn from this sentence? Don't the concepts then turn into their opposite so that the corrupt surface becomes the core, and envy clear-sighted? "Only the unloving sees the inadequacies," Goethe himself says. But suppose those inadequacies are part of the essence? Goethe's politics affected his work in many places, and it is idle to speculate what he might do today. This much is certain, however: at times, his insight attained a power which can even illuminate our own society: "Only the person who is shown benevolence by others is really alive." It follows that for most people, life in the present phase of capitalism is—death.

The New Objectivity: The "concrete" has become the fashion. But what is meant by this concreteness? Certainly not what the sciences have been investigating for the last few centuries. On the contrary! These days, it is felt that the sciences do not have much of a contribution to make to knowledge, and their bourgeois representatives applaud this development. What counts now is not the causal connections between things, those are not the relationships people want to discover. Instead, it is precisely things as distinct from those relationships, they themselves, their existence, their essence that is inquired into. The paintings representative of this new objectivity where one sees objects that are carefully set off against their surroundings afford a particularly clear insight into this endeavor. They are not afflicted by the sophistication of French Impressionism which resulted largely from the painter's inclusion of the connecting medium. The "synthesis" which is being created everywhere in the sciences sees itself as the ideational linkage of what was originally perceived as distinct, not as the description of the intertwined spatio-temporal connections of reality. And there also exists nowadays a doctrine about man. "Man" himself is being described here, his "essence," and the differences between it and that of all other living beings is stressed. Finally, and on the basis of such distinct determinations, his place in the hierarchy of the "cosmos" is shown. This newfangled abstractness of science which disguises itself as objectivity and so arrogantly disports itself as "concreteness" vis-à-vis the old formalism has a considerable resemblance to the conduct demanded of any "decent" person in good society. I am not to investigate the real relations between people, make any comparisons which refer to reality or discover causal chains. Rather, I am to take every person "as he is," I am to look at his character, his personality, in short his individual "nature." He himself, in his own being and apart from spatio-temporal nexuses, wants to be taken as substance. Relations are allegedly "inessential," irrelevant—they aren't part of it. The "personalities" wish to be seen discreetly and thereby take on that quality of interest and depth people in good society accord each other. "Seeing things as wholes," a method which recently has also metaphysically reformed physiology, is perfectly compatible with this abstract objectivity. It is its other side.

As this new philosophical anthropology defines the difference between isolated man and isolated animal, it disregards the fact that it is not abstract individuals that kill animals and eat their cadavers and thus cause the unending fear of death and torture of millions of those animals. Similarly, we are to abstract from the fact that the glamor of this charming woman is made possible through the misery of impoverished proletarians. We are to ignore that these prestigious people not only constantly exploit the wretchedness of others but that they produce it anew to again be able to live off it; that they stand ready to defend this state of affairs with whatever quantity of other people's blood may be required. We are to forget that at the moment this woman dresses for dinner, those off whom she lives start in on the night shift, and when we kiss her hand more tenderly because she complains of a headache, we are to abstract from the fact that in hospital wards, even the dying are not allowed visitors after six o'clock. We are to abstract, because today our philosophers everywhere are interested in knowing essences. In this pursuit, they dismiss everything external and accidental, any merely "factual" tie. The factory where one works for the owners, the hospital where one croaks after this sort of work, the penitentiary where those of the poor that were too weak to deny themselves the pleasures reserved for the haut monde are locked up, all this of course is "external" to this lady. It is "trite" to worry about it. It has nothing to do with her "psyche," her "personality." She may be sensitive, mild, witty, humble, profound, beautiful; or ambivalent, unsure of herself, depressed, disharmonious, hesitant, infantile. In short, she can have her own "essence."

The modern teaching about man, "characterology," and similar pseudo-sciences, do not focus on the outside of things, they penetrate to their core. There is just one exception. When people get their income in a way which appears illegal under prevailing social conditions and do not have the power to scoff at this illegality, their "essence" stops being a unity that can be understood in and of itself. Up to this point, it is therefore permissible to examine causal chains. Up to this point, but not beyond it, the origin of existence is to cast light on its content. The "magnificent" Mister X, chairman of the board and sportsman, will stop being magnificent the moment he cannot cover up the bribe paid an official by an even bigger one. Before this, the number of existences he ruins is of no importance.

Economic Psychology: To theoretically justify the continuing necessity of allowing our capitalists to retain in perpetuity the huge power and loot they derive as a constantly renewed annuity from mankind, it must be believed that the "economic egoism" of all individuals has to be stimulated to keep the whole economy going. But people forget to add that the "economic egoism" of the over-whelming majority of hard-working people is the constraint of hunger while those gentlemen do their interesting and satisfying, clean and safe work and are rewarded by living in palaces. To stimulate an egoist to such an extent that he will condescend to command an army of workers and employees, one has to give him cars, good-looking women, honors and security down to the tenth generation. But if someone is to work in constant danger in a mine day after day, and ruins himself both physically and spiritually, a steady diet of water soup and meat once a week are enticement enough. What a curious psychology.

Tricks: There is one trick Schopenhauer did not mention in his eristic dialectic. If one wishes to prove the validity of a tenet that clearly contradicts experience and is historically discredited, it should be made the subject of the most difficult and learned investigations. This will create the impression that the things one discusses with so much ingenuity cannot possibly be chimeras. Today, such subjects are the freedom of the will, the hierarchy of values, the transcenden-tal spirit, the ground of being, and many others. The blunt statement that these things really exist might fail to impress wide circles. They should therefore first be presented as important problems. Particu-larly when one has the power to make them the topic of lectures or treatises, they will appear relevant. All direct formulations must be avoided. The simple question about a Beyond, for example, should be replaced by the profound and more neutral-sounding subject: "About various modes and levels of being." The laymen will then readily believe that reality, this world, is only one among many, and the experts will have a new or, rather, their old problematics. The mist in which they lose themselves may not be a beyond, but it is a dream—and spirit realm. Anyone who has not mastered the subtle and quickly changing conceptual apparatus these people use will seem ignorant and unimportant. He has no say.

Another quite common trick which nowadays serves the same objective substitutes the easy proof of the contingency and relativity

of the positive sciences for the old and discredited proof of immortal-
ity and the existence of God. The former will tacitly be interpreted
to mean that there are many other, equally legitimate approaches to
knowledge, and that naturally gives our metaphysicians the upper
hand. As if any delusion could not be rehabilitated in this way. They
twist our lack of omniscience into a rope to coerce us into religious
belief. But this new proof which deduces God's existence from our
limited scientific knowledge is as unconvincing as all the rest. There
is the following appropriate answer to such "tricks:" Your problems
cannot be resolved by respectable scientific methods. So we want to
know at least why they should be kept alive. There must be some
social significance to all this humbug, otherwise professors wouldn't
be paid to teach it.

On the Telephone: If you happen to visit an acquaintance and he
is called to the phone, you may be in for an embarrassing surprise.
While answering the party at the other end with a friendly voice, he
indicates his impatience to you. He shows you how boring and bothersome the conversation is for him. His courteous tone which you
have often had occasion to hear under similar circumstances turns out
to be mere convention: your acquaintance lies on the phone. If you
are a frequent guest of this person, you will discover that the tone of
his voice can vary enormously. There is a range extending from
deferential politeness and ordinary courtesy to the noticeable expression of a slight impatience. The voice a person uses on the phone
reveals the variety of his relations to the world particularly clearly for
here his social position becomes apparent.

The discovery that most relationships are not genuine on his side,
and the insight that his behavior toward persons who might be useful
to him differs significantly from that toward those who expect something from him will perhaps prompt you to reflect about him, or even
to discuss this matter with him. It will then become apparent that
the constraints of the struggle for existence govern the relations of
individuals, and that the small income of your acquaintance adequately accounts for his behavior. To be honest with impunity, free,
open in one's conduct, to treat others according to their human
qualities is the prerogative of millionaires who no longer have aspirations. Too bad they so seldom make use of it.

The Contingency of the World: There is no metaphysics; a positive assertion about an absolute is not possible. But statements about the contingency, finiteness and pointlessness of the visible world can be made. The criteria of necessity, infinity, meaningfulness still implicit in such negations, however, cannot then be taken to guarantee the existence of the eternal in man's mind, as Kant did. Those criteria are themselves nothing but human ideas. Even the concept of an absolutely just and benevolent authority before which the darkness of this world, its viciousness and filth would pass away, and the kindness unrecognized and trampled by men might prevail and triumph, is a human thought which will die and be scattered with those who conceived it. This is a depressing insight.

A thought experiment: the contingency of the real becomes especially apparent when we closely examine the desire to live as well as possible. It can be understood in a variety of ways. It may mean, for example, that a person wishes to have known all pleasures, thought all knowledge, practiced all the arts, and would like to say as he dies: "I know life." But what does he really know? Conceivably, he might reawaken in a different world where all the pleasures, the knowledge and the arts of this one would be both quantitatively and qualitatively irrelevant, and after that death he might again come back to life in a third one, and so on in countless different worlds each of which overshadowed what was important in the others. In view of the infinity of the possible, this thought experiment shrinks his present knowledge to such a degree that the difference between the "simplicity" of the most wretched human and his own intelligence becomes as nothing. In relation to an infinite magnitude, all finite ones become infinitely small, however large they may seem.

This desire can also be understood to mean that an individual wishes to have lived a good, that is, a moral life. But he must understand that his conception of goodness is a human one, and that the moment may come when all his ideas will change. He must understand that this concept has not been sanctified by a supernatural power, and is not part of any eternity. All consciousness can change, there is no eternal memory.

The difference between a good and a bad life applies exclusively to the present. Here, it is decisive, but the present is also the only form of existence. In it, the difference between a good and a bad life means satisfaction or renunciation. And friendliness, decency, justice are also instinctual satisfactions for the person that practices them. They become illusions when they are understood as earthly means toward an eternal end, or as symbols with a deeper significance. Neither life nor knowledge have such significance. Not the afterlife of individual existence in a Beyond but the solidarity with men who will come after us in this world prompts our interest in the future.

This insight is open to the objection that our knowledge is incomplete. Perhaps a powerless and tortured existence that was full of kindness is not lost, perhaps it has an eternal tomorrow. We don't know. But neither can we know whether kindness may not walk in hell instead of in paradise in the future, and whether the government of eternity is not really as bad as it appears here below. The contingency of the world and of our knowledge of it, or the impossibility of metaphysics, expresses itself in the fact that all statements that transcend the temporal are equally justified or equally unjustified. When the theologians claim that there is a Beyond, and prove the perfection of this eternal something by pointing to the hope in our heart, they forget that fear and mistrust are equally good reasons for inferences about the absolute as is our trust in a divine justice. Why should the hopes of kind men which are usually disappointed by the powerful not be crushed at precisely the point where the highest power expresses itself directly? The senselessness of the world belies metaphysics, or rational interpretation. But it can only mislead the person that lives a human life, not from compassion for others but because he fears some master.

We can love human beings temporally and spatially remote from us, and wish them well, just as they might also understand us. Beyond humanity, that incarnation of finite beings, however, there is no understanding of what is sacred to us. To the extent that men do not themselves set the world aright, it will remain the plaything of blind nature. Kindness and justice do not dwell in the universe, the universe is unfeeling and remorseless. In the night that surrounds it, mankind as a whole resembles the girl from Lavaur who awakened from apparent death and found the entire population of her country killed. No one took part in her awakening, for no one else did her life have significance. No one heard her. Mankind also is utterly alone.

The Relativity of Class Theory: Theories have their source in the interests of men. This does not mean that interests necessarily falsify consciousness. Correct theories are those which result from the questions they answer. Our picture of the world will depend on what disturbs us, on the changes we want to make in it. Even in perception, in pure contemplation, the images are partly and subconsciously colored by subjective factors. And in scientific thought which always has some connection with a particular social or individual practice, the direction of interest is even decisive in the structuring of its object.

The insight into this is contained in the Marxist thesis of the unity of theory and practice. The practice referred to is essentially political practice, and the structure of the world-view deriving from this practice is the separation of mankind into social classes. To all those who are primarily concerned with the unhampered development of human potential and of justice, these classes must appear as the decisive structural principle of our time, for the realization of such goals depends on their elimination. There are other differences, other structural principles which, given the same interest in the free development of men and justice, may appear as fundamental as social classes. The difference between the sick and the healthy would be an example. Mankind is divided by a line which is ordinarily invisible for an active observer of the world. As unjustly as that between members of various classes, the line between the well and the ill excludes a number of people from the pleasures of this world and condemns them to the worst sort of misery. The distribution of property which is caused by differing physical make-up, the varying susceptibility to bacilli or accidents at work and on the street, is just as irrational as property relations in society. The results of these two forms of meaninglessness are equally cruel, and other principles which divide mankind might be added.

Nonetheless, the distinction according to social classes is superior to the other points of view, for it can be shown that while the elimination of classes would entail a change in the other antitheses,

the reverse is not true. Their resolution would not imply the elimination of classes. The considerable difficulties under which present-day
hygiene and medicine vegetate are not even remotely understood.
Although there is an abundance of all necessities, countries groan
under the burden of overpopulation. The imperialist society which
rules them and unscrupulously allows the talents of the vast majority
to be nipped in the bud no longer offers true freedom for the development of the enormous medical possibilities there are. Not only the
prevailing sexual morality but also the latent hatred against the suppressed class and the inability to feed the healthy affect the fight
against disease in all respects. Furthermore, the economic and political principle also proves more fundamental than the physiological
because the worship of power and the principle of competition of
capitalist mankind causes a good deal of the bitterness illness brings
with it today. Protestantism with its belief in reality as an expression
of God's power plays a role here. The elimination of classes is therefore the decisive principle—but only as regards revolutionary practice. Because of the irrationality of the world, this priority does not
apply to any and every assessment of the present.

Of course, we cannot view the present in a disinterested manner.
Political practice is not the opposite of pure contemplation. The
direction of our attention may be governed by other interests, other
suffering, another practice, and politics has no priority over truth. A
person who sees living beings in two categories, those who enjoy
pleasure and health and those whose entire experience is death and
illness, may be reproached for doing something pointless, but he will
not be open to the objection that this difference is less vast than the
social. But perhaps such a reflection is not as pointless as it may
appear. Being illuminating, it may contribute to a better reality. And
it is as deeply rooted in the hazy notion of such a reality as is the
theory of class society itself. It also exposes the injustice of things as
they are to the light of thought. The terror which prevails beyond
man's consciousness, in darkness, has its own specific hopelessness.

Moral Integrity of the Revolutionary: The bourgeoisie is "a wise
parent who knows his own child." Should it acknowledge the moral
integrity of a revolutionary during his lifetime, the enemies of the
bourgeoisie would be well advised to be careful of him.

Spiritual Suffering: Physical pain is worse than spiritual suffering. This is a debatable formulation. How can the corresponding degrees be compared? In man, spiritual suffering almost always accompanies physical pain. How can the two be separated from each other in thought? And yet the statement is true. Material wants, physical torture, imprisonment, heavy forced labor, fatal disease have more reality than the noblest grief. Neurologists are certainly justified when they speak of the horrible condition and the suicides of the psychologically ill. But nervous disorders or boredom is not what is really meant by spiritual suffering. Instead, we are supposed to believe that not only the poor and the hungry but also the Junker and the factory barons suffer severely, and that as their education and power increase, their worries increase along with them. Ultimately, they will be greater than any physical suffering. Poor devils should no longer believe this hoax. Proletarians certainly have a greater share of anxiety than Krupp directors. If they could only get out of their worst misery, the unemployed would gladly put up with the measure of spiritual discomfort these gentlemen experience. But even among worries, fear of material destitution of all kinds weighs most heavily. The spiritual suffering of the ruling class is nothing compared to the real wretchedness of the proletariat.

Two Elements of the French Revolution: Judged by what could actually have been accomplished at that moment, what makes the sympathetic observer feel ashamed is not that the French Revolution went too far, or that the implementation of its program only came about during a protracted period and after severe reverses. What does disturb him is the venting of what were precisely non-revolutionary, philistine, pedantic, sadistic instincts. As a practical matter, the revolution needed the support of segments of the petite bourgeoisie. But at the very beginning, the subaltern maliciousness of those strata made an ideology of the solidarity of the nation which the revolution invoked in theory. It is true, of course, that ideology contains impulses which not only point beyond feudal society but class society generally, but they are to be found in the writings of the "philosophes" rather than among the sadistic petite bourgeoisie which came to power for a time. Compared to them, it may indeed have seemed a salvation when the representatives of the developed forces of production, i.e., the bourgeoisie that was ready to take over, assumed leadership after the fall of Robespierre. The interpretation of the French Revolution by direct recourse to the philosophy of the Enlightenment distorts reality almost as much as does the insolence of a certain romanticism which only objected to the horror of the guillotine because it did not serve the Bourbons.

In today's Germany, the two elements of the French Revolution, pedantic philistinism and revolution, appear as distinct historical powers. If they do it in the service of the dominant bourgeoisie, the petit bourgeois and the peasants may rebel and call for the henchman, but the forces directed toward the creation of a more humane world are now embodied in the theory and practice of smaller groups of the proletariat. They are not concerned with the guillotine but with freedom.

Disapproved Emotions: No criticism will invalidate a scientific account as thoroughly as the reproach that emotions were the driving force behind it. Even though metaphysics has recently mounted a brisk and youthful attack against the demand that science be value free, emotions continue to be taboo. But what emotion does this judgment ban? Does anyone reject the pantheistic enthusiasm for Being, the reverence for an otherworldly realm of ideas, the contempt for the masses and their well-being, the regressive enthusiasm for the Middle Ages or antiquity, the antipathy to a "negative" attitude, the pathos of duty and conscience or the fervent propaganda for personality, inwardness, vitality or other legitimate feelings? Actually, it is only the sentiments of the ruled against the rulers that are disapproved in bourgeois thinking. It is not rare, of course, for our scholars to generate "sentiments" against each other and then engage in reciprocal recriminations, just the way members of the bourgeoisie compete one with the other. But the enemy against whose feelings all are united, and in whose exploitation all are interested, is the ruled class.

The demand that knowledge be dispassionate derives from the struggle of the revolutionary bourgeois intelligence for a science unfettered by theology. Today, it appears primarily as the calm matter-of-factness of the person who sees himself as part of the existing order, as the good manners of the *arrivé,* or the discreet eagerness of the individual who believes he will get somewhere. A little arrogance, a dash of the abruptness of "genius," indeed even theoretical and abstract "radicalism" are readily forgiven.

The demand for dispassionateness goes together with that for impartiality, objectivity. The latter also is the legacy of a period when bourgeois science was still a pioneer in the struggle of mankind, and originated in what was once an aggressive physics and chemistry. Of course, when natural science turned its back on ecclesiastical authorities and became experimental, it was itself extremely partial and emotional. In the so-called liberal sciences, i.e., the discipline and history of human civilization, impartiality today certainly does not mean the advocacy of human progress as it did among the physicists of the sixteenth and seventeenth centuries. Instead, it is the failure to accord central importance to what really counts in these disciplines —relations of domination and property. It is a narrowing of the horizon and has the dependence of science on capital for its cause. The honest description of the inequality that is maintained in our time to insure the profits of a small minority, and the analysis of the propagandistic and repressive machinery that functions to accomplish this purpose would indeed be partial, and are in fact disapproved. The suspicion that a bias against the prevailing order and scientific work are inseparable here may have lent a certain prestige to those philosophical efforts which are interested in setting up an antithesis between the liberal and cultural sciences on the one hand, and the natural sciences and ultimately science generally on the other. When it struggled against feudalism, the thoroughness and doggedness of research had been judged socially necessary by the bourgeoisie. Now, where they threaten the bourgoisie, they are to come to an end.

Not only in the sciences but also in everyday utterance, this dispassionateness and impartiality of members of the lower orders indicate to the ruling class that they are reliable. To have these qualities is a much more necessary condition for success in the capitalist system than is freedom from all those vices which are not downright criminal. There is a particular tone of voice which guarantees inner freedom from unauthorized emotions. The person that wants to train his child for a career in this system should see to it that his voice produces that tone when it becomes an adult.

Difficulties with a Psychoanalytical Concept: Whether a revolutionary lived a life that was "reality oriented" or not depends on the state of the class struggle. If his life was a succession of excessive suffering, failures, severe inner and external crises, prison and tortures of every sort, he may have been just as intelligent, consistent, sober and brave as in the fortunate event of final victory. If he was defeated, did his politics take reality into account? As regards the life of the proletarian, the historical future will decide. But what authority decides in the case of the fighter himself?

The analyst might answer that this is not a very important question. What counts, he will say, is not objective suffering but inner health. But can the fighter, let alone another person determine at any given moment how healthy, neurotic, at one or at odds with himself he may be? These bourgeois categories reflect their own world and not the struggle which proposes to unhinge it.

Such Is the World: Activity in a proletarian party has the abolition of exploitation for its goal. But the strengthening of this party is the mediate cause of increased pressure on the ruled class and the remorseless fight against all that are suspected of sympathy with it. The closer the decision comes, the more terrible the repressive measures of the ruling class. Civil war, toward which the party is driven in the historical dynamics, is fraught with all the abominations on earth. If the old order is victorious, terror and endless dread begin. For those seriously concerned with improving society, there has never been a way out of this dilemma. The act through which help is to come is condemned to increase misery. If the most cynical member of the ruling class reproaches the ascetic revolutionary for having caused untold suffering, he isn't really wrong. Such is the world.

Union Bureaucracy: It can easily be seen why the views of union functionaries should frequently be much more reactionary than those of bourgeois democrats. The functionaries constantly have to squeeze

concessions from the entrepreneurs. If they get less than they demand, they are blamed and get to see disappointed faces. They are
paid by the workers but due to the mechanics of the economic
system, what they do is never enough. Under such circumstances,
how can they fail to become annoyed with their insatiable, restless,
uncomfortable clients, and to develop an understanding for reformist
theories which tend to relinquish the claims of the working class but
not their own jobs.

The Backward: Over extended stretches of the world, capitalism
has put a stop to carefreeness. Carefreeness is filth, superstition,
stupidity, disease, slowness, apathy. Because it has no place in the
factory, the civilized world has developed a mentality which despises
it any- and everywhere. There is good reason for retaining this hostility. It should be made an element in a better society. Of course, it
will change its character in the process. For seen from the point of
view of society as a whole, it has something inhumane about it; it
means that ever more inescapably, only a small number of privileged
individuals can enjoy what remains of effortless pleasure, peace and
lightheartedness. It isn't that there was once a good old time of
easygoing ways: those good old times were mere dullness. But the
final eradication of a carefreeness which still survives in remote cor-
ners of the capitalist world is so cruel that it transfigures the shortcomings of the days of old. The mail coach was not romantic but an
instrument of torture. Inspite of the slower pace in by-gone times,
the discharged old master mechanic was just as much of a tyrant as
is his modern counterpart. The small cozy shops and inns which are
going bankrupt now became spawning grounds of stupidity and sadism toward the end. But it is the little people that swallow the dust
of the automobiles that replaced the mail coach; the old craftsman
perishes miserably, and the gradual ruin of unprofitable enterprises
is a hell in the midst of the modern economic process.

It is necessary to do away with carefreeness. But that is accompanied by enormous human suffering and the destruction of certain
values. The road free from the dust of cars, the slower pace in the
workshops, the conversations with customers and the boredom in the
small stores become precious to those about to lose them. Before, all

this was nothing. Now, where it all disappears, these aspects enter consciousness and take on the glow of things one must surrender, of values that have been lost. The philosophers whose thoughts reflect the social classes that go under in this process complain that "images and ideas" are dying. They judge the past from the vantage point of the present and believe that men formerly experienced these values. But it is only the pain an unceasing penetration of developed countries by capitalist production methods creates as a kind of endless repetition of the horrors of their introduction that turns those conditions into values the unfortunates are being deprived of. That's the reason they become the images and ideas whose death the philosophers mourn.

So the philosophers are mistaken. But the misery of the backward which technical progress brings and which gives rise to their false theories is no less real than the happiness of future generations which that progress may perhaps produce some day.

A Neurosis: There are thoughts which inhibit the capacity to work or to experience pleasure to such a degree that they border on illness. For that reason, psychologists call them neurotic. They are true nonetheless, and if many had them, and had them *all the time,* mankind might perhaps be better off.

Such thoughts are the following: I eat, and the crushing majority of mankind goes hungry; many starve to death. I am loved, but countless persons are hated and tortured. When I am ill, others take care of me and are ready to help. For the majority of men, illness affects their work, means less money at the very least, reproaches, public hospital wards, and misery. At this very moment, countless people in the world are being tormented, tortured, or killed physically and spiritually. That includes men, women, children, old people, animals—and their suffering is indescribable. It so *happens* that my condition is tolerable, the causes for this are not accidental, but they are unrelated to my value as a person; I am like all the rest.

That's how far Tolstoi went. His suggestions for change were bad, he did not clearly recognize the social causes of prevailing evils, and therefore did not see how they could be abolished. But is there a "way?" And isn't it compromised in advance because mankind can no longer help those who died along that way, once it arrives? Where is one to take courage and strength?

The Unfathomable: Whatever the scope and nature of the dependence of metaphysics on society may be, it is certain that the representatives of the official intellectual life will not saw off the branch they are sitting on. Although Schopenhauer could live as a rentier and went to some length in transfiguring that existence ideologically, he understood that the philosophy professors of his time openly or secretly supported religion. While their class had only a mediate interest in its preservation, that of the ministry which made appointments to vacant teaching positions was quite direct. He saw the extent to which the *thema probandum*, the compatibility of religion with the prevailing state of knowledge, either designedly or unconsciously affected even the remotest details of the system. But he overlooked the fact that religious ideas make up only a small part of officially sanctioned modes of thought and concepts toward which philosophy is tolerant or at least neutral, and that for the very same reasons.

To recognize the social alignment of its author, it is not even necessary nowadays to examine the content of a philosophical theory. The formulation of the questions and the more or less cultivated tone of the treatment betray the secure position to which they are peculiar. What is true of philosophy is generally true of the "liberal arts." Neither the talk about spirit, cosmos, God, being, freedom, etc., nor the statements about art, style, personality, form, epoch or even history and society show grief, let alone indignation about injustice, or compassion with victims. Their authors can remain entirely objective in this respect, for their material concerns are not those of the larger part of mankind. How can these people serve "eternal" human interests when they don't even understand the temporal ones? In spite of all the difficult problems the idea of eternity may involve, the wretched in their despair, not the officials employed for this purpose, are the most likely to produce it. Its peculiarity is that it manifests itself with greater purity and sublimity in the most naive, the most crudely sensuous hope, than in the most spiritual metaphysics and

theory. To resolve the conflict between that idea and reality, a mythology was required. The idea was therefore refined, stripped of its
substance, and raised above the realm of human conceptions. It was
removed from the excessively material ideals of the ruled and adapted
to the purposes of the rulers. For some centuries now, God has been
understood as wholly transcendant; he now is unfathomable spirit.
The reason for this may not have been so much that it is difficult to
reconcile the horrors of the world with the benevolence and justice
of an omnipotent being—theology has never found that a great feat
—but that there was a disinclination to confer on justice and benevolence the honor of being God's attributes. Such traits were not really
compatible with the image of rulers. To represent the all-powerful
God as fierce and terrible, like the powerful of this earth themselves,
was difficult, it would have driven men to despair. God was therefore
divested of all recognizable qualities, and a distinction was made
between His ways and those of the world. They became as arcane as
the business practices of factory owners and bankers. Under capitalism, people have their doubts about justice, benevolence and humanity, and our metaphysicians wouldn't dream of idealizing them. For
that purpose, they have jingoism.

DECLINE

Notes
1950-1969

Radicals: They understand the shortcomings of their wives, but mankind is expected to accomplish the miracle tomorrow. Is it that they love mankind too little, or too much?

Difficulties with Evil: Because English philosophy conceives of man as simply striving forward, as altruistic or even egoistic in the right way, it is true to say that it is superficial. But if the positivity of evil or even the depth of human nature is stressed instead, one becomes guilty of an absurdity. All speech is expression, profession, testimony, and one cannot profess evil. It is true that in every phase, our belief necessarily carries an opaque moment, an element of idolatry. If our speech remains aware of its vanity without however divesting itself of the naiveté of belief on whatever level may have been attained, if, in other words, it is cognizant of its natural impotence without becoming cynical and while continuing to believe in its unconditional truth, it will always acknowledge the necessity of evil. To maintain that evil is good is either to be understood metaphorically, as in Christianity, where it really means that evil *serves* the good. Then it is unfortunately untrue. Or it leads to gnostic dualism which demands that one abide by the unresolved contradiction, and expect eternal salvation to boot.

Expression and Grief: Writing may mean either that one makes observations, that one points to facts and thus contributes to domination, or that one expresses oneself. Since expression here is not speechless, it is necessarily reflected. Grief is something that complains about itself, a narcissistic, plaintive moment is intrinsic to it, even where it mourns others. This accounts for the narcissistic element in almost all poetry. And is there expression which is not pain?

In non-scientific literature, we have the choice between myth—the false—and lamentation, which is impotent. Positivism derives its strength from this dilemma. Even this reflection is subject to this constellation. Its meaning flickers.

A Kantian Sociology: One should write a critique of reason, like Kant, except that the processing factors, the mechanism which turns the material into a "unified" experience, would be the *social* schematism, not the pure forms of apperception and understanding. Even the order could be retained. The Transcendental Aesthetic would have to treat material production which directly structures the world for man. From it derive those general and specific modes of perception by which control is achieved, and also everything Marx called necessary appearance. The Transcendental Analytic would be the media of social intellectuality, from school to cinema. The sphere of reason, however, would be the tendency of society to adapt to ever higher levels—what Hegel calls the cunning of reason.

Beyond the Sexual Principle: In his theory of the Oedipus complex, Freud explains the identification with the father by the love for the mother. She belongs to the strong, adult male, and therefore one becomes like him. He can hinder the child, the competitor. One has to be like him to possess the mother. But there is a much more simple and plausible explanation: One becomes what one thinks about. The father—reality—demands, forbids, teaches. The immutable, that which denies—and which one would like to change nonetheless— forces us to identify with it so that we can bear it. This is the principle of thought and perhaps of all culture. From it, the control (over nature) also stems. Identification is the precondition for control but once control has been achieved, identification stops: what is controlled, but only that, becomes an object. (That Marx should have called the lack of planned regulation of economic relationships in capitalism the 'reification' of human relationships is terminologically misleading. On the contrary, it is a mythologizing process, an elevation to the rank of nature gods. The laws of the market are not just the day, the night and the thunder of the Victorian Age but also Moira, fate. It is only in the twentieth century that they become controllable things, objects of manipulation, and this is a result of the identification referred to). Love derives from fear, domination from love. We learn to love only what we fear, and we come to know only what we love. But we stop loving and fearing what we know. That is the history of civilization. Each of the terms contains the others, and the whole. The middle term, love, is identification, thinking.

On the basis of a passage in Plutarch, Bachofen reports that the men of ancient Lycia had to put on women's clothing when a death occurred. He interprets this custom as the identification with the mother who had given birth to the dead, and taken him back again. The entire event concerns only the mother, only she is really involved. To think of dying would thus mean to think of the mother, and to *think* of the mother to *make* oneself the mother. The bourgeois child makes itself the *father*. The process is more primitive than Freud described it; it is not as understandable and straightforward. To explain the assimilation to the father does not require the detour via the sexual desire for the mother (where that desire is inferred analogically from the genital relationships between adults). Fear of the father is the fundamental fact of civilization. In the relationships between mother and child, he is the intruder, the external force, the coldness of reality. All this, and also the connectedness of mother, homeland and death, Freud saw correctly. His prejudice (especially in his earlier periods) lay in the dogmatic postulate that the male and the female are distinct, ultimate powers, whereas the male child's sexual love for its mother is probably only a consequence of the assimilation to the intruder.

It was not until he wrote *Beyond the Pleasure Principle* that Freud had an intimation of these connections. Perhaps the title should read: "Beyond the Principle of Sexes." In that case, the classical myth about the birth of love through the division of the One would contain the truth about the non-libidinous longing (the death instinct) which can fulfill itself only through libidinous desire. Instead of self preservation and male Eros being contrastive, as Freud originally thought, these two would then constitute the unity of the creative principle (as is intimated in *Civilization and Its Discontents*). Through it, the utopia of reconciliation (which is precluded by the direct antithesis of Eros and Thanatos) would become a reality. Of course, one must be as guarded in one's optimism that the subjective striving for self preservation and objective fulfillment can be harmonized as one must be careful not to equate that striving and the male principle, or return and the female principle, too hastily. For death to which an active life in civilization takes us, simply is not the homeland but abandonment, not peace but disintegration, not rest but nothingness. This is the reason the Freudian antithesis of the male and the motherly is unmediated (Bachofen had seen that the paternal and the maternal are not genuinely interchangeable concepts).

In Hegel's philosophy of history, the subjective, the drives appear largely as the cunning of reason. They create identity, mediate the absolute in the sense of recovered immediacy. But that philosophy is so fantastically optimistic that it does not consider the possibility of failure. It actually experiences itself as the spirit that is already assured of victory. But particularly in our time, and from the perspective of western society, the possibility of failure seems to inhere in the very nature of the intellectual process. The tendency of knowledge to negate the identification which arose from fear overshoots the mark. Instead of mediating the immediacy of the identity of subject and object by remembering that the mediation is itself mediated, it forgets itself. It takes mediation, thought, or rather, their results, i.e., knowledge, so-called facts, as the primary. The naiveté vis-à-vis the product on the one hand, and the arrogance vis-à-vis the unilluminated on the other, the positivity of the modern spirit, is just another form of the dogmatic separation of subject and object carried to excess. The seemingly unproblematical unitary thinking of science is the old dualism of bourgeois metaphysics. Carnap implies Descartes, and logical empiricism the doctrine of two substances. "There is nothing but facts" either means "everything is object" or "everything is subject." The sphere of the undifferentiated is liquidated, and thereby thought about truth as well. The process is similar to what happens in art: as appearance becomes (seemingly) so transparent for itself that it takes itself only as appearance and no longer as reality; as everything magical, everything that is genuinely illusion disappears from art without a trace, art itself disappears. Applied to science: as we look at a thing merely objectively instead of being that thing, objectivity disappears.

Forward: To look forward is identical with freedom from mythology, from superstition—from thought about the dead. Freedom from self-pity, narcissism, obduracy may also express themselves here. Perhaps all backward looking loyalty is actually self-love.

Jewry, Truth, Madness: The clinging of the Jews to their old belief contains an element of insistence on the self—the fear of its loss— vanity. They paid a terrible price for this—and perhaps even more for the truth that is part of this obstinacy than for the delusion.

Mind and Time: Time is abstracted from in every sentence which aspires to truth, and that means in every sentence. For a sentence whose truth is gnawed at by time is not true. This is Hegel's starting point in the *Phenomenology.* The dialectic of sense knowledge is based on the fact that the sentence "now it is night" will be refuted by the day tomorrow morning. The sentence does not include time in its truth. The question is whether there are sentences which are independent of time. People first thought of mathematical physics— pure mathematics was too ethereal to represent truth. But Einstein did not free physics of this doubt, his criticism of traditional mathematics and mechanics is plausible. And the general theory of relativity is not at all absolute. But the *Phenomenology* takes a leap at the critical point (as might be expected). Reason does not overcome time in a rational manner but objectifies it directly. This is precisely the secret of the "leap" in the method, and it is repeated at all the other transitional points of the *Phenomenology.* In spite of the many individual steps which claim to be mediations, absolute spirit time and again irrationally posits itself as absolute. Things don't work out at the transitional points. The terrible Feuerbach already saw this. Mind is not outside of time, it cannot do without the verb, however much it might like to play it down as a mere metaphor. Death is not just *in* it, as spirit claims, but above it. According to it, death is not real —Hic Rhodus!

After Voltaire: In the nineteenth century, his fame conferred a kind of immunity on the writer. The absolute monarch was above the law, and an element of that condition had devolved upon him. He used the freedom this gave him as a representative of mankind, as it were. He could be wholly human. In him, society honored itself and overcame, if unconsciously and ideologically, the spiritual maiming of its members. In contrast to the July murders, majesty is preserved in Voltaire's victory over absolutism. That is the positive side of the bourgeois concept of greatness which has degenerated today. In the twentieth century, the representative function is abolished—parliamentarism is in its throes. Conditions are so multiform that their survival is conceivable only as the direct dependence of men. The Russians have liquidated parliamentarism and greatness at one and the same time. Unless he is a dictator, a living person may not be great, for the new government permits no immunity. The mere idea of an individual exempt from constraint, a person who might say "no" to the rulers, the idea of a criterion beyond their conventicles, is repugnant to them. Only the trademark of that government, the nation-devouring field marshall, is great. The writer regresses to the social position of the lackey. The process is the reverse of Voltaire's fame.

The Question of Philosophy: "If there is no God, I need take nothing seriously," the theologian argues. The horror I commit, the suffering I do nothing to stop will, once they have occurred, survive only in the remembering human consciousness and die with it. To say that they continue to be true after that is meaningless. They no longer exist, they are no longer true: the two are the same. Unless they be preserved—in God. Can one admit this and still lead a godless life? That is the question philosophy raises.

Temptation of the Philosopher: Temptation of the philosopher: he renounces thought because it cannot be proven, because it is always mere opinion. He goes in for healthy science. To finally get away from the sphere where one says how things "are," although they may "be" different; to finally pass from language to formula, like the physicist. Even the montage of facts is non-committal, plausible, mere expression. What a relief to get away from the constant torment of setting the goal and the method, the topic and the style, the object and the direction of interest, to be creative yet always close to the problem in all this. What objection can be raised against this unceasing constraint to be exact? Doesn't it follow the safe path of the external criterion and thus lead to precise knowledge? If it is true that even science submits to such philosophical constraint at decisive points, its enterprise with its fixed yardsticks designed for purposes of control and domination nonetheless offers so much tempting certainty that the philosopher will occasionally look into this world with envy. Here, mere ingeniousness, hard work and good health bring success, and the worry about the correctness of the undertaking itself can always be left to "others."

   The Forbidden Question: The peoples of the twentieth century are being kept in the dark about the most important social issue which may destroy civilization. The various social systems among which men must chose and for whose sake they would be ready to fall upon each other are not presented dispassionately and in detail, applied to each of the countries, or clearly set forth with their advantages or disadvantages, their favorable prospects and dangers, and this is true in both the western and even more emphatically in the eastern half of the world. But if they are not discussed, there is good reason to ask to what extent nations do in fact determine their own fate. In Russia and the sphere under its control, it is known that they are kept in blind obedience. But aren't conditions in the west also questionable in this regard? Aside from the positively or negatively tinged image of present-day Russia, does the average citizen and worker have any idea of the real risks or chances of socialism, were it to be accepted by the western countries and introduced there? People are not even adequately informed about the English experiment being conducted these years. Blame for this rests not only with the masses but primarily with those who have the intellectual and material means for enlightenment at their disposal. The most important problems of mankind continue to be taboo. They are repressed, and precisely because men suspect that they should be rationally discussed, they produce hatred against the person who they believe does discuss them. There develops an inner fury against life as it is, against the fact that all one can do is praise, and fanaticism against everything different. The "exchange" of students, professors and other privileged persons within the western countries is no remedy. Because of the negligible differences in their own homelands, the exchangees usually share the belief in the superiority of the social system they have in common. Expressly or implicitly, this fact creates the a priori of the relationships here discussed, and which becomes even stronger through intercourse.

Psychoanalysis as the Cause of Its Necessity: Therapy in psychoanalysis means that inhibited affects are given the chance to express themselves. It wants to eliminate the threat, the door or the lid as it were, behind which those feelings simmer. Therapy assumes that will clear the air. But isn't it a fact that that door only compresses because it is made of the wrong material,—of prohibitions one no longer believes in? And doesn't the ignorant assurance by which the therapist feels qualified to remove the obstacle prove the meaninglessness of the prohibition which, like its force, produce the neurosis? (Aren't force and meaninglessness ultimately one and the same?) Rationality is not a formal category, it has a content. Reason is the name for what is reasonable. If the analyst leaves it up to the patient whether or not a painful tie to a child or a marriage partner should be broken off, he negates a taboo which has already been eroded by the progressive disintegration of middle class mentality. Dangerously careless—a little Nietzsche—he pushes what is already falling, and thrusts the dagger into the heart of his patient's partner. He encourages that side of the family conflict to which he can present his bill to act as unscrupulously as is customary these days, and calls it therapy. The more solid taboo, however, the still intact taboo on incest and perversion, is allowed to stand, and the desire to break it is "analyzed."

The reason of the analyst reflects the relations of domination in society. Everything those in power might be reproached for is negated as superstition though he may blame them for their occasional bad conscience which stems from the fact that they have not all been cured yet. He leaves those defeated by life without the hope that therapy is not the highest judge, for to him life is that judge. And all he could say to someone dying in spiritual anguish is that he failed to go into analysis in time.

After the Movies: Mindful of art—and the theater in particular —we reject the film. But even when we have seen one which does not affront our demand too seriously, and especially after a good play, we easily feel a familiar grief. Either we could view the content only historically—for what applied to Nora is true of Iphigenia i.e., that the meaning of the situation does not square with our existence—or we could respond directly, and in that case we feel that our existence is at odds with life as it really is. In either case, the absolute hope in which to confirm us is the most certain sign of the work of art, is stifled. We do not feel it but its remoteness, and a sense of abandonment penetrates us even more profoundly than before.

The Pragmatism of Religions: The thinness of the world religions, and even of famous philosophies, is that all of them not only function secretly and not even so very secretly as ways to manipulate nations —which is known—but that they were originally intended as leading strings. This was least true for the poorest and most naive believers, and perhaps for Jesus of Nazareth. But in the case of the Buddhas and Mohammeds, things are different. What surprises the unprejudiced observer is the profound pragmatism at the core of world religions, the lack of illusions. Substantial differences in legends and cultic apparatus notwithstanding, this turns them into products which can hardly be told apart. Basically, they are all as synthetic, artificial, manipulatory as the trashy sects like Christian science. Perhaps the present should be given credit for the fact that even believers suspect this today, that even the most sincere adherent takes religion pragmatically. Of course, the suspicion cannot be rejected that already the martyrs felt as they went to their death that men could not possibly be guided without religion. Were they perhaps martyrs—of progress?

Note on Dialectics: In dialectics, all opposites go back to a single, fundamental contradiction. Indeed, every specific contradiction in the course of development is a form of this same decisive contradiction. The philosophical problems tied to the concept of dialectics as a whole, such as the question of reconciliation within or beyond history, the relationships between history and reason, logic, nature and spirit, closed or open dialectic, ultimately refer to this contradiction and can only be understood through it. It is that between truth and fulfillment. Whether the absolute is the same as what all beings long for, whether the good and utopia coincide is so profoundly indeterminate that its determination will shape the entire system. In Hegel's logic, the answer to that question is settled in advance. It is Christian civilization. The Hegelian system is based on the hypothesis that reconciliation is certain, that being is also good. It rests on the Christian concept of God. Even in Marx, who denied Hegel, the theological character of history, the unity of theoretical insight and its political application or, rather, the certainty that it could be applied, is the a priori of his thought.

To the great thinkers in their self assurance, the death of created being is of no moment. But for us, dialectics is no game of whose outcome we are assured. It is serious. If the contradiction is not reconciled, we know that the entire effort of thought was useless. But this brings us suspiciously close to the proscribed "bad infinite." Is the tour de force of his hypothesis perhaps the price Hegel paid for his consistency so that the honest "postulate" and the regulative idea would ultimately be terms more appropriate to our situation than the concept that is reconciled with itself?

Myth and Enlightenment: We are always mindful of the fact that as contrasted with the spiritual God, mythology is a false religion. But as we face the totally dark world, the threatening and the insipid one of the primitive, it yet contains something positive, something that confers meaning, the beginning of relativization, negation.

Reason of State: Perhaps it is the meaning of the ever increasing power of the state in our time that man will be able to rise above it, once he has internalized it through the pressure it exerts on him. The free burgher came into existence when the Middle Ages had broken the tribes of the Gothic invasions by the frightful discipline of the allied ecclesiastical and secular powers to such an extent that the individual had internalized the dignity that subjected him as human dignity. Perhaps a similar process, albeit on a higher plane, and involving the entire human being and all of mankind, is occurring now, in this horrible epoch. That would provide a general explanation for the greater intensity of suffering, and a specific one for the despair of those who were already civilized, and must now go through the mill again.

Temptation: The temptation a woman has for a man, or vice versa, is always that in this embrace, the world might transform itself and the absolute become reality. One never knows if the totally new might not occur in this union. Thus love is always—sacrilege.

The Promotion of Science: One should look at the administrators of science, the agents of foundations—their sober, bitter glance, and behind it one will see their principals sitting on their backs. The contradictory unity of their objective power and subjective uncertainty in our present society is reflected in the administrators who hate the new and adventurous like the plague and rely on large congresses, even in the sciences. That's where the money of the foundations goes, and science shows it.

The Busy Man: At times, I am surprised how easily people will accept the refusal of a request, an invitation, a professional offer when the person they have turned to states that he is too busy. The reason for this is the feeling that a lack of time is indicative of considerable professional qualification, perhaps even of wealth. The person that turns down the offer shows that he does not need the other one, and that produces respect and love. I know people who are instinctively aware of this and refuse even when they have nothing else to do. They thus give themselves an air of importance and, at the very least, they get themselves asked again, and even more insistently. But even if that should not happen, they have the pleasure that comes from the social value of their own person. But then I know others who, though also busy, are so accustomed to identifying with others that they will not easily say "no," although the request is purely formal. (I am abstracting here from the material interest that is predominant in relationships.)

Hegel Criticism: A criticism of Hegel must not set in at the point where he defines spirit as both itself and other. Precisely what can no longer be grasped as theory, as thinking (and also what cannot be grasped by thought) the so-called element of practice, the active, the will, are part of spirit provided it is not conceived as abstract, as one element in the division of labor. A correct critique of Hegel should bring out that he is determined to justify a priori all actions and their results, provided they have a lasting effect in the real world. For this very reason, the practical is once again absorbed in the theoretical, and the difference is not sublated which is precisely what happens in action, and not only in the action of thought, but obscured or, better, implicitly deleted. Between the purely theoretical and the childlike on the one hand, and the practical on the other, however, there subsists a similar affinity as between the practical and the paternal-maternal. The theoretical corresponds to being protected, the practical to the protective. But what protects must also be saved, otherwise reason only sees regression in the world and becomes false reason. To say this sounds strange in a world where the leaders and magnates, adulthood and protection are worshipped as it is. But this is precisely the reason that we run the danger of hypostazising the other. Spirit is reflection—self referential, and always has a narcissist, infantile moment when it does not go beyond itself, even when reflection says: I am ashamed of my humanity. If you are ashamed—you might go no further then merely taking note of it!

Personal Property: A time will come when it will no longer be comprehensible that an individual might dispose over his property as he pleases. The *usus ius usus abususque* that was granted and preserved by society and expressed indifference toward it will appear as an insane contradiction. But that time will also no longer suspect that it was precisely this right that made the individual king a symbol without which society can never become humane. For to be human means to be king.

The Special Exclusiveness of Love: The unity of the general and the particular becomes apparent in love. In your love for this particular person, you love what is in all human beings, indeed in all created being, for one can only love mankind or life in the concrete individual, and to love mankind exclusively is a contradiction in terms. It also becomes apparent that the separation into body and soul is an act of abstraction which must be retracted for one does not love either the soul or the body, or the one plus the other, but this forehead and this mouth and this walk as those of a specific individual. But it is in this limitation, provided that it be conscious of itself as such, that love for the whole exists—it is a kind of mediated exclusiveness. Spinoza, who was both more severe and milder than Bruno, comes very close to this knowledge but as a stoic, he will respect the individual only *because* the whole is mirrored in it. And it is precisely the "because," the reflection as the condition, as the a priori justification of identification with the particular which deprives the particular, the ephemeral, of its weight. For then, love is once again love for the general which has lost its content by the intellectualization of the particular.

It is not very different in Christianity. The only way to avoid the exceptionally bad contradiction that lies in the demand for neighborly love "for God's sake" is to do what great theology has always done. God must be emancipated so completely from His creation that He would be endowed with all the richness of the living world even if none were to exist. The moment God is in need of so much as the single grateful glance of a mortal creature to be wholly God, even the great love "for God's sake" will not be love of the Absolute. God's insufficiency which manifests itself here and which patristics was right in stigmatizing as a heathen imputation—the gods who need sacrifices—is acknowledged in Judaism when it speaks of God's feelings, wrath and grief, and in Christianity in the doctrine of God as the son of man. Both posit the suffering, the dependence of God, except that in Christianity the whole question has been settled in advance. One might say that the resurrection—a perennially accomplished fact—had rendered it theoretically innocuous (This is the reason for Eckhart's alternative.) We experience the contradiction that love for the general only realizes itself in love for the particular when the general is renounced. But it is equally true that love for the particular can only be preserved if the limitation, the exclusiveness which separates it from the general is experienced as accidental, and we love life in that love. Otherwise, exclusiveness becomes obtuse. Precisely because this forehead and this mouth are unique, they are only an example. Unless I experience this through them, my love remains a mistake.

1956

Freedom of Thought: There may have been some truth in the polemics against the state as nightwatchman (Saint-Simon, for example). But since that time, the Leviathan has become such an enormous monster that we no longer may say, write and think that it is one, even where it provisionally pretends to be nothing more than a nightwatchman who sees to it that the citizenry has its peace and quiet. Such freedom exists only in a general way, as when one implies, for example, that one opposes social security. To want to be an individual, to want time to think quietly, to want the freedom to say what one thinks even though it be wholly contrary to the demands of the moment rather than supportive of them now seems almost as perverse as promiscuity did a hundred years ago. It is part of this condition that the serious assertion that there is no freedom of thought already leads to ostracism or worse. For only certain abuses of the freedom of thought, i.e. the responsible consideration of what the monster happens to disapprove of at any given moment, will obviously lead to the perverse assertion that only the few things which happen to be forbidden are worth being thought about, and that that thought should be protected. As if freedom of thought did not mean precisely that what is forbidden is thought through and not repressed or projected, and whatever else goes along with that. It is this very reflection about the forbidden that the state should protect, were it not that the state has long since begun protecting something other than man. Who would dare pursue this topic—who are you that you should use this tone? The evil and the malice in this tone are unimportant, not because you are impotent, but because the inflection of power is wrong, whether it be in the mouth of the powerful *or* in that of the impotent. What is wrong is that you, who survive, participate in the suppression of freedom, that one cannot angrily denounce the withdrawal of the freedom of thought when one goes along with it, and goes along with everything that is part of it—the whole operation —bragging, eating meat. You repress too much to be entitled to accuse. You despair because you cannot tell the truth as easily as you wish. A critical tone is much too easy a way out. You make no distinction between your personal annoyance and the advocacy for all who cannot speak.

The End of Speech: We deplore the fact that one can no longer talk. People are mute, however wide they may open their mouths. But we forget too easily that language is dead because the individual speaking to another no longer has anything to say as an individual, as a thinking subject. He is someone who "has no say," i.e., he is impotent; he can accomplish nothing, his word leads to nothing. "It's just talk" means it has no consequences, it effects nothing, it doesn't matter, it doesn't *do* anything. When two persons talk to each other nowadays, their speech may be a link in an established, fixed chain through which power communicates itself, as in the speeches the marionettes from the East make at United Nations meetings. But the exchange between two citizens produces no sequence of causes and effects in the world as once it did when argument and counter-argument led to the new. This was true not only of the barter contract as the distinctive basis of the economic movement (or the social contract which, seen retrospectively, from the point of view of the market economy, appears as the creative act par excellence) but in every respect, even in power politics (not to mention the religious sphere). Today, speech is vapid and those who do not want to listen are not really so very wrong. For the pathetic leaders of mass society, words are instruments of manipulation, their hypnotic hammer which enforces obedience through the muzzle of radios and, along with other methods of torture, in the loneliness of places of detention. And words vegetate along the periphery of a declining bourgeois civilization, ghost-like remnants of what once was culture. But the intimidated, perplexed progeny of the educated only let themselves be haunted by this specter because they already sense the dawning of a new day when the psychoanalyst will be replaced by Big Brother. They seek direction because, in their talk with others, they can no longer find a way of their own, a clear path for themselves. And that ıs the reason it is pointless to listen today. Speech is outdated, and so is the kind of action that once resulted from it.

Educational Reform: In *my* platonic academy, the lowest grades would be taught the critique of political economy, and would have to draw all the consequences that follow from it. They would be brought up to be active dialecticians, and introduced to practice. In the upper grades, they would have to understand Mallarmé, but without forgetting the other.

Psychoanalysis as Judge: The psychological novel and its sequel, psychoanalysis, stress, or, more precisely, hold responsible the inner motivations of individuals. They make the person, not the objective constellation, their principal theme. However the subject may justify itself, it is condemned in advance: its justification is seen as rationalization. It is an old legacy of Christian psychology which is supported by the Enlightenment and comes to us from St. Augustine via Pascal, Vauvenargues and Freud, but ever more abandoned by hope. With every step of this inner sounding, the otherworldly salvation for whose sake it was begun becomes more irreparably confounded with the abstract process through which it is to be attained, and finally the goal is completely forgotten and the process, analysis, is worshipped for its own sake. The ultimate phase whose trivial anticipation we find in the antics of Horney's "self-analysis" is the "self-criticism" of Stalin's half of the world. Here, exactly as in Freud, the examining magistrate and ultimately—anticipating and introjecting him—the self confronts the impotent subject with the allegedly immanent consequences of the thought it once had, the act it once carried out, however innocent it might have been. Whatever might be said, it will be considered as a rationalization of the proscribed intent or—more crudely in the case of Stalin than in Freud's—an evasion and a lie. With both, the facts to be proven are already established before the process begins. Under both, one is condemned in advance. But in the moral phraseology, in the insistence with which a confession of guilt is demanded, the existence of the "soul" is acknowledged, even under Stalin. At least in those cases where the gallows does its work for all the world to see, the "pater peccavi" must be pronounced. Obedience, self-abasement, remorse, the readiness to do penance, those venerable ornaments of Christian psychology, experience a peculiar renaissance and thus reveal something of the secret of their earliest social achievements. The terror of the external powers has been transformed into, more precisely supplemented by, voluntary discipline. Nietzsche knew what internalization has always been about. Question: is "self-criticism" a terrifying beginning, or a terrorful ending?

On Anti-Semitism: The Jews are the enemy because they witness the spiritual God and thus relativize what puffs itself up as the absolute: idol worship, the nation, the leader. The support non-Jews must look for from medicine-men the Jews find elsewhere. This is why their mere existence—the fact that they are "God's people"—becomes a stumbling block. They must be eliminated, and the more absolute a system aspires to be, the more urgent that necessity becomes. For every Jew is experienced as a member of the Jewish people, the people that almost two thousand years ago lost their state and that, though scattered, were held together by their idea of God. It is thus a people in the highest possible sense of the word, the sense of a substance all others feel their own people cannot equal. And precisely for that reason, they frantically insist on that absoluteness. In his own isolation which the other vainly tries to break out of by making an idol of his nation as the collective to which he belongs, he sees the Jew who need do nothing, not even go to the temple, not even speak Hebrew, who, even a renegade, remains part of his people. And the other, in his separateness, sees him possessing something he craves—an essence. That people experience Jews largely as Jews arouses the thirst for revenge which even death cannot slake.

Perversion, a Dreadful Vision: What an enormous mass of repressed desires for instinctual satisfaction other than the regular, genital variety must live in men since they are always ready to burst out in fury when they hear the word perversion. Since the beginning of the Middle Ages, the victims of tyrannical regimes have fared badly when the perversion motif occurred to their persecutors. No torture is too horrible, none satisfies the masses, for none is strong enough to extinguish the fire inside them. None can compensate them for their own renunciation with which they have not come to terms. The pleasures they imagine in perversion seem so superhuman to them that the tortures imposed in retribution must exceed the human measure. And yet there is hardly a crime that causes as little suffering as perversion except where violence is involved. But isn't that true of any transaction? Just as the murder committed in the course of a robbery is the non plus ultra of fraud, so sex murder is the non plus ultra of sexual passion. It has as little to do with atypical sex as "your money or your life" with the imperialism of big business. Even less.

The World-Historical Personality: One's ideas about the "grandiose," "profound" personality of Stalin and similar types are terribly exaggerated simply because these men have a great deal of power. That someone can climb that high and then cause so much evil does not testify to the grandeur of his character or even his thought. One underestimates how far someone can get by brutality, once he has reached an important position. As a person, Stalin is probably nothing more than a brutal gangster chief who cannot tolerate criticism and treats others like dirt unless they happen to be more powerful than he, and that could only be the case outside Russia. He is extremely uninteresting. Only the terror he spreads is superhuman. Compared to this world-historical figure, his colleagues Al Capone and Mickey Cohen seem innocuous indeed. Anyway, what can one say about world history, particularly in its written form? The more horrible its subject, the more mendacious its annals.

Employer–Employee: The entrepreneur is threatened by bankruptcy after a long series of mistakes which can hardly be distinguished from unfavorable events for which he bears no responsibility. He has to begin all over. The employee makes a mistake, is dismissed, is constantly exposed to reprimand and even punishment. One wonders about the enormous difference in self-confidence, its effects on even the smallest details of character and lifestyle.

Thinking and Having: At the core of what we call thinking, we have "weighing," the calculation of risk and possible gain, the interplay between retaining and increasing one's possessions—a contradiction which is the lifeblood of thought. "Perhaps I should take that risk, it might turn out" can be conveyed by a gesture, which, if as a child one never saw one's father make, one is not a complete person as we understand it, one has been cheated. For that gesture, pleasurable because of the very contradiction it harbors, and made by a man who can forbid himself and others many things, first illuminates the meaning of that strictness which is itself a millenia-old legacy. It is possible only against the background of a love for what one has. Nowadays, taking risks has become empty and formalized because that background is gone. If love no longer ties us to what is, we cannot truly want what lies ahead. That is the reason the apologists for the prevailing order in our time, men who merely glorify it by murder and out of hatred for something else, are always prepared to go along with any revolution. They know nothing of history.

Church Fathers and Prophets: For Christians, the main point to the story about paradise is original sin. For Jews, it is the expulsion and the desire to return.

On the Nature of Man: The bloodthirstiness of peasants and others when a wolf or a mountain lion pounces on a sheep at night shows that the greed for raw meat, the desire to rend, to attack, has only been inadequately overcome. By calling the marauding animal a "beast," one strikes a vicious, brutal blow at something outside, at what one cannot eradicate within oneself, and which predates civilization. Beyond that, this bestial hatred of the wolf makes clear that one secretly perceives stuffing one's own belly—the only use the sheep are meant to serve—as the horrible practice it really is. Through their daily contact with them, those who breed domestic animals discover something of their individuality, their trusting life. The resistance against murdering what one protects, against its sale to the butcher, is repressed into the lowest layers of the psyche and rises with bloodshot eyes when they vent their fury against the illegal glutton that is so much more harmless than the treacherous shepherd. In the murder of the wolf, one silences one's own conscience. The opportunity is favorable: one sees oneself as the protector, and even is one at that particular moment. That protection is also murder—

qui saurait y remedier—and only the bloodshot eyes betray that more is involved here than the dialectic of civilization.

On the Criticism of Ideology: The simpler official ideology, the more complicated its derivation has become nowadays. This insight tells us that thinking has become unfashionable.

Fear and Morality: Try to really divorce your obedience to God, the observing of holy days, for example, from the *fear* of the Lord —but do it all the way. Provided they do not in themselves appear appropriate, you will discover that being dead-set on observing the commandments turns into something like pity for God—or let us call it "voluntary reciprocity." And it shows. Am I to postpone some work which is useful to me and others, simply because God rested on the seventh day? But don't be misled: Kant was right when he said that obedience to God became respect for the moral law, and what is true of that respect applies very precisely to the fear of God without fear. If one cannot see the usefulness—and we are abstracting from usefulness here—there is no reason why morality should be what it is, and not something else. What remains is simply that something happens for which there is no reason; the detachment from the pragmatic, from what has effect and validity in this world. While such detachment in and of itself gives no concrete indication about what is to be done, tells us nothing, and certainly provides no hierarchy of values, it yet seems unambiguous in a certain sense. This comes from the suspicion that the world as it is at any given moment may not be *right,* and even from the suspicion about all good motives. (Kant saw very deeply in his mistrust of all good motives.) If we cannot naively believe in the revelation, the coldness contained in that detachment becomes a danger.

Against Doctrines of Essence: In the sphere of the concept, it is the same as in music. What an element is only becomes apparent in its progression. It is true that three successive, identical tones are not nothing but something. But a three-part rhythm, something complete in itself, and the beginning of a Mozart melody, are two different worlds, and one should not believe that the former is really the fundamental, the "natural" one, that it serves better to define the "essence" than a definite melody. This error probably underlies almost all doctrines of essence, even if one tries to define man's essence through his existence as an individual. But for that very reason, the statement an abstract philosophical doctrine makes does not tell us very much unless the place and tone allow us to infer its inevitable political consequences. One must know the entire melody. That all thinking will thus always remain fragmentary is no objection to the demand that it be carried as far as possible.

Equal Rights: Everyone Becomes the Same: Equal rights for men and women in marriage is welcomed by the men that run things today. For it means that competition, "human relations," alienation, in short, isolate human beings even within the so-called social cell, that a microscopic utopia remains unrealized, that even on the smallest scale, a sworn community no longer exists, that man stands naked before the machinery of the general. The reader will note that our rearguard action makes us allies of the church. As so often in matters of freedom, it used the father confessor to weaken in advance and to thus make acceptable the sworn community in that it tolerated within limits what is being liquidated today because it escaped control in bourgeois society through the invocation of privacy, freedom and humanity. As long as it extended only to the privileged segment of the bourgeoisie, a measure of tolerance was possible. Today, where society is being "democratized," that is becoming dangerous. Everyone is answerable for everyone else. Let no one claim the bedroom as a haven for freedom of thought!

The Accessories: Whatever may happen, we must not complain, for we are sitting quietly and comfortably in our armchairs, we dine and discuss although we know that hell is loose. We are devils too, even we.

Living, Thinking and Money: People so often say that temperance has become unfashionable in the technological age. That's quite true. In a certain sense, happiness, indeed the capacity for intellectual pleasure, presuppose temperance. But we cannot live moderately because without money, without more and more money—and Hobbes already saw this—one is defenseless against brutality, death, terror. Without a great deal of money, there is no security and therefore no real life. And the amount of money needed to protect oneself, to live and to think—and isn't that part of living—no one has who has what it takes to live and think.

Bourgeois and Peasant: It is well known that the bourgeoisie became the victim of its own means: money, or of abstract power, purchasing power, that it generally understood all ends as rationalizations, ideologies for a hypostatized exchange value. The mechanism that plays the most important role here is the dwindling of memory. It manifests itself in the kind of mentality that is peculiar to the bourgeoisie, i.e., skepticism. The negated myth is not sublated but cancelled, liquidated, forgotten. Not having been surmounted, it survives in the lower regions, and finally the thoughtless victor becomes the victim. This is apparent in the very conception of man. The bourgeois perceived man's nakedness, his rawness and stupidity in the peasant, he acquired his self-confidence as the town dweller who, though not of the nobility, was certainly not its underling. The consciousness of the bourgeois carries the traces of his rise: he identified with the nobility; laboriously, through work and saving, he supplanted it. And unlike the nobility, he despised the peasant. The successful businessman shrugs his shoulders at the little man, and even that insignificant gesture reveals the identification with his class, the detachment from the person who is not really part of town life. Like the peasant, the other is just a human being and therefore mere cattle. But since this other which is still crude and uncivilized is wholly negated, simply left outside and forgotten, civilization becomes its own opposite. It merely fought primitiveness and did it everytime a child was raised, but at the end of the epoch, it is about to succumb to it again because it survives unmodified in bourgeois man. The French got furthest, especially the Parisians, and Goethe dedicated his life to this question. Almost all his great works are attempts to make civilization concrete. Rousseau and Stifter can be understood from this perspective. Hollywood, on the other hand. . . .

The Future of the Bourgeoisie: Marx conceived of socialism as the higher stage of society where everything that had developed in its bourgeois form would be sublated, which means that it would both be stripped of its absoluteness, and preserved. In Russia, we have the elements of prehistory but they are discontinuous, gigantic distortions. This is most apparent in the trials. At least in principle, it was the glory of the bourgeoisie that it granted the accused or suspected individual the freedom to confess his guilt or maintain his innocence, and the state had the duty to prove the truth to him and society. The Soviet tyrannies acknowledge this principle except that the state, that radiant vehicle of whatever happens to be the most infamous clique, hunts down the individual. The intellectual wreck who is compelled to confess there is the caricature of the human being the bourgeoisie —acting from self interest, not deeper insight, and yet quite emphatically—wanted to respect and perfect. In so-called socialism, the things that once took place in the basements of its metropolitan police stations now confront the bourgeoisie as its own caricature, and the bad conscience which caused decent people to overlook such blemishes in better times now stares into the magnifying mirror in the East. If, in view of such results, the bourgeoisie fails to search its soul, if it does not at least infer the mote in its own eye from the beam in the mirror, the Russian caricature of socialism will become the model for the last phase of bourgeois society. Hitler and his Mediterranean colleagues were the beginning.

Critical Analysis and Pragmatism: To look East is to become aware of the terror of military dictatorship. Does the horror one feels imply one's being part of the integrated West, since the integrated West is the only opposing world-historical power? Is criticism without such integration not just wind, like the impotent individual from which it comes? Does it not become empty opinion, since, historically, there is substance only where there is power which can put something different in the place of what is being criticized? And isn't the converse also true? Isn't criticism of the West *nolens volens* eastern? Can there be criticism without a historical base? Isn't a vain utopianism the price one pays for the loss of the pragmatic element in criticism, the prospect of the concrete possibility of implementing it? There certainly can be no true criticism without an intellectually grounded hope which derives its legitimacy from realistic possibilities, and differs from merely arbitrary, vague wishes by being precise. But criticism is the soul of historical experience itself. Without it, there is only followership, and aren't practically all who talk about history these days mere followers? Without precise criticism whose source and sole guardian may be the individual (though its subject can be mankind) it would not even be possible to meaningfully consider whether West and East might ultimately not be the antinomy they want to make us believe in.

Need: Long before Hegel, it was known that industry artificially creates the needs for its products. What escaped the thinkers was the disappearance of natural need itself. They saw the contradiction between the created, so-called "cultural" minimum and the restraint that was forever being demanded of the masses, the contradiction between the interest in increasing demand and that in declining production cost, the contradiction between the mass as consumers and wage earners. But this phenomenon has long since receded. As the great economic powers became institutions, and countless economic functions were taken over by the state, the form of demand also changed. Anyone who wants to exist in this society must have the living standard which the situation dictates. As a consumer, as someone who himself becomes the producer of his abilities in his role as employee, he must constantly keep up, renew, supplement, etc. his "private" means of production without which he is useless, and that includes bicycle, car, radio, his apartment with all its gadgets, prescribed clothing and whatever else falls into this category. He stops being a consumer and becomes subject to a levy. The difference between purchase price and tax, public and social property decreases for the amount he pays for the upkeep of the road and his own means of transport are both equally involuntary, except that he himself has to operate the latter. What is the latest need at a given time may still require stimulation, like the really cultural one for television. But that is true for only a brief period. Once the time of inflammatory speeches returns, it will already be subversive not to look obediently at the tube. The tube will be a must. This example is instructive. In a changed society, all these gadgets, from alarm clock to phonograph record, will become elements of a comprehensive hypnosis, brain-washing. It all began when needs were created. Once created, it turns out that their very nature makes for nothing but their own production. The hypostasizing of means, the process of reification tends to direct man's will to nothing but its own production—empty desire. It is untrue that the machine itself gives orders to those that operate it. It only commands in the absence of a subject to take charge of it. Today, individuals are nothing but the compulsion to serve, and dispositions are blind and anonymous—in spite of business and political leaders. Only with the creation of a disposing subject would freedom—and need, be posited.

Two Aspects of Materialism: Tolerance—since everything has to be the way it is. Protest—against everything being the way it has to be.

Holiday Mood: The concept "holiday mood" denounces the everyday, just as it denounces holidays and the life that splits up into the two. That happiness is conceived as a mood that must be tailored to a span of time shows what it really is: prescribed happiness. But the everyday is entitled to the buffoonery of seriousness which knows that happiness cannot be found in it. That's how human beings have arranged their life in our time.

Concrete Wonderment: Wonderment has come into the more concrete branches of philosophy. Anyone who first notices how the split between feeling and reason, love and interest, human relations and a contract of employment is connected with the transition of the family from a closed household economy to the "private" sphere of the competitive society will feel as if the scales were taken off his eyes. He learns that Romeo and Juliet mark a turning point in this story, and thus discovers the meaning of literature. He sees the "sanctity" of the natural community passing over into the unity of the two lovers, the individual coming into existence with romantic love.

A Question Addressed to Psychoanalysis: Is a love suspect because, being sublimated, it may revert to vulgar instinct and even aggression? Can one tell its origin and possible future, or does the transformation of the vulgar drive into something other involve not only a change of its object but of the essence of the impulse itself? Does only the moment count, or is genesis also part of the truth?

Tradition: Children have a more significant, profounder experience of the customs of adults than those adults themselves. This is necessary if customs are to survive. But our generation is about to abolish children.

Market Research: A decisive fact for so-called market research in our society (that one can no longer print a decent book, for example) is the passing of wealth from private individuals to concerns and corporations. As long as the individual still had money, he could deviate from the dictates of mass culture in his private life—and if not he, then his sons, daughters and other dependents. Today, he buys a Mercedes on his expense account. Books one need not have read no longer arouse interest, and this is even truer of expensive convictions. And the young have to hurry up and earn money. Thus it comes about that a society which daily decimates its forests to create forests of newspapers, mimeographs theoretical thought. Otherwise it becomes too expensive, relatively speaking.

Human Grief: The happiness of men is no more noble and no more profound than that of animals, but it is less innocent. But men's grief is both more noble and more profound—through grief, men become more innocent.

What a Person Concerns Himself With: That the "economic" interpretation of history is so close to the bourgeois tendency to debunk, to always look for a "motive," gives pause. It wasn't originally intended that way, but just look at the imitators. What is being debunked usually gets what it deserves, but that doesn't mean that the debunkers become more tolerable.

Charm: Whenever someone uses intelligence and conviction in a civilized discussion to get others to accept his point of view, he is usually told that his success is due to his charm. A person who says that cannot imagine that one can be a human being without immediately using that quality as a technique. For him, all being is instrumental.

Undeserved Good Luck: Someone inherits a great deal of money. How nice that without having "deserved" it, he can live without working, without pain. That's when people start screaming "how unjust!" Don't you realize that this is the tiny bit of justice still left in this world? Good luck that wasn't deserved?

The French Revolution: That the great French Revolution left such a profound impression is partly due to the fact that the sanctity of the French king was etched more deeply into people's hearts than that of other princes. That this king could be beheaded, that those who did it could be victorious in spite of that fact, caused an uncommon strengthening of the consciousness of freedom, and brought comfort to resentment.

Progress, Justice, and the Decline of the Self: Mach wrote, "the self cannot be saved." The statement was meant epistemologically, and the development of society made it a fact. That its strength, intensity, duration, complexity and substance depend on what is external to it the idealist Fichte, the herald of the self, had already seen when he made the person dependent on property. Since then, there has not only set in a general trend toward the dwindling of personal property but other, equally necessary conditions are being affected by the process of industrial development. The role of a changed environment—from assembly line to computer—and the disintegrating, atomizing effect of the mass media, are known. In addition, there are social facts in a narrower sense. Because people constantly move within cities, or from one city to another, they no longer have a permanent home, and change has a differentiating effect on the individual. Altered relations between the sexes, the fact that marriage can be more easily dissolved, mean that people no longer share experiences in a closely knit life, no longer age together or reciprocally constitute their selves through knowledge of each other. This is equally true of other relationships, friendships and professional associations. Along with these material preconditions of the self, the human ones disappear as well. In the atomized social reality, the atom is split as it is in the physical world. Yet both dissolve something that had been mistakenly hypostasized. What is being destroyed through progress are mythical entities. It is justice that puts an end to them.

Happiness and Unhappiness: Happiness is infinitely various; unhappiness differs only in degree.

The New Illiterates: It's not so long ago that being able to read and write was a privilege—even in Europe. Today, it seems natural that it should be the rule. But style, skillful expression, the order and disposition of thoughts are still a privilege. All of this becomes questionable as automation sets in. There will be an elite that knows how to push the right buttons, and that will understand the machinery. We are becoming illiterates again. Our skill dates back to the day before yesterday. The attempts of artists, from the automatic literature of the surrealists to the newest music, will be of no avail. We are hopelessly falling behind. Thought must adapt itself to the medium which mediates it, and in the long run, the medium is more solid than a logic that is alien to it and wants to use it, albeit by a sophisticated adaptation.

Bourgeois Dialectic: We must not be ungrateful to the bourgeois order. Its greatest shortcoming is not the misery it contains, for it could overcome that, but rather that it is liquidating itself through the operation of immanent laws. The most important intellectual debt is that our thinking carries the signature of freedom, that—however great our fear of the end—there is a sense in which we do not feel it, for our reason has not been intimidated. If we want something higher than this bourgeois order it is only because, even as it was just beginning to gather strength under feudalism, it taught us to be critical, and also critical of ourselves. We want something better but we must be careful that its arrival not stifle that will.

1957–1958

On Scientific Theory: The particular quality and the instrumentalities of the social need to control nature change from one period to the next, and the facts of the natural sciences bear its stamp. The facts of the social sciences bear the stamp of interest in the structuring of social relationships, be it in the strengthening of those that already exist, or in their transformation. If these sciences want to overcome their abstractness and become conscious of themselves, they must reflect about those functions which form, structure, and constitute their material. More important than anything else here is the machinery of the mode of perception at a given time, the work of the intellectual apparatus through which it isolates the phenomenal world of possible experiential nexuses so that those living at a certain time, in a certain society, can largely understand each other. Kant took it to be his business to define those functions which are common to all periods, i.e., the forms of every conceivable intersubjective reality, of any and every experiential nexus. We are concerned with the differences. The average empirical sociologist these days is totally naive vis-à-vis the prevailing schematism. Through the concept of "facts," he posits as absolute both a form of perception which is conditioned down to the most insignificant detail, and all the conscious and unconscious interests which organize the world, and then calls "theory" the systematic presentation of these "facts." But such theory lacks self-awareness. It is stupid.

Transposed Roles: Descriptions of the decline of culture in mass society are readily criticized for being romantic. But actually the account of what is disappearing expresses what is negative in the present. It denotes the misery of things as they are too exclusively to also lay claim to setting forth the splendors of the past. Because they feel this, the reactionaries today are against the past. The roles have been transposed. To praise the old becomes suspect, and confidence in the future the conventional thing. The analysis of the suffering from which this new romanticism springs reveals the pressure of reality. As long as that pressure does not become the object of direct, unblinking reflection, accounts of mass society will be no more than a form of distraction. The misery in a remorseless industrial society is disguised as grief over culture. This is an alibi for those intellectuals who do not want to see that misery for what it is.

Ladder: What was attained in an earlier phase of culture only because archaic cultural contents and myths were overcome and therefore seemed mediated—"spiritual"—is taken for granted, immediate, during a later phase. The earlier stage therefore seems more "cultivated," i.e., more spiritual, more inward. Rome looks back on Greece, America on Europe. Nonetheless, Rome and America are also right to feel more "developed." To become oblivious to mediation is an element in the capacity for social achievement.

Closed Society: One reason that romantic love seems old-fashioned is that it promotes opposition to society. In its isolation, the union of the lovers is also self-sufficient, universal and exclusive, particularly when it even sees marriage as a concession. In an attenuated form, the same holds true for the family in the old sense. It is a society within a society.

Respect and Fear: How closely respect and fear are still allied becomes apparent in the fact that one respects only what is. The less substance or power a thing has, the less venerable it is. It is the secret of European culture to have propagated the idea that eternal justice, the good, has a meaning. People thus came to love justice and the good although it is really the stolid, the stable, the persevering that has substance. This distinguishes the European, Western situation from everything Eastern. Whether the problematical is beneficial, whether it ultimately fosters what is humane is something I do not know.

Dialectic of Enlightenment (1): After the bourgeois epoch, it is probably not its sublation but the relapse into the immediate that will occur. It will be accompanied by the greatest mechanical precision of the process of reproduction. Men no longer experience themselves as individuals, in need of a goal that transcends their existence. Le Grand Etre and Hegel's objective spirit have become unnecessary. And man no longer thinks of himself as finite, as being unable to live without an infinite, or at least some, meaning. Instead, he is unreflectedly "positive," an element of social reality. Mediation goes by the board. Dialectic of the Enlightenement.

In the Circus: Through the image of the elephant in the circus, man's technological superiority becomes conscious of itself. With whip and iron hooks, the ponderous animal is brought in. On command, it raises its right, its left foot, its trunk, describes a circle, lies down laboriously and finally, as the whip is being cracked, it stands on two legs which can barely support the heavy body. For many hundreds of years, that's what the elephant has had to do to please people. But one should say nothing against the circus or the act in the ring. It is no more foreign, no more inappropriate, probably more suitable to the animal than the slave labor for whose sake it entered human history. In the arena, where the elephant looks like the image of eternal wisdom as it confronts the stupidity of the spectators and where, among fools, it makes a few foolish gestures for the sake of peace and quiet, the objective unreason of the compulsory service which serves the rational purpose of the Indian timber market still reveals itself. That men depend on such labor to then be obliged to subject themselves to it as well is ultimately their own disgrace. The enslavement of the animal as the mediation of their existence through work that goes against their own and alien nature has the result that that existence is as external to them as the circus act is to the animal. Rousseau had an intimation of this when he wrote his prize-winning essays. Civilization as stultification.

Love and Experience: The lover loves the beloved as he sees her, and this expresses his own personality and history as it does those of the society to which he belongs. What seems good to him in the beloved also denotes his own idea of the good and of the world as it should be. But his conception of the good is also affected by the beloved. There are people who can offer no resistance here and quickly adopt the qualities of their partner. Experience in the emphatic sense is the productive, reflective process of the assimilation of the new that lights up in the other.

The Devil: I have made a discovery: that the Nazis kicked the Jews to death, that the hireling who lashed the Jewish woman in the face when she cursed him as she, as entire swarms were driven into the gas ovens has its origin in the perverted longing for the kindness that has power—in the provocativeness of the good. In that lash of the whip lies the inability to love the good that is impotent, the despair that it has no power. The devil.

Don't Think About It: As causes of the difference between men, wealth and other sources of happiness were abolished in the totalitarian countries of the East. A bureaucratic hierarchy was then established. But in a just society, that hierarchy also would have to go. Only personal differences remain—and could those be preserved without socially established differences in happiness? If that were to disappear, wouldn't differences in education in the widest sense of that term also become a thing of the past, and everything become a question of skill, psychological talent, streamlined conformism? Competition for friendship—and friendship for what—in a just society? Until that society has become a reality, one should not think about these questions.

On Saint-Simon: Saint-Simon says that no one should starve, that everyone should be rewarded according to his capacities and achievements. But what happens if people are perfectly content with not having to starve, and don't ask for anything more? Either that is made so unpleasant for them that it comes to the same thing, as welfare in this society, or one has to talk people into wanting the better consumer products, luxury, and that is also being done today. But if they are permitted a reasonable morality which may make even a modest existence a happy one, the power of society will be a thing of the past. Machinery, airplanes, indeed the natural sciences themselves derive from the compulsion to have a career, to "get ahead." For its sake, one forgets about life. Without the whip of competition, people begin to think.

The Error of Idealism: The concept is abstract, in spite of Hegel. Insight into another's torment is not the same as personal experience of it. Indeed, memory itself, however vivid it may be, is pale. That is the error of idealism, particularly of the German variety. There is a gulf between the positing of the ego and horrible reality, and there is a gulf between the life of the concept, and nature and history whose image it is. This is the argument against any form of rationalism. The concept is inadequate. It may reach all the way to heaven, as its advocates believed, but it is incommensurate to what is, and that didn't occur to them.

The Individual and Society: When all the gods have been toppled, there remains as the substance of the self the choice between —no, not even between a career and possessions, for they will amount to the same thing. What does remain is the automatism of choice by the abstract individual, the functioning of those social mechanisms which condition it, and for which it is a mere vehicle. This is the result of a society which is rich in itself but not for men. They always hanker after something. Will it be the eternal pattern that men must be broken to be human beings but don't become human beings because they are broken? Is it conceivable that they might be brought up like the sons of wealthy parents who now and then turned into something, or like Emile or Buddha? But then mankind would come to an end, for such men are ill-suited to preserve the race. Nature cannot rely on them, they are too intelligent for it.

Wrong Ascesis: What once went beyond rational motivation—the attachment to things and people, the cultivation of relationships which no longer have a practical value, the keeping of a promise which cannot be enforced, the listening to the nature stirring within —all this must yield to the increased demands of making one's way. Ever more exclusively, the power of society forces the young into the channels of civilization. How they conform, how seriously they commit themselves to production, how considerable an effort they make to adapt to, to identify with, the division of labor! The intelligence of the mechanic, the calm, stable patience of students becoming experts, all of these things are assimilations to instruments whose quiet power has its own dignity. Look at American students late at night, in libraries, on trains and airplanes, and how they conform to the formula, the compulsion of mathematics. It makes no sense to wish they were romantics. But isn't overcoming the childhood still stirring within us a renewed repression of the animal, the highest form of the divesting oneself of animal innocence that went along with the enslavement of animals? Isn't emancipation too radical—or not radical enough (for there is no going back)? Even in the finest specimen, aren't we reminded of the slaughterhouse rather than ascesis? Max Weber was in error. He considered saving—and that was correct as far as it went—but gave no thought to liquidation. Genuine ascesis presupposes knowledge of the other.

Critical Theory: Right away, people always ask what should be done now, they demand an answer from philosophy as if it were a sect. They are in distress and want practical pointers. But although philosophy presents the world in concepts, it has in common with art that by an internal necessity—without intent—it holds a mirror up to the world. It is true that its relation to practice is closer than that of art, it does not express itself figuratively but literally. But it is no imperative. Exclamation marks are foreign to it. It has replaced theology but found no new heaven to which it might point, not even a heaven on earth. But it is true that it cannot rid itself of that idea, which is the reason people always ask it for the way that could take them there. As if it were not precisely the discovery of philosophy that that heaven is none to which a way can be shown.

Contradiction of Love: Nowhere does the dialectical nature of reality and its concept become as clear as in the nature of the virtues. Love and loyalty demand hardness against others. If one is not hard, one cannot love. Perhaps love cancels itself.

False Appearance: If it seems today that the great achievements, telegraphy, and the telephone, airmail and radio, are at everyone's service, and that the trained voice of the telephone operator is there "for us," it must be added that all of this is there for industry magnates. It is at our disposal only as long as the men in charge do not lay exclusive claim to it. In the voice of the telephone operator, in the figure of the airline hostess, one senses the conformation of the world to large enterprise. They speak to us as the employee, the secretary, speaks to the chairman of the board because he sets the tone. "We" profit because this entire apparatus cannot also be specifically designed for the few important people. That would be too laborious. The tone changes at the counters of the Social Security Administration.

On Hegel: The history of creation according to which man is meant to be the lord of nature would refute Hegel also. Although for him reason does not coincide with the deception of all creatures, as in technology and the sciences, the all-penetrating concept, spirit, which recognizes itself in what it confronts, ultimately remains subjective. It is the spirit of men, their institutions and their society. The only objective thing, the other—what he calls the "mystical,"—lies in the circumstance that the struggles of nations in world history cannot be resolved by rational agreement. That is reason's only limitation. The world comes into its own when it is adequate to men. Hegel is superior to the Enlightenment because he knows that knowledge requires self-estrangement, the entering into things, although it is true that they finally reveal themselves as knowledge, as the "concept," the subjective. He is inferior because he believes that adequacy has already been attained.

Without Measure: As if the drive behind the heroic acts of the martyrs of progress, Bruno, Vanini, Galileo, were not similar to the urge of other criminals who act from passion. To pursue a longing that is forbidden by the law, be it that for love, happiness, or truth and its propagation. To let oneself go. To strain in order to let oneself go. To be blinded. To be unable to resist doing or willing. Doing what one should not do because one follows the light. All this is found along the edges of society. Only blindness or the lack of love, whether in crime or uprightness, in the pedantically evil citizen or in the evil fool, are different from this. What is good or bad is not measured by the handy law, however necessary it may be. A toast to those who can take it as their guide, and not wither.

Schopenhauer And Nietzsche: Schopenhauer was angry with the world because he saw that all life obeys power, that surrender to the thing, identification with what is not the self, seems barely to lead out of the magic circle of egoism and into nothingness—and that is a myth. Nietzsche, a German philosopher in this respect as well, also found appetition, the drive toward expansion at the cost of everything weak, the core of existence, although he suspected that this was not the final word. In contrast to Schopenhauer, he resisted the misery to which we all succumb in the end: he would not allow it to force him to negate all being. He knew that it was precisely such negation which is the consequence, the prolongation of the entire horrible mechanism, the opposite of philosophy, the opposite of freedom, thinking, imagination, spontaneity. He noticed that pessimism presupposes the very things it denies: the beauty of the world, the splendor of life, and discovered the bad contradiction in the work of his teacher. What he brings up against suicide, the argument by which he shows that it makes no sense, applies to the pessimistic position generally. But that his affirmation sounds more desperate than spontaneous gives pause. For in his work, pessimism is not just sublated but more terribly, more madly persisted in than in the writings of its founder. Nietzsche's psychological, social, historical insight is superior. There probably is no such thing as philosophy, it is always just a myth.

Hegel's Trick: Our imagination is limited in its capacity to transcend reality. Either there are many more lives after this one which are similar to it, or there is eternal bliss or hell, i.e., quantitatively and qualitatively greater suffering and joy, or an intermediate condition, purgatory. Hindus and Christians have experimented with all this in their thought, and sects have elaborated this or that aspect. Medieval philosophy also, and even St. Thomas, have made their contribution, and told us that the sight of the damned delights the blessed. But since that time, philosophy has merely added that we may well know nothing of that other which constitutes the meaning of this life. That was done by Kant, and all the rest resigned themselves to this reality. Indeed, positivism even called this resignation a myth and put it ad acta. By using the term Absolute, by predicating its immanence in the relative and the dignity thus confered upon it, Hegel used a trick to create the impression that the Absolute in itself, i.e., abstractly, has its own significance which it could infuse into the non-abstract in the dialectical process and this inspite of Kant and all insight into the nullity of the abstract. He believed that being, which he had recognized as nothingness, could ultimately be proven to be that abundance in which nothingness inheres as merely a moment, as the passing away of individuals which it needs for its splendor. But as the individuals pass away, so does the splendor. Facts exist and pass away, and one could say that existence and transitoriness remain and do not pass away. This is really what Hegel means by the preponderance of the positive in which the negative merely inheres as an immanent, propulsive force. That is the reason the concept, life, love, are to endure and to unfold pain within themselves. But the thought that pain, decline, horror recur and that the concept, life, love are mere corollaries in this repetition destroys the system. The inadequacy of Hegel's doctrine does not lie in its nominalism—that would be an absurd philosophy—but in the defectiveness of its ideas. If it is true that the positive, the most highly developed moment, first makes the negative the negative; if it is not, conversely, the happiness only the most experienced can know that causes the sadness that is adequate to the whole, it is equally true that the philosophy that wishes to affirm this conceptually, the reference to this positive as meaning and significance, distorts it into a horrible lie. Rather than truth, the highest is the unrepeatable—the absolute, happiness, love. It is what the concept is not.

Mediation of Progress: From the point of view of the backward, the progressive always looks superficial. But when confronted with civilization, the backward degenerates into hocus pocus, the ritual dances of the primitives which amuse the explorers. The backward is narrow, twisting streets, antiques. It's what the great philosophers are for the travellers of history, or Paris for the tourists. The path leads from the immediate to the mediated, from sensual pleasure, cannibalism, to belief and on to mere contemplation. Once that has been attained, it turns out, as is only proper, that cannibalism is foolishness, i.e., life seen wholly through the wrong pair of glasses. The contemporary American businessman views the old-style European thinker as a plague, a magician, a phony really, and since America has actually gone beyond Europe, the thinker becomes what the businessman sees, a charlatan, and his truths incantations. This identical process recurs in all areas. From the sacred temple prostitution which was itself quite derivative, a line leads via the great demimondaine to the Russian Ballet and the Folies Bergères, and from there to Hollywood musicals. But once such mass productions of empty appearance have conquered the world, even the streetwalker becomes ugly and indigestible. As the mediation of the immediate becomes apparent, it loses the appearance which once enabled it to bestow happiness.

Morality: Conscience as moral authority is the specific contribution German philosophy made to European culture. Neither the Mediterrenean nor the Anglo-Saxon world really know morality as duty, as a commandment that translates itself into acts. Education in England always retained a feudal, esthetic element—the gentleman and the lady. In America, there is the law on the one hand, and religion on the other. In Mediterrenean countries, we have a religious or secular natural law. And the Russians today see morality as ideological foolishness when they are confronted with it. They are altogether incapable of understanding what it is supposed to mean. How can there be an authority that is independent of the party? They haven't yet reached that point.

Humanity: Our practical philosophy is humanity. That men do not suffer misery, that created beings can develop, is the purpose of action in general. That the protection of freedom may cause the restraint, the suppression of its enemies results from the contradictory nature of reality, but here also the sole guide is the humane goal which must not be devoured by the means. Admittedly, this sounds banal, but we know no other criteria of equal rank. The western world defiled them when it offered friendship to Hitler until he laid hands on their own material interests. It dishonors itself in every smile at the murderers in the Kremlin. It would be friends with them if only their stance were not so threatening. The western world will perish because its own material interests are more important to it than the protection of mankind within and beyond its borders. And to counter the danger that its judgment may be presumptuous when it arrogates to itself the decision when and how mankind is to be fed, instructed or protected, there is no higher appeal than that to the solidarity with the suffering which must be abolished. Not war, but the terror in war and other conditions such as despotism is the greatest evil. And it is that appeal which decides whether or not it is right for nations to go to war to do away with tyranny elsewhere. But usually tyranny will come to an end when the destitution that sustained it is abolished. If only I knew a better term than humanity, that poor, provincial slogan of a half-educated European. But I don't.

Democracy and the Mass Media: The democracy whose electorate is not both enlightened and humane will ultimately succumb to the most unscrupulous propagandists. The development of the mass media of propaganda such as newspapers, radio, television, polls and their connection and interplay with the decline in education must necessarily lead to dictatorship and the regression of humanity.

Hegel and Marx: It is not until they discuss the role various strata play that Hegel and Marx begin to differ as regards social reality. In both, it is the meaning of existence that the individual involve himself or even guide his group in the function history assigns to it. Independent of that group—abstractly—the individual is nothing. By making his function its own, the Absolute realizes itself in and through the individual, as the meaning that accrues to it. But they differ in their definition of the strata and their function. For Hegel, every social group is a positive, "moral" element, provided it is part of the structure of the whole. From family to nation, all units involved in production and reproduction, and directly or indirectly part of society, have their validity, and that includes entrepreneurs, workers, farmers, employees, bureaucrats, professors, everything. That is essentially the meaning of their being recognized as "estates." What Hegel sees is not so much their transformation as their permanent share in the whole whose preservation gives them, and through them the individual, their meaning. Both Hegel and Goethe would have taken America's side, their philosophy is pro-American. Aside from the feudal lords who are dying out, Marx only acknowledges entrepreneurs and workers. Actually, the time when the entrepreneurs were a positive element is already up although—and *for the time being*—they can still represent the positive in that they have an essential part in the present economic period. Categories such as "employees" have no reality for Marx, and the role of the workers is that of the proletariat. They do not fulfill their world-historical function by running machines but by preparing themselves to replace the present form of society by a new one and to concurrently negate and transform their own existence. The concept "proletarian" cannot be separated from this negative, this self-negating element. (And this is also the reason the social democratic and Russian glorification of the proletarian as "the working human being" conflicts with Marx.) According to Marx, it is thus not its absorption in its social function but the transformation of that function that is the "absolute" meaning of the social being of the individual during this world period. And this transformation results from what he called the dehumanization of the proletarian, i.e., from the fact that, more and more, he is cheated out of an independent, free, self-governing life. The "historical act" which makes him the executor of the Absolute derives from this. Two critical questions must be asked here. First: how can the idea of an absolute be substantiated at all if it is inconceivable that our philosophizing is grounded in it? How can an awareness of his negativity not just as misery but as negativity relative to an absolute determination ever disclose itself to the proletarian unless there be a dawning of the wholly other, the new? And could not the new turn out to be nothingness after all? Secondly: Although at the cost of an unending further reification, an improvement of material conditions is currently under way in the social system. Is this development to be viewed as making for further dehumanization or as its, albeit questionable, remedy? Marx would not have disputed that such improvement should be endorsed for it mitigates the raw misery that attends the struggle for a better life. But would dehumanization not become an increasingly less conscious motive in such an eventuality? Did Marx believe that prospect for change is obscured because with the disappearance of the most visible forms of dehumanization, reflection about humanity, this bitter desire for it, would disappear along with them? If this were really the case, the assault of the technicized barbarians of the East would mean the end of society as it developed up to the bourgeois period. As after antiquity, a new beginning would have to be made, and a new principle would have to be found for it.

Vain Love: Kant is a rationalist, and thus at one with any form of positivism. Any transcending love is delusion. Woe unto me.

Small Talk: Language loses those meanings which go beyond the purely functional, pragmatistic, instrumental. Concurrently, the individual declines. The less typical the autonomous citizen, the individual, becomes of society, the less he has "something to say," be it reactionary or progressive, oppositional or conservative, the more the non-technical uses of language become mere show, recommendation for a career, for membership in groups, like clothing, table manners, habits. When people get together, there is small talk; the content is inconsequential. Those who hear or make declamations full of pathos or attend festivities, gatherings, religious services, also realize that substance is of no moment. What counts is observing customs. Nuances come into play when specific, personal interests which one can know or guess at play a role. No one is so naive as to consider what language says, let alone to take it literally, at least no one that is up to date. Children already *learn* language in this way, they do not understand that it could be different. They only know purposes, not meanings. The television or radio announcer, the film stars see to that. That they are not perceived as the characters they play but as the more or less current idols, and that this perception includes their private lives and all the rumors about it, is a repetition of the language system. *What* they represent means nothing. It is pure superstition to expect that a child that hears this voice, sees that smile, or listens to synthetic good humor for hours on end each day, or at least each week, should ever discover that they are something other than means. Everybody regresses into cleverness. Cleverness is more characteristic of the animal than insight. Animals are clever. For them, the rustling of the foliage is no intimation of autumn or transitoriness but a hint that the enemy is approaching. In the construction of the sputnik, man does not triumph as a rational being but as a race of predators so clever that it has become insane.

The European Spirit: The philosophers in the nineteenth century, Hegel and Nietzsche, wrote: God is dead. It would be truer to say that thought has died. Its historical role, the overcoming of superstition, the loosening of the bond by which religion kept men subservient to the first and the second estate, the emancipation of the individual citizen, is over and done with. Continuing emancipation, its generalization in a society of abundance where it preserves the individual and his spiritual capacities, has failed. Thought has a critical, negative, liberating function without which it cannot survive. The soul of great philosophy, the strength of truth, its historical claim, is enlightenment and the individual. Since bourgeois society did not succeed in developing beyond itself without atrophying the individual spiritually, thought goes under along with the citizen. Its death is imminent. Already, it has ceased to exist. What mind remains is the instrument of natural science or, rather, the mere ghost of mind. It will disappear.

The Three Mistakes of Marx: The three mistakes of Marx are, firstly, for him, the history of those few European and American peoples with bourgeois and progressive economies is society as such, history as such. But the most one can say is that they cause a frightful commotion in the present age of the world. Secondly, being himself a child of this same bourgeois, progressive, idealist ideology, he believes that consciousness, determined throughout history by its dependence on material conditions, would become "free" the moment men mastered them, including economic ones as the last link in their chain. Although the economy would remain a realm of necessity, consciousness would be as free, absolute and unfettered as even Fichte had hardly dared maintain. According to Marx, not to mention Lenin, all misery and horror along the way toward that goal must be put up with for that reason. And the sacrifices offered on the altar of freedom would be no less than those brought on the much more modest altars of the pagan gods. Thirdly, he imagined that peace among the classes would also be peace among men and with nature. The right order would only require sublimation but no repression, and therefore no hatred, no resentment, no psychologically and therefore socially conditioned evil. This idea, which results from the earlier two, is his finest thought. Then, men would not just help each other but also nature. Ultimately, they would not play, as Herbert Marcuse thinks, but go to their death as they surrendered, gave themselves over to, created being. But such decline would have to announce itself, and thus man would return again to a more barbaric, more cruel, more primitive state. As the more highly developed, nobler individual has less resistance and succumbs to death, so mankind would perish if it fulfilled its destiny, for it itself is nature. Resurrection is the prerogative of gods.

Stripped of its idealist delusion, Marxist materialism is closer to Schopenhauer than to Democritus. Marx would probably really have believed that a liberated mankind would send rockets to the moon—because it was curious, or pour passer le temps. But it turns out that rockets are part of the realm of necessity. What remains to freedom is solidarity with life, the struggle for what is right, not only in society but in nature at large. Happiness does not thrive when it keeps unhappiness company. Although he said that one should push what is already falling, Nietzsche knew this better than Marx. When one can see, one forgets oneself, and forgetting oneself, one finally stops seeing. The right state for mankind that Marx is thinking of would also have to be its briefest. The philosophers were wrong to believe that truth is what is most stable, most solid, most dependable. It is the vanishing moment, appearance, or so it seems to me.

Marx as a Phase: Marx's doctrines were meant to be a moment of social practice. As the theory of the proletariat, they would lead beyond the bourgeois, capitalist, market-oriented order toward a higher, socialist one already implicit in the former. That was around the middle to the second half of the nineteenth century. When Marxist doctrines are presented in western countries today, and the fact that they have become historical since that time is not made clear; when, even worse, they are understood as a sort of guidepost or as slogans, though history has long since moved beyond the period when they had practical significance, they turn into a kind of ideologization, into the false consciousness that demonstrations, propaganda or political strikes can promote something other than the interests of the potentates in the East or the speedier rise of fascism in the country in which they occur. Marx's theories are phases through which thought has to pass, as it had to pass through Nietzsche and Kant. It makes as little sense to hypostasize them as it does to hypostasize the *Critique of Pure Reason* or the *Gay Science.* Indeed, their hypostatization is even more inimical to free thought. For albeit in truncated form, it seems that the doctrines of Marx and Engels are intended to serve as the technique of domination during the next few centuries, just as the truncated teachings of the gospel have served since that other migration—the Gothic invasions—at the beginning of the Middle Ages when Jesus was picked by other nations from among the Jewish prophets, like Marx today from the array of European philosophers. Marx's theory becomes the turbulence which seizes the masses, just as Pauline Christianity finally seized the masses, but don't ask me what despots lend a helping hand in such cases.

Subject–Object: Freud discovered that a line extends from the typical handling of all objects in the environment to the kind of touching of the beloved that is a look. If the first grasping which cannot yet differentiate between subject and object is inhibited, the subject will never be able to lose and recover itself in the object by passing through the opposition between the two. Human life does not develop.

Upshot of the Great Tradition of German Philosophy—In Abstracto: If mankind ever became conscious of itself and determined its own destiny with the greatest possible freedom, only the whole-hearted effort to mitigate the suffering of all other created being would remain its task. If it ever came to pass that mankind as a whole could have experiences, it would arrange the world as a thoughtful father once managed his family and his wealth because his happiness lay in their prosperity, his misery in their ruin. But unlike family and possessions for that man, created beings would have an additional purpose for mankind. For to the extent human development can be conceived, its end is not something other but unity with, devotion and magnanimity toward what lives in darkness. That mankind still survived at that time would be due to the will to self-sacrifice, for without the protest against the clinging to it, human life becomes inhuman. And a protest is not made when life is only sacrificed to make it more secure, as in war and technology. Only when life is made the highest good will it be loved so deeply by all that its surrender stops being foolishness.

Mass Democracy: Democracy in the age of mass propaganda will not respect the constitution. Poor human rights that are anchored in it, poor freedom which democracy is meant to protect. But democracy exists for the sake of the majority, and human rights apply to the individual. Has there ever been a time when the individual was secure? Relatively so in the industrialized countries of the nineteenth century perhaps, but only perhaps. And freedom after all is the freedom of the so-called people, not of the individual. So don't worry as long as it is the majority that opts for constitutional change— change against the individual. That's why democracy leads to its opposite—tyranny.

Against Philosophy: Philosophy is the futile attempt to achieve recognition for a kind of knowledge which is more than merely instrumental. It is the attempt to produce truth which not only has no practical purpose but cannot even be used in the ordering and application of the knowledge one has. It is truth as such. Behind it, there lies the theological good of eternal salvation which philosophy, the heir of Christianity, made its own. But because that theological goal cannot be verified, it strays about in a labyrinth of pious hopes though that, of course, is something it has in common with all men, provided they can talk at all. The dialectic which leads to no positive result only seems to be a way out. It is true that it is the meaning of the determinate negation that a negated thought becomes the inhering moment in a differentiated, richer intellectual structure. But if such structure has no chance to prove that it is superior to reality, there is no certainty, indeed no likelihood whatever that it is more than the originally negated thought. Validation may be sociological or psychological, that more complex structure may increase the capacity for pleasure, provide a better overview, win the consent of individuals or entire groups, but in and of itself, it has no truth, however seductive it may sound. Recourse to the immanent logic of the work of art is useless, for philosophy lays claim to a different kind of truth. What remains is insight into the impotence of all that is spirit and is not content with mere power. That is the truth, and at this point, materialism and serious theology converge. It is also the reason why real philosophers today are against philosophy. The insight into impotence is no exception. It is vain itself, no different in this respect from any language, any thought, unless it understands itself as observation, and the world confirms it. Then it is knowledge, like the law of gravitation.

The End of Morality: Morality is disappearing. It was the autonomous version of faith and is now being replaced by the increasing scope of social and governmental directives. But that is true not only for individuals in the West, the only place where people had come that far, but applies to European nations as well. They are being controlled by combinations run by stronger peoples. As a result, individual and national sovereignty and their corollary, the illusion of human responsibilities, pass away. Even the so-called neutral countries know sovereignty merely as the freedom to deal with their subjects as the government in power may please. In their foreign policy, they have to maneuver, take their cue from others. Inside their borders, they can rage as much as they want. The great nations don't care, for with the decline of cultural ideology, they have also abandoned that of a civilizing mission. That is called colonialism, and proscribed. But precisely now, where the horror of colonialism dissolves before the equally horrible rebellion of the suppressed colonial peoples, the good image of that responsibility of the white nations that once served them to rationalize the accumulation of capital rises on the horizon. As global organization or global destruction, the world is making ready to get along without morality. The two are close to each other. Because it leaves the backward where it is, progress tends to issue in catastrophies.

Egalite: That the distinction between the scum and decent people is not supposed to apply in a democracy does not mean that the scum no longer exists. Instead, the difference is being liquidated in its favor. The distinction seems to be rooted in injustice, for decency as a moral condition requires a differentiating instinct, perhaps even independent judgment, the result of the experience of many generations. But it is difficult to determine whether the morally more highly developed individual—and he need not be the wealthier, more powerful by any means—also necessarily suffers less than the rabble. As society arranges itself in such a fashion that both have the same chance, the difference will become anachronistic and illusory, and nobility as a character trait will become hollow and ridiculous besides. It may be true that even the good in a person rests on unconscious, narcissist instincts or on drives which were experienced as pleasurable during infancy, and therefore become character traits. But in the new social reality, human energies are so decisively reduced to conscious interests that the more noble person is either considered merely foolish or seen as someone that knows how to conceal his interests more slyly. Observers have a stake in imputing such craftiness to every finer gesture. Resolute in their vulgarity, they feel profoundly disquieted by the genuine presence of something which constitutes a claim to culture only when it is mere show. Here we have the reason for the exaggerated praise of every decent impulse whose motives cannot be questioned. Exaggeration is at least to leave a lingering doubt. Perhaps the whole thing isn't what its recognition makes it out to be. At the same time, such behavior is being taxed with living up to the exaggeration, and thus suffers the punishment of a rigorous future control for the good it did in the past. It is part of the eradication of noblesse that it is all the more vociferously hailed in mass culture.

The Price of Self-Control: That society where it is most progressive nowadays reduces individuals psychically to such an extent that it castrates the inner life, the autonomy of its members, has its ultimate reason in the odiousness with which the human race has instituted self-control as a quasi-natural process. The destruction of the inner life is the penalty man has to pay for having no respect for any life other than his own. The violence that is directed outward, and called technology, he is compelled to inflict on his own psyche. The wealth men increase by their machinery, the violence of machin-

ery, becomes totalitarian rule in society, and everywhere and psychologically, the reduction of intellectual life to the adroitness needed for
self-preservation, i.e., poverty of thought. People that merely want
themselves quite literally destroy themselves. Life revenges itself for
the offense it commits against life. While the negative symptoms in
society today are symptoms of decay, it is destruction, not so-called
constructiveness, that is the final goal, and one must be a devil to
promote destruction. What triumphs in history is only what isn't
worthy of it. *Ecclesia triumphans* would be the grimace of the dying
god it uses as a trademark.

Evil in History: According to Kant, the radical evil in human
nature is that man is unique among living beings for knowing the
good, yet doing the bad. Knowledge of the good is part of knowledge,
and immanent in all of it. If there is such a thing as progress in
civilization, knowledge will necessarily spread among men. More of
them will be in a position to have a greater and clearer idea of the
good than in barbaric phases of history. Unless this also means that
doing the good, the moral condition of men, increases in the same
proportion, progress will therefore be moral regression, an increase in
evil. But if men do not become better as they become more knowledgeable and thus more able, it means they become worse. This is
not merely a mathematical relationship or a manner of speaking but
a real historical process. Unless it expresses itself in a significant
change in its subject, the progress of knowledge calls for rationalization, ideological and even physical regression. As their telescopes and
microscopes, their tapes and radios become more sensitive, individuals become blinder, more hard of hearing, less responsive, and society
more opaque, hopeless, its misdeeds (those just committed and those
that threaten) larger, more superhuman than ever before. Radical evil
asserts its dominion over all created being everywhere and reaches as
far as the sun. At the same time, it lacerates itself, waving itself, men
and mankind as its banner, because an elite in the know merely uses
mankind as a propaganda slogan, to outsmart the enemy. And the
duped blink their eyes when they hear the word. The evil person has
forgotten what longing is. He only knows its opposite, assent to what
is.

What Is Religion? What is religion in the good sense? To sustain, not to let reality stifle, the impulse for change, the desire that the spell be broken, that things take the right turn. We have religion where life down to its every gesture is marked by this resolve. What is religion in the bad sense? It is this same impulse but in its perverted form, as affirmation, prophecy, that gilds reality in the very act of castigating it. It is the lie that some earthly or heavenly future gives evil, suffering, horror, a meaning. The lie does not need the cross, it already lives in the ontological concept of transcendence. Where the impulse is honest, it needs no apology. No reason for it can be advanced.

Too Abstract: In its struggle with the powers that be, the Enlightenment represented the truth. After the bloody victory of the French Revolution, it was no longer the opposition, and that had been its lifeblood. Its theses remained the same, but because they were no longer a protest against the power of injustice, they became an insipid epistemology which was not even correct. Deprived of the tension that develops in its struggle with reality, thought loses its power. When it is isolated, removed from a historical context, a mere "thesis," truth no longer accrues to it. In and of themselves, even the highest ideas are nothing. That is the meaning of the sentence about pain and boredom in the preface to the *Phenomenology*. It also solves the puzzle why other art is boring. Abstractionism had a language when it defied naturalism, and even impressionistically and expressionistically progressive naturalism. Now that the works of the nineteenth century have become petrified museum pieces, abstract art pales, turns into a consumer product, an ornament. It is becoming insipid and conformist, however rebellious its gesturings. "There should be a spot of color on this wall," says the up-do-date bank director. "Look, how funny," says the American employee of a Picasso, "that woman has three eyes, doesn't she." The artists won, but it was a Phyrric victory. In times such as these, art survives through its defeats.

Empty Mediation: The insistence with which epigones point to the mediation of all phenomena and by which they mean that perceptions, for example, or human qualities, are historically and socially conditioned, misses the mark. Such insistence was crucial during the struggle against the scholastic concept of nature, and finally against Nominalism up to Hume. Modern positivism would not dream of pretending that "facts" are ontologically primary. It couldn't care less, it sees itself as an auxiliary science and leaves absolute truth where Nietzsche threw it. What is problematical in positivism is that it does not get exasperated about itself, that it secretly agrees with theology that one has to be positive. Theology says, in the end, there will be justice. And positivism tells us, things are getting better and better. Thus both make their peace with things as they are as their logical presupposition. In view of that position, it is anachronistic, it misses the mark to repeat that everything is mediated and has developed. For such repetition takes theology seriously at a time when its own adherents—again in league with the positivists—have quietly seen through it and understood that it is an element in a functioning economy.

Unmasking the Concept of Ideology: Direct relationships, the personal relationships between men, if you will, have always been mediated by social ones. Not just how one person saw the other, but how he conducted himself toward him, what he did for or against him, whether he liked him or not, how he talked to him and what he said, depended on the social reality. But relations of dependence have become more comprehensive. At the present time of decline, the cynical recognition of materialist motives in their dealings with each other increases as people repress their awareness of the general structure of domination in society, and this results from the economic situation. When one person invited another it once, if only symbolically, denoted the friendly gesture of generosity, the curbing of bourgeois avarice, the secularized, bourgeois equivalent of sacrifice. It exalted the person invited. In the gratefulness for such hospitality, there still lingers the long forgotten intimation that the gift makes a god of the person on whom it is bestowed. Today, the company pays expenses. Apart from those that look for people they can invite because they want to have a meal on their expense account, or because it is tax deductible, or from those luckier ones with so much money that hotel bills remain subliminal, it has become the general ethos to ask only those that cost nothing. Sacrifice also was brought because one expected results. But it was once the greatness of the bourgeois era that it adopted the rite of bygone ages although it did not believe in its efficacy. Stripped of its purpose, it thus assumed a significance of its own. It became like a work of art which only reveals its import because it is no longer an object of immediate use. Nowadays, the reification, the hypostatization of psychic impulses is not overcome, but eliminated. Instead of informing the social totality with their own sublime configuration, they become transparent to the prevailing knowing cleverness, are seen first as ideology and then as oddities, and are finally withdrawn. As human relations disclose themselves as the simpleminded purposefulness they are, the chance that the appearance which once veiled it may become truth in a new world recedes.

Hated Mirror Image: In spite of feudalism and a slave economy, European civilization—and probably the others as well—was based on business, and anti-Semitism is partly the result of this fact. As the oldest representatives of culture in the Christian world, the Jews are experienced as testifying to what one is oneself but refuses to acknowledge. Their every gesture affirms that justice is an equitable trade, evokes one's own mode of existence and, even where it serves a lie, compromises the lie that pervades society. This is the reason the Jews had it easier in materialistic America than in idealistic Germany. It is also the reason they are endangered everywhere today. The justice which manifests itself in their nature and without their will is a protest against both the state capitalism in the East and the monopolistic society in the West. Jews are rooted in trade and liberalism, in the relations between individuals, in the bourgeoisie. To whatever extent the life of any one among them may fail to conform to this pattern, their existence points toward a society of free and equal men, not to a people's community.

1959–1960

For an Association of the Clearsighted: One should found an association in all countries, particularly in Germany, which would express the horror of those without affirmative belief in either metaphysics or politics. As a humane practice in insane post-war Europe, the latter would seem impossible to them, and the former galimatias. For those who are appalled by the economic miracle, the mendacious democracy, the bribery trials with Hitler judges, the luxury and the misery, the rancor and rejection of every form of decency, the admiration of eastern and western magnates, the disintegration of spirit, the slide into parochialism of this old civilization, such an association would be a kind of home. They would plot no revolution because it would end in naked terror. But they would nonetheless be the—admittedly impotent—heirs of the revolution that did not occur, these pitiful clearsighted ones who are going into the catacombs.

In the Name of the People: In Germany, people are wholly without consciousness of the fact that judges and the bureaucracy are public organs and must therefore look out for them. Judges are authorities and therefore somewhere up there—responsible to no one. When a case is discussed in the papers, no one feels that the court is acting in his behalf, that he has to see to it that the judge does not transgress his powers. He is an official, a member of the ruling class, indeed its incarnation. He speaks the truth. From childhood on, the feeling obedience arouses has taken the only path inviolate power leaves it, identification with power and revenge on those it marks. The reactivated emotions take the prescribed course, use the prescribed rationalizations and simultaneously serve as laxatives for the envy that accumulates day after day. All turn against the accused, especially when the crime involves money or brutality, for these things are in demand among people that must cower. The accused is alone, an element in the instinctual economy of psychological cripples who consume him, waiting for another to come along. They are already looking forward to the even tastier dish the uncurbed prosecutor and judge will serve them up the next time around, for no one is immune, as they put it. When a baron let himself be bribed by a meal and was put on trial, we still felt faintly ill at ease. We will no longer be disturbed when things finally turn against the truly corrupt once more, the profligate and the racketeer. What is happening now gives us the requisite good conscience or, more precisely, it is ex post facto justification of the persecution of those moneyed people and intellectuals and empowers us to engage in others still to come.

Instinct of Self-Preservation: It is the curse of mankind that it cannot rise above the animal. Everyone wants to live, eat, drink well, make things pleasant for himself, and that includes sex. Everything else is a detour toward those ends where someone may get lost and take the detour for the goal. The production of the true and the beautiful is a means toward well-being and readily tends to see itself as the end. The important difference between it and the butcher's trade is not that it becomes a means but that, taken in itself and when it does not lead to a greater quantity of blood being spilled, it is less a technique of domination. Freud was right in opposing a mendacious psychology by differentiating between self-preservation and libidinous instincts. The latter are plastic, the former brooks no delay. But insistence on the libido easily makes one forget that self-preservation is primary. Freud no longer saw the connection. The derivatives of the partial drives as he called them, narcissim, avarice and ambition, lust for power and cruelty, are just as much transformations and fixations of phases of self-preservation as of sexuality. Indeed, sexuality is probably that tendency toward self-preservation which is innate in the species and transformable in the individual. The transformability of sexuality shows that the individual only exists to reproduce the species. He can give up his own life because he is no natural end, and he can posit himself as absolute because he does not count. Religion propagates the fantasy of a well-being at an infinite remove. But beyond the restricted scope of well-being that the species grants the individual in his historical situation, there is nothingness.

Both domestic and foreign policy must also be viewed from the perspective of such insights. All the efforts of industrialists, union leaders and the clergy principally aim at their own well-being and its preservation which can only be assured through the consolidation of power. Secondarily, such efforts are made on behalf of groups whose claims must be taken into account. The same, though more obtrusively, applies to the East and the so-called developing nations. But when an individual risks his life for a group, he either hypostasizes a rule that holds for all herd animals—the one counts for less than the many—or he falls victim to the rites instituted to honor this kind of conduct. He takes them absolutely seriously. Even compassion and love are hypostatizations of the self-preservation and love of self innate in man. The lover loves himself in his love, as he does in wholly different acts. But when the insight into the greyness of all motivation is insisted on, art and philosophy and what is noble in an action all disappear in the generality of the natural drive. That is true, and yet at the same time an obvious untruth. A Beethoven symphony is not just self-preservation but also liberation from its sphere, just as surrender to another is also liberation from the narrowness of the self. Transcending oneself expresses what holds everyone prisoner, and something other lights up as appearance. But the freedom which thus discloses itself does not abolish the real imprisonment in the circle of self-preservation, though that is the goal of reason. It merely makes it conscious. Freedom means that imprisonment seems mere appearance. That is the only consolation left to powerful, impotent man, who is really no more than an animal.

History and the Future of the Individual: Through Christianity, the idea of the absolute importance of the individual came to prevail in European civilization. It was mediated by the concept of the immortal soul. Because God was eternal, so was the destiny of each of His children. That this result actually entered consciousness and was not lost in the available galimatias which could also be construed as a consequence and was expanded upon at some length by the theologians, is due to real needs, the specifically European development of technology, production and economics which cannot be wholly separated from Christianity, and which issued in the freely managing individual, the entrepreneur, and the bourgeois form of society that goes along with it. But as liberalism necessarily becomes outdated in monopolistic capitalism, so does the idea of the importance of the individual. Christianity is no longer a progressive element, its function now being largely to further integration into the monopolistic reality. Here, it has to compete with fascist and nationalist ideologies which do that job equally well, or better. To be intellectually progressive would require a consciousness which, though aware of the transitoriness of the individual subject, yet insists on its uniqueness, and develops a society where it, though insignificant, would be the purpose of the whole to serve which would make sense to it for that very reason. In such a case, an ex post facto historical justification would accrue to the individual and its sublimation in the myth of the soul. It would be something like the totem, the image of the animal that is exalted as it is being domesticated, the worship of the lion and sheep in hunting and breeding. The elevation of a concept into the religious sphere usually indicates its impotence in real life. To make something an object of worship is the first step toward mastery. But mastery over something may either mean overcoming or liquidating it. It seems that in the West, the concept of the individual is becoming a token coin. "Everything depends on the individual," and "the value of the personality." That's all part of the veil that hides the rule of the billionaires which no longer has a historical future.

The eastern monopolists are no more moral. On the contrary. But they stand at the beginning of a historical period, and as they create a kind of antithesis to Christianity by making society rather than the individual their god, it is possible that a society that has come to terms with itself, that works for all men, might someday arise from the bloody reality, much as the bourgeoisie issued from the horrible struggles of the Renaissance. In such an eventuality, there would be no liquidation but a sublation of the concept of the individual. In some measure, this will depend on historical constellations. Will they enable those European intellectuals who originated the modern ideas of the East in Marxism and technology to retain their ideas, to inject the new which will also create havoc in Europe? The new will come from the outside, and will be devastating, for Europe did not realize it within itself. It thus has to come out of barbarism and spread in a barbarous manner, and it is possible that the idea of the indefectibility of the individual will be lost again for mankind.

Function and Limits of Bourgeois Culture: Men having been unreflectively caught up in the collectivities and hierarchies of the past, it became the historical function of bourgeois culture to teach them individual self-consciousness, to educate them to the insight that thought dwells in everyone, that its dignity imparts itself to all. The limits of bourgeois culture are that separateness and particularity harden and turn into a lie. Self-consciousness is consciousness of life, abilities, impulses, experiences which derive no less from social structures, from a nature which favors or is adverse to them, from history and the present, as they stem from the as yet indeterminate, seemingly free subjective energy, the élan, of the individual. The one on the other side of the fence has always known this, the poor that saw the rich, the native that saw the colonialist, the sansculotte that defeated the aristocrat and vice versa. Foreigners also perceive each other as individuals, except that they attribute greater importance to the natural and social determinateness of their vis-à-vis, from language to armaments, from dress to skin color, than to so-called individuality.

But in practical life, all are strangers to each other. National, religious and other groupings therefore address their members by the relevant collective designation and not as distinct, individual human beings. Bourgeois culture which incorporates the opposition between man as such and man as conditioned normally ignores it in everyday life by adding the two without regard to their sign. It adds the individual and the social, the general and the particular. According to it, the individual is himself plus a historical, supra-individual one, plus the influences of the world in general. In philosophical theory, bourgeois culture makes short shrift. Subjective idealism spares only the subject, philosophical materialism only the object. Logical positivism, which learned something from these difficult discussions, puts an end to the concepts of subject and object, eliminates them as practically useless. The impenetrability of the question about the individual which recent ontology has hypostasized and falsely dressed up as a kind of magic, as the being that has become eccentric "being in the world," is also a reason why positivism is so convenient and plausible. To deny the problem or to make it into a divinity and oneself its prophet are the two sides of the same refusal to overcome it in practice. The absoluteness of the particular subject is retained as the fundamental thesis of bourgeois society, but at the same time, its determination through other things, its relativity, is acknowledged. But the unmodified retention, the absolutization, gives the individual in theory what practice must deny to it. The less the bourgeoisie succeeded in validating the political emancipation of individuals by subjecting society to their conscious, common activity during its time of dominance in the West, the more compulsively it clung to the ideology of the freedom of the individual.

The dogma of the inviolable sovereignty of the nation is part of this. For the French or the Germans to stop being led like children, to become autonomous subjects who can address each other by the names of their peoples instead of their own, France and Germany would have to become the concern of individuals to such an extent that they would cease being France and Germany and become moments in a world as it should be. Instead, the bourgeoisie made impossible the rational, autonomous negation of the individual which would make him part of his own society he would then have a share in determining. After the horrible prelude of fascism, this now results in the bourgeoisie's being confronted by the caricature of the negation of the individual, the collectivism of the East. Fascism expressed the inability of the bourgeoisie to overcome the false absoluteness of the individual. It was a final stage. The Russo-Chinese despotism is a beginning which does not contain bourgeois self-consciousness. To the West which missed its chance, it can only appear as fascism did, as the blind denial of individual autonomy. The future will show whether it can turn the particular into the general subjectivity and yet avoid the decline of that public order whose establishment—orchestrated by horror and proceeding according to the new technology—is now under way. But individuals in the bourgeois world must learn that the formula: I am autonomous, I am free, my own end, is no less abstract, no less false, than the claim of the Russians that their society is the true reality. Nor is it less false than scholastic realism according to which only the general, i.e., the church, exists, while yet the doctrine of the immortal individual soul obtained directly alongside that teaching until nominalism, the precursor of the bourgeoisie, reversed that relationship. The belief of the individual in himself has become sterile. It was a moment of the bourgeois process of emancipation and, as such, a moment of truth. Today, that doctrine prompts the answer that the individual must die without the possibility of an active absorption in a meaningful totality, that he must die as he is being led in modern wars, in which brainwashing or physical force make him participate as if they were his own, which he lives and in which he dies, and driven by conditions he unconsciously helped create.

As long as death is not overcome, man will always die like an animal if the end comes from out there, opaque, and death will be senseless even in conscious self-sacrifice. But as the world men create for themselves is itself chaotic and senseless, not identical with them but something merely external, life and death will become increasingly nonsensical. At the same tempo and to the same degree as bourgeois culture passes beyond the point where it can still become more than it is, it and everything in it become more false. This expresses itself everywhere. Art, literature and music were once a critical moment whose impotence was not an intrinsic despair; today, even despair becomes ornamental. Architecture, the high rooms, the furniture intended for a particular person and to which memories could attach, had exalted him, albeit at the expense of the masses, for they seemed to make what were means, house, chair, bed or rug, into ends. Through them, through the way each in its particularity could enter the long days of childhood, the individual discovered his uniqueness, to which they belonged. Today, everything becomes instrumental in turn, and nothing remains to exalt the subject one is, neither food nor dress nor ornament through which to recover oneself as distinct. The subject becomes the object of a process of production it does not control. Now wholly means, it is lost in the mass that is led by the most clever and brutal. In the absence of forward movement in the history of individuals and nations, regression sets in.

Love and Selfishness: The element of selfishness present in every kind of love for others plays different roles and can change its function and strength in each. The expectation of divine reward in Christian charity may become irrelevant in the course of years, either because it is replaced by the pleasure taken in the gratitude of those provided for, or by habit, the tendency to repeat. Real compassion may also become the principal motive. Depending on the personal and social situation, sexual love may be governed by blind drive, narcissism or tradition. But it may also transform itself into life in the other and total identification, and differ from its Christian counterpart only by the greater intimacy implicit in its limitation to a single person. And yet there is an element of truth in the vulgar disparagement with which the young cite Philemon and Baucis when they hear of such love. The strength to react to attraction, and to which the infinite complexity that marks all living beings has disclosed itself in that one person in a long, shared life, has also become so modest that that one person answers all its needs. The cynical reaction of the young expresses the suspicion that, objectively, and in spite of all its nobility, exclusiveness also means indolence. No love is pure.

The Truth of Positivism: Philosophies with a content are always symptomatic of social tensions. They announce historical struggles, revolution and reaction. The second half of the European nineteenth century tended toward a formalistic Kantianism, and even that merely as a feeble answer to Vogt and Moleschott. Positivism fits in with the boom after the Second World War. Neither those on top, nor the workers want anything other than what is, and therefore the imagination which philosophy develops has no strength. The difference to earlier periods is merely that the dreams it can weave will no longer see the day of their fulfillment. Contentedness with what is not only comes from a lame will but the feeling that nothing further can be expected, at least nothing that depends on oneself. European history is finished, and therefore positivism is right. There is no escape except machinery. All concepts that are irreducible to facts are meaningless.

Spirit and Freedom: The work of the mind as an end, not as mere means, is losing its meaning today. The happiness that once attached to it, and that communicated itself to both the originator and the recipients, ultimately derived from the relativization of death or, rather, from the fact that in the so-called primitive stages of civilization, its finality had not been understood as yet. To concern oneself with a beyond where one might hope to attain to a higher life once afforded pleasure, as does everything that has some connection with future pleasure. Like the ominous, happiness tinges all thought about it. Declining Christianity had its most intense experience of that happiness when the new science was already monopolizing the universe as a field for earthly theory and practice, yet the belief in the other was still strong enough to produce the logical contradiction that there was a place of salvation beyond the natural infinity, a place not only for ideas, as in Plato, but for paradise. It is spirit that addresses itself to such an impossible possibility, and German music and philosophy once expressed it. There is no happiness in thought or the imagination that does not derive from an anticipation, however remote, of concrete pleasure. Even the most sublime longing owes its existence to natural instinct.

What is true of spirit also applies to freedom which is both identical and at odds with it. In historical existence, it was aspired to and loved as the way toward the satisfaction of needs, a means which seemed an end because it first had to be fought for. Freedom on earth took on the glow of spiritual paradise, just as paradise had once made its own, and then reflected, the glow of the firmament more brightly than the real stars from which it had originally come. At the beginning, in Bruno, the new science for which freedom was being demanded still thought it bore allegiance to God and eternity. Only in the eighteenth century did it dismiss that idea; it called it a hypothesis and discarded it. Freedom as a political principle derives from this secularization, constitutes one of its moments that later developed and became a giant. The ideals of liberal politics still invested material goods with what was remembered of their spiritual counterparts which themselves had originally derived their power from the projection of earthly aspirations. Now, where the machinery of the consumer goods industry and mass propaganda stills needs at their root as it were, mediation through spirit and freedom falls by the wayside; they no longer arouse interest. Consciousness returns to itself as the organ of the struggle with nature, to the satisfaction of physical needs as to the specific weapon of the human race. The individuals in the West come to resemble those in the East. Technology has made superfluous the freedom which its development required. Indeed, it seems the process is reversing itself. In the East, freedom is about to become a good to be acquired but in the West, where it is supposedly an inalienable possession, it declines. Being no longer used for any-thing as a means, it stops being an end. It is not sublated but disintegrates. But what was always considered means, all that is needed to sustain life, and especially the means of those means, machinery and means of transport and everything that serves them, has become an end. In his categorical imperative to use man as an end, Kant took it for granted that man always uses man as a means in any event. He was right. To be a means is a condition for being an end, and it is this paradox of autonomous thought which thought now experiences in itself. Of course, Kant postulated a highest good, which he took to be autonomy and which included both freedom and justice. Should society also need these as means for its survival, spirit would have a future other than disintegration.

Being Led Along: One of the insignificant symptoms that shows how industrial concentration destroys the individual's capacity for making decisions is the packaging of the products of the phar-maceutical industry. In an earlier day, pills were put into small bottles or tubes which were placed inside paperboard cartons. Included was a description, sometimes in several languages, which gave composi-tion, effect, enumerated indications, and informed about dosage and use. Today, one gets a clumsy plastic apparatus which is larger than its contents justify and leaves barely enough space for the brand name and a terse comment. Big industry no longer needs to give the consumer detailed instructions; it only has to spur him psychologi-cally, through big advertising. The rest is up to the physicians with whom industry is in league, as in America. There, it supplies the patient with the smallest possible quantity of any product and even omits the name so that the physician has to be consulted again when reordering becomes necessary. Consumption increases nonetheless, for everyone is attached to his health. He has to keep his body, his own machine, in good repair so that it can function like all other machines. Industry uses physicians as partners of a sort; it is not the patients that avail themselves of the services of industry. Conditions are analogous in other branches of the consumer goods industry. As allegedly autonomus patrons, people are encouraged to become dependent as they are being supplied with ever more functional objects which tell them ever more precisely how they are to be used. It was difficult to draw water from the well. On their way there, women could not understand that necessity might change. The modern housewife knows this kind of laboriousness from paintings and the opera, but the freedom the taps in kitchen and bathroom afford her and her family is used up by countless other chores during work and leisure, and they resemble the turning of the tap like peas in a pod. The necessity to adapt to them is no less imperative, and the path along which no gadget or traffic signal absorbed the attention no longer exists. As woman becomes a subject, she becomes less of one.

Too Late: For over a hundred years, German politics has existed under the sign of the "too late." The slogan of unification which still accompanies events as a call for re-unification (as if past experiences did not deter all Europeans from such a repetition), already served the abortive revolution of 1948, at a time when Holland, England, France had been united long since. The genuine innovation Prussian Germany introduced into the world when, shortly after Italy, it could proclaim through a series of wars: "it has been achieved," was the arms race as an indication of the relationships between nations. It was the cavalry helmets of the chancellor and the Kaiser, the Kaiser as strategist, but unlike Napoleon Bonaparte, for he did not understand more of strategy than others but merely wanted to get his share of glory quickly. The fleet and colonialism, the inglorious revolt that followed the unprovoked World War One, were all too late. Historically, National Socialism may be a model. Although it followed the example of fascism in historically similar modern Italy, it may show the way France and indeed the balkanized European continent might take, for those countries must become more authoritarian as the power of the East grows in all areas and the United States come to an understanding with Russia, forcing them perhaps to defend themselves.

But National Socialism came too late in a two-fold sense. Like the backward countries today, the proletarian nations as Hitler called them, it wanted to catch up with America by drastic remedies, and that meant gigantic factories, new cities, freeways, teamwork, the unscrupulousness of the early magnates. But also, and as part of this, it made Germany catch up with what had long existed elsewhere, bourgeois society without Junker and radical workers' movements, and the intervention of the state in the economy. The nationalist fever was to promote rationalization, economic success and world power status. Roosevelt could fight the crisis with his New Deal, but the German bourgeoisie had traditions and communists to contend with, and that was the social and cultural lag which turned the last caricature of bourgeois revolution, the clean up in the twentieth century, into an image of hell. The present is training in imposed democracy, and democracy has no historical future.

The Truth of Religion: Someone wrote about Tolstoi that he became devout when he was too old to enjoy life. But religion as consolation means more than might occur to a minister. It is not the truth of religion that dawns on the person in need, it is the need that constitutes its truth, not only individual, but social need as well. Since the decline of antiquity, the history of religion has had a clear structure. Phylogenetically, it followed the ontogenesis of the religious consciousness of a child from a good bourgeois home. After the world was first experienced in religious categories, the way monks and parents wanted it, doubt set in as growing knowledge came into conflict with those categories. The gods vanished with the fear which is, according to Lucretius, their origin. The townsmen had to èarn their livelihood, obedience alone was no longer a reliable guidepost, they had to deal with the world themselves, and interest in the here and now intruded between the firm rule governing life in this world, and the expectation of life in the next. Just as the child, once it has become an adult and free, gives its own children a religious upbringing because that is expedient, so, after every revolution, the bourgeois encourage the dependent masses to persist in their religious faith. If today, need constitutes the truth of religion, its state is no worse than philosophy's. Philosophy also consoles, and even when its attempts to reconcile religion and science, or to at least assure the former an undisputed existence alongside the latter, failed, there was at least the consolation that there is none. Wherever reason tries to rationalize the expression of hope or despair, as with Kant's possible postulate or Hegel's negation which finally must derive its force from the idea of a truth that can no longer be negated; where it reveals itself, as it were, either as means or end—the one implies the other —where it believes it overcomes reflection by reflecting upon itself; where it re-interprets expression as truth which is always the case when it does more than merely function—it becomes consolation, like religion.

It is not only the sexual impotence which the above-mentioned Tolstoi critic had in mind that stands in need of consolation. From youth on, in many respects and at many times, everyone is old and impotent. In happy times, during a period of boom and full employment, philosophy loses interest, of course unless, like fundamental ontology, it can serve as a latent stimulus to heroic deeds to be accomplished. The real malaise of intellectual youth is that it is too saturated with technical knowledge to feel that philosophy is more than a congenial illusion, a kind of drug. Today's youth knows more about philosophy's advanced age than Tolstoi did. But this knowledge, this entire reflection about the impossibility and obsolescence of philosophy is subject to the very verdict that is its substance. Formalistically expressed, it tells us that skepticism is self-invalidating, and this applies no less to the denials skepticism makes than to the things it wants to turn against. Philosophy against philosophy is unthinkable, it proclaims the truth whose existence it denies. Is the positive true then? Because skepticism contradicts itself, does it perhaps follow that non-skeptical philosophy, religion, some belief or other, are right? There is another possible consequence, and that is silence. Whatever is being said is not said because the one to whom it is addressed, the non-finite, doesn't hear it. The people to whom we talk are mere objects we set in motion by words, or by using our arms, by weapons or machines. To the extent that philosophy wants to be more than directions that can be confirmed, i.e. science, it disregards speaker and listener and posits itself as absolute. Language in the emphatic sense, language which wants to be truth, is chattering silence. No one speaks, and it speaks to no one. Therefore nothing is true. Not even that we are in darkness is true, not even that that is untrue, is true. And the posturing of negation and renunciation as philosophy, i.e., logical positivism, which makes a virtue of mathematical necessity, lives on the appearance of something which it is philosophy's sole content to deny.

Mind, Art and the Bourgeoisie: Since the Renaissance, the new science has been the vanguard of the bourgeoisie. The more its truth spread, the more general persecution became, the more dedication adherence to it demanded. Thus reason became a goddess and its devotees, the free intellectuals, a group of sworn torchbearers. Thought is the pioneer of liberal society, it espouses it as long as it has not yet reached its goal. Adherence means that intelligence is adopted as their cause by those who have not yet caught up with it. At the end of the bourgeoisie, the time of decline, the intelligence which has outdistanced understanding has lost its progressive social function. On holidays, the bourgeoisie praises the spirit but its representatives now preach what already exists. They have turned into makers of more or less refined ornaments, of luxury goods for the rich and the not so rich, as demand may dictate. But there are others who continue pursuing the immanent logic of the spirit. Forgetful of themselves, they withdraw from the bourgeois crowd. In a manner of speaking, they run ahead where no one has the interest and therefore the understanding to follow them. Just barely considered elegant during halcyon days, such intellectuals are seen as unreliable customers in troubled times. It is therefore all the less compatible with their cause that they should claim to be custodians of possessions allegedly sacred to all men, and deferentially offer their services to a society that cannot follow them. They are beacons, but in the prevailing darkness, they have long since lost those entrusted to their care, and tell themselves that it is the others' fault. They offer the bourgeoisie the merchandise whose correct use would lead to its transcendence. As artistic, literary, philosophical experts, as ornaments, they have been integrated into the division of labor though their trade is to break out of it. The deception shows up in their product, however. As it becomes coherent in itself, it also becomes mute, and that it requires commentary is proof of that fact. It must ingratiate itself with a world that condemns it. As the bourgeoisie comes to its end, the advanced intellectuals can no longer tell the truth whose purpose it was to help the bourgeoisie come to power. Truth is finished, and the proof is that it still pretends to exist. The time for a transition to a higher form of society where freedom is coupled with justice, to a higher bourgeoisie, in other words, which would contain the earlier one within itself, is long since gone, and the barbaric beginnings of socialist authoritarianism in the East took cognizance of these intellectuals only during the very first phases, when bourgeois liberalism was at stake there as well.

Progressive intellect has its place in the liberation and transition from feudalism to the emancipated existence of the competitive, politically self-determining entrepreneur who organizes the masses into a nation for his own purposes. That was the meaning of great music and great literature whose immediate comprehensibility coincided with its profitability. Today, the pieces of the past are performed in museums, and the contemporary ones as rare plums for the families of managers. Their incomprehensibility is no longer pointed. The occasional malaise of the public before avant-garde works of the turn of the century and the twenties results from the unconscious suspicion that the perfection of the bourgeois way of life still conceivable then was replaced and foiled by world wars and fascism. This hidden guilt feeling produces the quality of embarrassing obsolescence that marks certain products of that period. In the case of paintings, ominous meanings can be obscured by high prices. With music which is being revived because the organizors want to cash in on the boom that is more difficult, and literature lies between the two. Kafka's conservative pieces can be reinterpreted as cheap fun in literary histories and for mass consumption. In spite of his conservatism, Karl Kraus is only read by students. Although reactionary, Schönberg reminds the listener too much of opportunities that were missed. He is not as free of content as abstract, contemporary paintings which, though not specifically created for the office of the chairman of the board, are yet mute enough to find a place there. Today, abstract art is to surrealism what positivism is to the Enlightenment. It no longer has any enemies.

Dialectic of Enlightenment (2): The dialectic of the Enlightenment consists largely in the change from light to darkness. This means not only that the disintegration of mythology is accompanied by the disappearance of experience and the capacity for it. Because of the spiritual passivity which befalls men in the new economy, the exclusive concentration on money and job, the sophisticated cleverness to which the psychic mechanism of individuals is reduced, there is no limit to what the most transparent delusions can do, the moment they appear on the horizon and pass the screening of the mass media. All mendacious values create the ties which this or that power constellation needs. Durkheim says that the loosening of the social fabric favors the suicide of the isolated individual. He might have added that as that disintegration progresses, the lies designed to patch up that society become less necessary. Who wouldn't rather believe in the national community than commit suicide unless he is already so crazy that he shrugs his shoulders even at that. Schizophrenia, the logical development of the rejection of any and all demands for love or respect, the final destruction of mythology, is ultimately a more humane mentality than the readiness to give one's unprincipled allegiance to an idea which is a substitute for the capacity for solidarity. In periods of decline such as the present, the higher truth lies in madness.

Enlightenment and Religion: Those who enlightened the nations said that the concept of gods or a god served to explain the unexplained, creation, the functioning of nature and the destinies of men in society. The more knowledge of nature advances, the more just and transparent society becomes so that no socially caused differences, no socially caused suffering would require divine intervention to explain them, the less people would need religion. But one might answer these men that the question concerning the truth of religion can be asked unambiguously only when it has been freed of its ideological function. But, they might reply, would we not need religion then because man must die, and all other created beings suffer at the hands of nature and especially from a pitiless mankind? Isn't religion always needed because the earth remains a place of horror even if society were as it ought to be?

The Delusion of Happiness: Two old people, two young friends, two lovers or whoever exalts the other through words and gestures and makes life more beautiful against the dark background of reality live in a self-created world of appearance. Language is true or false. The expression that rapturously sublimates the other is a judgment—and a false judgment—unless it defines naked fact. Even the confession "you are good," "you are beauty itself," is appearance though the lover perceive the beauty which escapes the indifferent, for the more clear-sighted eyes cannot redeem that "are," cannot prove what was posited in a moment of happiness but signifies more than that moment. The answer that truth only lies in the moment, that it flashes with an ephemeral glow and disappears without being destroyed, without denying itself, is the belief of the happy person, and a delusion. It is as much of a delusion as the scream of the tortured who accuses the world. As it dies away, its truth also fades. Expression is appearance because there is no God to hear it. Only as long as someone has the power to hear and perceive, only as long as reality confirms us does resistance against it have the truth which is its substance. By its very nature, resistance is doomed to impotence. There is no absolute that takes it into itself and preserves it. Pain and the negative remain abstract, even in the Hegelian myth of totality.

Rationalization of the Ratio: Progress means chucking the superfluous. The more detours it makes unnecessary, the more it is progress. That it is the discretion of each individual, the freedom of each to starve or to earn a wage that drive them to their places of work is a detour. It can be eliminated by central planning. Thinking can be done away with, and that in a three-fold sense. First, reflection need not be complicated by the individual's apparent freedom. A comprehensive social program assigns the work everyone must do. Secondly, there will not be so many individual entrepreneurs. An authority with the power to enforce its decisions will run the economy and do away with the crises of the past. Thirdly, no longer will everyone or a large number have to know something about a great many things. Instead, the individual will have competence in a narrow sphere, and even coordination will become an increasingly specialized function. Thinking administers. It should be rationalized, and thus rationalize ratio itself. Thought turns out to be a myth, and the happiness it brings primitive magic. Grow up at last, you lazy fellows. You are still free spirits, no more than the successors of the theologians you ridicule.

Weatherbeaten Tablets: Nietzsche spoke of the decadent. He knew that the world to which he still belonged was coming to an end. Seeing the pallidness of values that claim to be objective, he became aware that they were relative. So-called meaning, everything that went beyond their daily reproduction in the lives of individuals, that gave life a reason, proved hollow in his time. As something objective and independent of the will of the subjects, values had demanded the negation of individual pleasure and had therefore shown themselves poor consolation for people for whom it was economically or psychologically out of reach. So Nietzsche set men a new goal, the will itself, the strength to be independent of even the highest degree of pleasure one might be capable of. But Nietzsche did not know why the old world was coming to an end. It has run its course because it no longer has a historical function in the geographical and social structure the world now has. European culture withered because it had no future, for individuals stop developing when a collective task with which they can identify no longer exists. In Hegel's philosophy of history, nations that have accomplished their mission are no longer treated. They are a theme for the philosopher as long as the world spirit is with them. The chapters on the Orientals, Greeks, Romans, and the Germanic tribes discuss the period they are the most advanced. Then the thinker falls silent, and even the desperate act that posits values of its own invention no longer avails. The tablets are weatherbeaten before they are broken.

Come and Go: The underdeveloped nations, as they are called today, look greedily at the highly industrialized ones. But the grief over their privation is attenuated; they know they have the strength that will ultimately bring them to the level of those that have made it. The backward individual in the countries that have arrived fares differently. Like some of the older, retrogade cultures, he has perhaps resisted his envy. The satisfaction in the world of the spirit, the

compensation through myth and imagination which owe their existence to historical stages where a high degree of social and subsequent
psychological differentiation were wrung from a more uneven distribution of wealth are no longer his. He has no reason to share the
confidence in the future shown by the backward nations. Mesmerized
by the consumer goods paradise, he can think of nothing but the
disgrace of not being part of it. His privation, though perhaps less
acute in absolute terms than was common once, measures its force
wholly by reference to the present. He is no newcomer but an old
one that is disappearing.

Outdated Protest: The element of protest in the naturalistic plays
of the turn of the century and even the twenties, including the
theater of Brecht, has lost some of its force. It strikes one as vapid
because the fact that one can lead a respectable life only by cheating
—by what is called conformism today—that injustice and blindness
are part of a career, has become obvious. In everyone's psychological
situation, the ideas underlying the protest appear as ideology, and
that situation derives from the social and historical reality. Justice
which goes beyond things as they are becomes mere abstraction
because the old nations have abandoned their historical mission.
Whether, after barbaric beginnings, the new ones will assume it some
day, is uncertain. But there is no question that the resignation of the
West, which made history happen during the last few centuries,
leaves it up to them.

False Return to Religion: Critical theory saw the social role of
religion as the projection of earthly conditions into a beyond. The
purpose was domination. Today, that projection has become transparent and weak. The rockets that are sent into space have an effect
on the realm of the blessed. But the projection goes on, it continues
to function according to the law of inertia. Identified as a technique
of control, it becomes an element in full employment and also serves
in the preparation of the next attempt to avert the fate of Europe
by war and to fulfill it in spite of itself. As religion has become hollow
in this way, what it once contained becomes apparent, the longing
for the other compared to which this world showed itself as the evil

it was. However vigorously it may have checked its indwelling protest against things as they are, religion also had to sustain what was always kindled anew until that protest became the theism and atheism of the Enlightenment, divested itself of the form of religion and helped another kind of social life to be born. Brought on by nature, like hunger and thirst, that protest yet aimed at something beyond nature, and that was a just, a right order. That the prevailing, worse order aroused and justified it, yet simultaneously denied its fulfillment, gave it its productive force, and it is this force which has run down in the West.

While in the East, the pressure of terror already senses a future resistance which, after migrations and catastrophes, aims at something socially higher, here, all illusions vanish. The materialism into which men are forced in the East exercises great power and sustains a considerable obtuseness, but it also bears the stamp of the provisional which may last a thousand years, as it did in the European Middle Ages. Here, everyone knows that the idea can do nothing but complete its withdrawal from their world. The firmer structure in which western society seeks a refuge is imposed on it by its competition with the East. But the West cannot preserve its own thought, the freedom and the right of the individual, inside that structure. Instead, it will have to surrender it in ever new dictatorships and in alliances with them. Rather than quite consciously bringing to fruition the Enlightenment into which religion had passed, rather than transforming the illusory freedom of the revolution into justice, western society has given up. The return to religion does not mean that it believes in heaven once again, but that it lacks belief in a better order for the world, that it wants nothing but itself. To transform oneself into something higher, to want oneself in another, is the substance of religion, and this society lost it when it made religion as something unchanging its cause. Something unchanging can be exchanged for another equally so, as happened in Germany with Arian Christianity, as happened in every nationalism. After the debacle, the rightists in Germany went back to being religious Christians, but they hadn't changed. The game can go on like this until the continent passes into other hands.

Mass Media: In this doomed civilization which attempts in precipitous haste to counter the threat of a new, even more overpowering migration than those from the third to the sixth century by producing the means to annihilate life and by patterning itself on dictatorships that bristle with armaments, there is no purpose other than money and power, and so madness erupts. If one wants to hear its daily voice simply turn the radio at any time whatever, one is flooded by a carnival of unleashed hucksters and a sprinkling of outmoded jazz and boogy-woogy in between. That is in America, the progressive country. The expectation that things might be better in parochial Europe is disappointed at the first sound. It is worse. The lilting melodies, the lying good cheer, the folklore of the backward nations betray by their gesture of innocence and harmony that they are the masks of envy and malice. The more profound someone's thirst for revenge, the more sensitively he reacts to pain and dissonance in kitsch and art. The daily voice of the nations proclaims that they no longer see a task ahead, that spirit has abandoned them. The time of a new migration is dawning.

North Atlantic Pact: In the Second World War, England and America were still fighting anti-democracy, totalitarian aggression as such. They allied themselves with Russia when it was attacked by fascism although with his infallible instinct, Stalin had initially recognized his affinity with Hitler. Like the Russians, the Germans were newcomers, though older ones, and that's why both were nationalists from rancor. Today, when the Germans have been defeated, the Anglo-Saxons no longer confront just the awakening Teutons but two awakening continents. They can no longer afford hostility toward anti-democracy but must join up with the authoritarian states on the right in order to resist the Asiatics. The alliances with the most reactionary governments in the world, the invitations and offers of friendship to the totalitarian gentlemen on the opposing side the moment they make a friendly face, make it abundantly clear that the slogan "war against totalitarian barbarism" has become the rationalization of very tangible interests. The mass murderers are patted and embraced, and it now takes a massive insult before one will walk out on them at a conference, and even then one does it reluctantly. A reign of terror no longer means that one will not hobnob with the tyrant unless his own people drive him out. Battista, a friend until just recently, is no longer welcome, and Krushchev would certainly be shown no hospitality if he had to flee across the border, like the former. Dictators are not judged by their acts, but their fate. That is one of the indications that the objective contents to which the so-called free world is pledged, are disappearing with dizzying speed. The sense for them is about to become extinct—it is extinct. That is the result of the years since the end of the Second World War, the fifteen years during which the Anglo-Saxon world moved from the struggle against National Socialism or, rather, the German danger to England and America, to alliances with its like all the world over. That development was foreshadowed in the politics of Chamberlain and his ilk: they had no objections to Hitler's concentration camps, his designs on Russia. Today, they would help him. The unique Roosevelt is no more—and would have no chance to be elected in any event. That's over and done with.

Philosophy and Ideology: The *Critique of Pure Reason* tells us something about ideology, the analysis of necessary appearance. Kant himself said this about the Transcendental Dialectic, but it applies equally to the Transcendental Aesthetic and Analytic. What the senses perceive through the spectacles of space and time, reason, the powers of pure, original apperception, turn into the world which we take to be a reality that is independent of us. Appearance is necessarily seen as thing in itself. And this inversion is not only necessary, but socially necessary. In spite of all later efforts to get away from it, Kant defined the synthetic activity of the mind as that of the personal subject as the activity at work in every single self, and this derives necessarily from the state of a society which is determined by the activity of a multitude of individual subjects with similar powers.

Because of his critical theory which relativized everything, Kant seemed the "all-destroyer" in spite of a conciliatory doctrine of ideas which permitted belief by depriving it of its allegedly firm foundations. It was not long until the successors had drowned out the critique by the positive doctrine of the absolute. By making unconditioned the subject whose characterization still wavered in Kant, they repeated in philosophy the process Feuerbach had identified in society. Here, the father becomes God and the civil family the holy one. The final chapter, the determination to remove all hesitation, all contradictions from Kant and to draw all logical conclusions led philosophy back to ideology.

Schopenhauer the Bourgeois: Schopenhauer's pessimism stands a notch above European philosophy because along with his insight into the mechanical character of all events which he shares with the empiricists, skeptics and philosophers of the Enlightenment, he also understood and expressed something that is identical with it, the desolateness of the whole. The shortcoming of his thought is that he identifies with that curse. The evil pathos that everything that happens to life is no more than it deserves is a peculiarity of his lucid style. In his discussion of the drive to being and well-being which is the essence of all creatures, there is an undertone of grumbling denunciation. Precisely because it moralizes, his language contradicts the morality it proclaims. He makes compassion the foundation of the good, indeed the source of insight which is more profound than knowledge. But compassion can only be felt by someone that can love happiness. Schopenhauer had a glimpse of this when he said that the joy of others which we can share is the highest form of compassion. But even here, there is the jeering note that those capable of feeling it are so few. He is a bourgeois, and the mood from which his thought flows is coldness and avarice. Only one person knew this, and that was Nietzsche. Schopenhauer is a stranger to exuberance. That is the stigma which attaches to the truth of his work, the opposite of Spinoza's, whose ethics reflect on happiness and scorn compassion. But how much better a person he was than Schopenhauer.

Philosophy of History, a Speculation: Foreign policy is the continuation of domestic policy, and what the populations in the age of radio and television find out about it is mass propaganda through distraction. The West wants commercial ties, the diplomats in the so-called under-developed countries act as the representatives of the consolidated business interests of their native lands, and even espionage serves mainly to outdo the competition. The East wants to increase productivity. It hasn't come nearly as far as it would like, and so it takes primarily industrial products for its exports. In their dealings, the men in charge there try to counter the danger that the greater productivity of the western enemy may entice foreign countries to the other side; besides, their own geographically preponderant condition to which the world will someday succumb, must not be whittled down by so-called encirclement. Ultimately, everything, including strategic considerations, adds up to the guaranteed, secure standard of living, except that in the East, because it is lower there, a stronger impetus, an idea, the communization of the world, stands in back of that goal. There has always had to be an insufficiency of some sort lest ideas degenerate into clichés. And here we come to the core of the question concerning the substance of mankind, the actual speculation about the philosophy of history. If prehistory comes to an end because food, housing and clothing are no longer and nowhere a problem for anyone, will the higher, the real history, culture as it is called, begin, or do the movies and the stars in the countries that have arrived show the kind of regression that will then set in? I believe that mankind will only have so-called nobler needs, needs beyond its natural ones, if these remain unsatisfied. Perhaps I am wrong. That would mean that the idea is not tied to a lack, love for justice not to prevailing injustice, magnanimity not to misery and power. The very existence of non-human nature which man could care for without therefore being threatened by it presupposes a fraternal longing which could hardly be understood, were it not for the suppression among men. Even the violence which inheres in education really loses its ground when everything is available and misery at an end. It seems that regression is the only goal of progress. As long as there is suffering that progress can alleviate, however, that very thought is infamous.

Happiness and Consciousness: Consciousness and happiness go together, for unreflected happiness is no happiness. Only if it was labored before does breathing become a pleasure. As long as freedom is yearned for, it appears as happiness, and not only misled but also autonomous human beings risk their life for it. Once won, it is forgotten, like breathing. The brightness that enters the room through the opened blinds, the view from the window in a still dusky interior, afford the experience of light. In the picture windows and glass houses, it is about to disappear, and even the talk of housing authorities that mankind needs buildings with air and light is tied to recollections, the memory of slums, although there it was not windows but toilets that were in short supply. Life continues through change but the course of progress which destroys present and future happiness is essentially nothing but this unending decline unless what is past is also preserved. The proverbial official in his dark office who looked out from behind his small window and closed it abruptly when the clock struck was an object of scorn and envy, and both with good reason. An object of scorn, because he dwelt in bureaucratic darkness; of envy, because he could shut out the world. Today, he and his like sit in the glass house, checked by all that pass, and the end of the working day is quietly respected by the public. Things have improved. The official sits in the light, and the people no longer have anything against him. But with the removal of the evil, something positive has also disappeared, the bliss of darkness, the freedom to lock up, the freedom to scold with a good conscience.

Autonomy: If the autonomy of the individual stops at the point where what is socially determined begins, does it exist at all? Kant thought that reason had an interest in it. What he calls reason, however, is transitory, its ideas are a product of history and will be outdated by it. And the same holds true of the interest, of all interests whatever. Both in their origin and their goal, all feelings are social. Gratitude is shown the person who has power, i.e., money or influence, or at least some quality that carries weight under present arrangements. And the person showing it makes a naive or calculated use of the ability he inherited from the beginnings of the herd. What is called beauty in men or women is as dependent on the structure of an epoch as is the value of physical or intellectual strength. Its specific quality is itself determined by conditions, and its possible effect—and therefore its value—will vary widely and depend on the availability of foodstuffs, the intensity of the struggle for subsistence, and the state of technology. Personal courage, which is so closely tied to what we mean by autonomy, and increasingly necessary as intelligence or superstition grow, has survived into the present from the feudal times that cultivated it. Defense ministries and certain careers still have use for it, and therefore it is not merely reproduced on the stage. In the youthful gangs, it seems to grow by itself, together with defiance and scorn of the world which no longer offers honest motives except power and consumption. The chaotic despair of the young, and the resigned alienation of those who withdraw from the declining collectivity, i.e., the most obviously conditioned phenomena of our time, appear as the weak traces of an impossible autonomy which never existed in fact.

About Smartness: By "smartness," people mean the ability to adapt to the way things are, to make one's way—action guided by the profit principle. To be dumb means to find the universal principle repugnant, to be motivated by other interests, or to be simply unskilled in the manipulation of the inner and outer mechanisms of self-preservation in the social hierarchy. There is an infinite number of causes of such ineptness, from excessively greedy ambition to a schizophrenic detachment which is not conducive to learning surefire methods. In the middle of the scale lies surrender to appearance, the exclusive addiction to art, philosophy, political resistance. There are smart geniuses, and there are dumb ones. The material the smart ones use to express themselves is the reality of the moment. They show what one can achieve in it, what one can do with it. But the material of the others, stone, language, color, sound, and history itself, requires imagination and enthusiasm. The entrepreneur of genius and the revolutionary are no less obsessed than the poet, except that the former dedicates himself to the here and now, and the latter to the other, unless he is smart like the business man and turns his production into an enterprise. But it is also true that the entrepreneur of genius has a greater affinity for ruin than the man that will only bet on a sure thing.

On the History of Sexuality: The circle the Enlightenment describes as it returns to myth becomes apparent in the history of sexuality which is coming back to its origin. In the Middle Ages, love, romantic love as it is called, sprang from the same historical constellation as trade and science. The individual took on significance. Not in the beyond, but here on earth, his acts became consequential. But as secular politics became absolute, historical events began to depend ever more closely on the circumstances of reigning families themselves, and the bourgeois townsmen took them as their model. The significance of the heir, however, which determined rules of female conduct in both cases, affected families directly in only one way. It brought strict order but no love. The appearance of love as a social phenomenon is probably the result of the negation of discipline, the rebellion against the interests of the family, against an order of relationships which had taken on the glow of sanctity. As the exclusiveness of sexual surrender was no longer imposed from without but desired for the sake of the partner, sexuality was freed from a means-end nexus that had been transfigured as eternal custom, and it was only now that the person acquired on earth the infinite value it had lost in the beyond after the importance of theology had receded. The mortal danger which recurred every time the taboo was broken, the mastery of the fear of the sacrosanct, and of external resistance, lent sexuality the sublime quality that turned it into love. As fear and resistance dwindle, as the social bases of the family change, sexuality in the form of love becomes less and less able to structure the entire life in all its detail toward one end, the tie with a single other person. The bond thus created loosens; the past is no longer carried as fully into a future, and the future becomes more nuanced as a result. A motive for sublimation, an element of civilization, falls by the wayside. The increasing likeness and changing functions of dress among the sexes are an outward sign. They symbolize the liquidation of the sexual taboo itself. The backward nations, the bushmen of Africa who are about to repeat this process at greater speed, dress up; the whites undress. They are moving toward a kind of monogamy which probably differs from promiscuity by its greater convenience under prevailing conditions, not because it is a more intense experience. It will be easy to make it an element in the controlled traffic in which the Chinese are being trained in our time. The only difference is that it is a beginning there, a regressive phenomenon here. What seems a circle when viewed in isolation and from this continent may be a moment in a development. The European Enlightenment might be fulfilling a historical function which is no longer visible from Europe where we seem to have come full circle.

Pro Patria: That one should be ready to die for one's country is no general moral commandment. It is valid only if the order there makes the equal treatment of all a principle, and grants each as much freedom as is compatible with the rights of others. When that sentence refers to war, it is valid if one's own country is threatened by others who wish to endanger that condition. This can be inferred from the state of their own institutions and the intent to conquer and subject they may prompt. The citizens of totalitarian states at war with free countries are not obliged to fight. The fatherland in abstracto is no true idea. Of course, what man is meant to be also remains abstract and untrue unless developed. Depending on the degree of technological maturity and the amount of tension between nations, the condition of general freedom tends to limit the power and the pleasure it brings to an ever smaller circle of persons while the rest are kept under control by food for body and spirit. If, on lower technological levels, freedom must be restricted for its own sake, i.e., to attain higher skills, it is also mandatory to do so on the highest if regression is to be prevented. It is not merely power in the hands of a few that augurs it. The poverty in the hearts of nations with a high standard of living is also a symptom. The smaller the number of those that hunger impotently, the less voice they have, the more strongly they repudiate the few at the top and the many that forget them. Freedom in abstracto is no truer than the fatherland.

If a good cause demand that men risk their lives, there are usually those ready to do their share. More often than not, the good cause fails. Later, very much later, a historical situation develops where the survivors are to be rewarded. Then it is the wrong ones, for the right ones are rarely around when things go well, otherwise they wouldn't be the right ones. Reality, even the better reality, passes them by. Like the worse reality in which they risked their life, it is friendlier to those that have a greater affinity with power than it is to the just that become its victims.

On the Capture of Eichmann: A minion of National Socialism called Eichmann who had been specifically assigned to exterminate Jews in Germany and the countries occupied by the Germans was seized by Israeli citizens in Argentina and taken to Israel. The inten-

DAWN & DECLINE

tion is to place him on trial there. Estimates of the number of Jews murdered at Eichmann's orders range from three-quarters of a million to four or five million. He was proud of his role in the "final solution" and in the right, according to prevailing law. If the court in Israel wants to be just, it will disqualify itself. The formal grounds for the trial are obviously untenable. Eichmann did not murder in Israel, nor can Israel wish that the seizure of political criminals in the asylum they should or should not have found become the general rule. Punishment is a means by which a given state enforces respect for the laws within its territory. Its purpose is deterrence. All other theories of punishment are bad metaphysics. It is madness to assume that the punishment in Israel could deter possible successors of Eichmann. Whatever may happen to him in Israel will prove the impotence, not the power of Jews conscious of themselves and their right, the arrogance, not the customary conduct of governmental authority in Israel. Everyone knows that it is with an eye to New York that the Israelis' totalitarian airs, which are reminiscent of Mussolini and the Russians, were let pass once more. The reasons given for this legal action are no less inadequate. Allegedly, the trial is to enlighten the youth of Israel and foreign nations about the Third Reich. But if such knowledge cannot be communicated through the pertinent information available in scientific and generally accessible works in all civilized languages; if the relevance it should have for present and future generations has to be created through an outpouring of accounts of the trial and international sensationalism, it is in bad shape. The consciousness which needs new headlines to be impressed with the death of the Jews under Hitler has little depth. It will not remember. The real consequences of the publicity given the extermination by the trial, the political and socio-psychological effects on peoples in our time, are unpredictable. Both among Israel's youth and the sympathetic masses in other nations which one hopes to win over, the unconscious suspicion that the slain are being used for political means, that they serve tactical and propagandistic ends, will constitute an obstacle, however legitimate the national purpose may be. The resistance of the good against the destructive powers will be paralyzed if it must avail itself of weapons which the enemy uses as a matter of course. Criminal trials based on political calculation are part of the arsenal of anti-Semitism, not of Jewry.

The calculations of the Israeli authorities are false. Persecution and mass murder are pervasive themes of world history. For a brief span, and after they had been defeated by internal or external enemies, political systems which used them to acquire or retain power were abominated by the nations of the world, and then they returned in similar form. For decades, no one was free to declare his loyalty to Bonaparte, not to mention the great Revolution. At the time of the economic miracle under Louis-Philippe, the coffin was brought to Paris in triumph, and finally the infamous Napoleon ascended the restored throne. There were countless victims, yet toward the end of the century, France was considered the guardian of freedom. The power of oblivion is all-inclusive, it has grown with growing intercourse among nations, and the trial won't be able to change that. One news story succeeds another in the limelight of press and radio, and meanwhile the ominous effect builds up in the dark. Expiation is referred to as the ultimate or the primary reason for the trial, as if it were a perfectly human need. I have a profound mistrust of the term. It seems to be a screen for impulses that fear the light, that come from an alien world, it reminds one of the Teutonic past, ages and ages ago, and of the Inquisition. But the notion that a human judgment, a sentence, could make Eichmann expiate his deeds is a mockery of the victims, a horribly grotesque mockery. It would be easier for me to understand the frank desire for revenge, however inadequate that would necessarily be in view of the crimes committed. If someone who had lost his father and mother under Hitler had tracked down the villain in Argentina and murdered him on the street, he would be no tactician but a human being everyone could understand.

But however ingenious its preparation, the trial in Israel is simpleminded and shocking at one and the same time. The intent to eliminate Eichmann if he participated in plans of international fascist agencies would be perfectly legitimate. But the desire to get at him not only betrays a lack of political know-how but insensitivity. No people has suffered more than the Jews. Suffering is its destiny's basic motif, and it has made that suffering a moment of permanence and unity. Instead of creating malice and viciousness, suffering trans-

formed itself into a kind of collective insight and experience. Suffering and hope have become inseparable for the Jewish people. At one
point in its history, the European peoples sensed this and by profess-
ing the tortured Redeemer, they made the torment the Jews suffered
because of that eternal future they would not let go of a part of
history. Jews are not ascetic, they did not worship suffering, they
experienced it. But more than is true of others, it is connected for
them with the memory of their dead. It does not make saints of them
but imparts to them that infinite tenderness which can dispense with
the consolation of eternal life.

The Jew who sees Eichmann and understandably looks forward to
seeing him suffer has not yet become conscious of himself, not because his desire offends against his religion, but because it contravenes his entire heritage. To punish Eichmann without need
amounts to inflicting on him a measure of what ennobles the dead.
The Israeli politicians are not only short of intelligence but also of
heart. They neither know nor feel what they are doing. I plead the
incompetence of the tribunal and for the return of Eichmann to the
country from which he was taken. Nothing good will come of this
trial, neither for the security and position of Jews in the world, nor
for their self-consciousness. The trial is a repetition: Eichmann will
do harm a second time.

Spirit: The substantive moment in a spiritual whole is abstract.
Taken by itself, the doctrine of a religion tells us little about it.
Torquemada and Victor Hugo professed the identical faith which
was yet something else, its own contradiction. For one believer,
religion in today's Germany means allegiance to a strong cause,
having a roof over his head now that Nazism has collapsed. With
another, it is a substitute for independent thought, a reason not to
bother too much with the suffering of others and the world at large
but to stick to his own business. With a third, it is the motive for
self-righteousness. There are a few where attachment to religion is
the same as the memory of childhood, the love for dead parents, a
kind of gratitude. Such people come from protected bourgeois
homes, from an affluence still recent enough not to turn into hardness
and routine. In their case, it is difficult to distinguish religion from

kindness. Because of their religion, the Jews in imperial Germany whose wrathful God was like that of the others in demanding an eye for an eye, a tooth for a tooth, not infrequently developed a sense for the splendor of kindness which was certainly as pronounced as that of the German Christians whose god, after all, is love.

But it is no less untrue to deny that content has significance in the meaning of an intellectual structure. The child that does not experience the happiness of having its mother's words and gestures impart to it a teaching for which heaven is not merely a space for rockets but a promise of salvation will get to know new friends and substitutes only in atrophied embodiments. Expression cannot truly be detached from what is expressed. Only in abstract science, and even there only where it is mere execution whose meaning is tacitly presupposed, can form and content be separated without becoming something else. Logic in itself is untrue, as is everything that merely needs but lacks it. What is true is the whole, which ultimately eludes us, thus making all the work of the mind both abstract and untrue, however true it may be.

Permanent Education: Mankind is still being educated. Education means learning, submitting to rules which are first imposed and ultimately to be internalized. Once that has happened, they will be followed automatically, like walking erect, adding and subtracting, observing the laws. In our time, it is being demanded of Euro-American society that it compete with other nations and civilizations and finally become a member in the world. As this occurs, it must eradicate individualism within its own borders, for world-historically, individualism was merely a means toward technicalization which ultimately benefits all. Increasingly, the reason for an individual's culture disappears for it carries a hint of Pharaohs and slave owners. The freer mankind becomes, the less meaning individual freedom will have. Not to see this was the error of Karl Marx. His system is undialectical. During the final change, the last great change from quantity into quality where the freedom of part of society is to become that of all, the quality remains the same in spite of all his ambiguous talk. The freedom of all men is that of the citizen who can develop his abilities, much as Goethe already envisaged it. The founders of modern socialism did not consider that those abilities themselves are part of the bourgeois form of production, of science and technology which society needs in its growth and its struggle with nature. Fundamentally, they were idealists and believed in the self-realization of the absolute subject. By way of Hegel, they returned to Fichte as the metaphysician of the French Revolution. But freedom is not an end but a transitory means as the animal that is man adapts to the conditions of its existence. The purpose of its education is probably nothing but reproduction under conditions of minimal resistance. All systems are false, that of Marx no less than Aristotle's —however much truth both may have seen.

1961–1962

On Kant's Moral Philosophy: Kant's maxim that you should never use a human being or, rather, the humanity in him as merely a means but always also as an end is the highest moral principle. But if there is none higher, what is the "end?" Precisely that you should always act in such a way. The moment one infers—as Kant did—that the world should be arranged so that everyone *can* act like this, something has been read into the principle that isn't there. Actually, it leads to a progressus ad infinitum which keeps repeating that the end must be the end of man and not the means. We are not told what the end is, and if changing the world were proposed as the end, we would pass from the formal, where Kant would prefer to remain, to the substantive. What determines how the world would have to look for that kind of action to occur? Is there more than one possibility? Isn't Schiller right when he interprets Kant to say that man can also be free in chains—precisely because the maxim says nothing about any content. One has to pass from formalism to dialectic. Even in moral philosophy, the consequence is really already assumed: you must treat man as an end because the world in which everyone can act in that way is just as much an end as man.

Kant's philosophy is the most sublime translation of Christianity into the language of the liberal bourgeoisie. The *Critique of Pure Reason* establishes the dualism of God and the world, of thing-in-itself and phenomenon, of idea and knowledge. Both opposites really mean the same thing, for in the infinite progress of theory, it is precisely the idea that is to reveal itself as the thing-in-itself. Quite consistently, it therefore pervades the progress of cognition as its guiding principle. It is present in every step thought takes, as the thing-in-itself is present in every given fact. (Schopenhauer sensed this when he objected to the word "given.") The *Critique of Practical Reason,* the categorical imperative, expresses the command that men should be respected not for themselves—for that would be inclination—but from respect for what is present in everyone as a demand, for the sake of God. The *Critique of Judgment* attempts to answer the question which preoccupied Kant until he died. How do transcendence and immanence, idea and reality, God and this world fit together, how can they be reconciled with each other? That is protestantism which, given the world as it is, can no longer define God. It is the doctrine of the unknown God whose existence is nonetheless understood as the cause of everything. Kant differed from Scholasticism in not daring to see unity in a world that accomodates man, in what is a fundamentally good order (although a good mankind at an infinite remove, a mankind that would be realized by history in spite of all misery, all struggles and wars, indeed by their agency, the cunning of reason, is really the story of redemption in the secular garb of the competitive struggle). (How modern, this thought that the competition among nations, with that among individuals as its model, will lead to Eternal Peace.) It is not in the encompassing order that the unity of reason and reality can evidence themselves. Only in the cognitive effort of the intellect, in the nature and quality of living beings, in art, can unity, appropriateness and perfection unfold. And it is therefore consistent that the step from the imperative to action, the concept of mankind as end in contrast to mere means, indeed the concept of an end, should also not be consistent and valid. If it were, Kant's philosophy would lead back to Scholasticism, to a time when the world seemed in order.

Nietzsche and the Jews: Nietzsche had a sharp eye. He attributed a kind of importunate familiarity to the Jews. This is true. The very long time they lived together in a hostile milieu produced the gesture

of collusion, the "between you and me" which the speech of Jews so
readily takes on, even when only inconsequentialities are being discussed. There is no transition between formal or what might be called
soulless speech, and this attitude. There are no degrees, there is the
one or the other. Language is either addressed to those outside,
beings who do not act like human beings but to whom one must talk
if one wishes to live, or to one of those to whom one belongs, and
who have a heart. "Between you and me" is the stylized phrase which
indicates that one now speaks in the community, among human
beings. It does not mean what it sounds like in German, and as what
it is also misunderstood by Jews today: "don't let this go any further."
It does not refer so much to the two speakers as to the people,
seriousness, and truth. "I am now speaking as one speaks where no
one lies." From the very root this confidentiality springs, there came
what Nietzsche saw as the "dangers of the Jewish soul," the "insolence of kindness," the parasitic adaptation. The Jews that remained
Jews—who were made not the persecutors but the fellows of the
victims—have evoked an inclination to sympathize with those that
fare badly. Quite apart from the satisfaction that lies in being the one
that gives, that stands higher, is the more powerful, there is not only
unselfishness but also a sense of kinship in such compassion. The
settling down in the world of the others, however, derives from the
habit of feeling "among ourselves" whereever one may be permitted
to remain because there is only an outside or an inside but no transition. Wherever Jews become humane, they conduct themselves as
among those who, for millenia, have been the target of the world's
hatred because they had an idea in common. At least their conduct,
their language have this objective meaning. What their own thoughts
may be in this is something else again. As among other nations,
language can preserve its meaning even if those that use it have long
since become strangers to it. French carries humanity within itself
even when murderers speak it, and Jewish gestures contain a great
history even when they are a rascal's patrimony.

Stages of Myth: Apart from the conscious manipulation which
merely makes use of it, human beings are objects of suggestion, and
autonomy is a limit concept. The position a person occupies from

merely passive to independent thinking and acting depends not only on himself but on the larger situation. The old doctrine of predestination returns on a higher theoretical level. The difference between American and European citizens lies primarily in the fact that the former created their institutions through rational reflection, and as appropriately as possible. Usually because of religious conflicts in which they proved to be the progressive party, they had left the highly developed countries of Europe and came to America, and finally arranged their lives without fanaticism. It is symbolic of such civilizing progressiveness that after the detachment from England, after the realization of independence, no serious conflict immediately arose to interfere with the unification of the individual states. And during the three-quarter century that followed, there was only the Civil War. Although they made efforts to create a federation and were confronted by an extreme external danger besides, the conduct of the European nations during the last few decades seems eminently pathological by comparison. The reactions that developed as individuals and collectives lived together on the old continent was mediated less through insight than through myths. Respect for history and origin, devotion to the nation, old metaphysical concepts to which religious history turned in modern times, are preliminary stages in the development toward rationality, just as the tribal god is the early form of the spiritual one. Men have no power over them. But at the same time, and as a consequence of scientific and technological progress, European ideas have become hollow and barely serve to cover up the naked struggle for power. Because in Europe, myths have not disintegrated and are yet outdated, cynicism has become the general mode of conduct, and for that reason, the professions of faith that prevail are largely fanatical. Deep down, they are not believed and anger over this is enflamed by the person who demonstrates that they need not be.

In America, on the other hand, the artificiality of myths is apparent. Instead of preceding rationality, they followed it. The law, the state, the homeland were made eternal ideas, yet one knows that what those ideas refer to was created by men that loved these things. They are recognized as historical products. But here also, the modern economic process curtails thought, and the time may come when indolence and fear will prompt individuals and the mass to abandon themselves to fanaticism. That would be the end of the world which calls itself the western or the free world. But perhaps both forms of conduct, the mythical and that founded on reason, will ultimately become so much a matter of routine that a mediating consciousness of whatever sort will no longer be required, and only the mechanical self-preservation of the species will remain. The Americans are closer to this than the Europeans, and the Asiatics might complete the process even if a large part of the species has been exterminated in the meantime. In that case, the Euro-American epoch would primarily have served the purpose of furnishing the machines, the elongated arms of these creatures that make them so dangerous to others.

All Are Criminal: The expectation to be allowed to live peacefully in the world as it is, the matter-of-factness with which even the so-called intellectual settles down as a good citizen when he has come into money by writings that denounce that very life, a rich marriage or an inheritance, such expectation belies the spirit which recognizes the world for what it is: the perpetuation of suppression. The human species which devours other animal species, the nations with bursting granaries that allow others to starve, the decent folk who live next door to the prisons where the poor vegetate in stench and misery because they wanted a better life or could not stand it any longer— they all are criminal if crime means an objective abomination. The self-assured gestures, the worldly-wise superiority or the mendacious modesty of some are immeasurably less appropriate than the helplessness of the fantast whose bewilderment only increases as he discovers more about the world. Only a reprobate can live as a realist.

Vain Hope: The hope of introducing justice into developed, civilized society is self-contradictory. The same economic laws which make the big bigger and the small smaller even when the majority of them gets more to eat cause technology to progress in such a way that what the little people have to offer is devalued and becomes abstract. The economy might also develop differently; it could promote the independence of the individual. That this does not occur means that justice can only be attained by increasing injustice. The error of social optimists, and that includes the classics of liberalism no less than Marx and the modern realists, consists in the belief that finally, when everything, indeed all of humanity, is technologically fully developed—and this cannot be brought about because the conflicting national collectivities have to persist—it would not be some important people but the united wisdom of all men that disposes over the concentrated means of domination. As if wisdom, peaceableness, love and experience could weather the process which is the precondition for such frightening concentration. Quite apart from its theoretical impossibility,, the idea makes no moral sense. The intensified subjection of nature casts the glow of madness on the idyllic society of the oppressors. The extrapolation of the process of an earlier liberalism where the citizens become more powerful and initially more peaceful, 'more civilized' toward each other, does not really get to the bottom of this "toward each other." In their private life, they were more civilized, but not in their business. They were more civilized at home, not in the market place. In the economic sphere, every improvement had to be wrested from them, and if no power were left to do this, they would lapse into savagery or apathy, or both—they would not enter the idyll of freedom.

On The History of Autonomy: What Kant called autonomy refers to every individual's capacity to arrange his own acts in such a way that the rational state of mankind is integral to his goals. Although situations may arise where personal advantage, indeed one's own life, come into conflict with consideration for the whole, such conflict is not necessary, for the right relations between men allow for self-preservation and the protection of personal interests. That is what the "at the same time" means in the formulation of the categorical imperative and according to which the others are never to be "mere" means, but also ends for everyone. But there is no way of laying down in advance that the relationship between the individual and the collective to which he happens to belong, primarily the nation, must be harmonious. On the contrary. Autonomy implies that relations to one's own nation must be questioned in every historical moment, and this is true of both finite and infinite intentions. Precisely for this reason,, autonomy is becoming increasingly less relevant in our time.

It constituted a moment of the bourgeois tradition, a time when the development of society depended on decisions taken by many individuals, and as autonomously as possible. Because of technological and world-political events, the interests within the power constellations have become so uniform that the significance of the autonomous decision of a multitude of individuals has stopped being a dynamic, necessary moment. The bourgeois achievement of autonomy is not becoming part of the future phase but atrophies because the well-being of society does not require it. At first, autonomy seems dangerous, and finally merely whimsical. The question remains whether the prosperity which can dispense with such means still has a goal other than that of the natural species. It doesn't. Prosperity is no goal but the effect of a natural dynamic which only appears as "historical" properly so called when it is veiled by ideology. There is no goal.

Manners, Higher Culture: In bourgeois society, all the good things which once existed because they were believed have become questions of prestige, advertisement, mere to-do. What else can one expect? It is surprising they don't disappear. Art itself is degraded and becomes mere polish when the last glow of the belief in the unbelievable has left it. "Art for art's sake," *l'art pour l'art*, was already the resistance against the breakdown of cultural norms, as it was the resistance against the positivism behind it which tolerated art as a leisure time activity because it wanted to avoid the embarrassment of having to dismiss Shakespeare, Goethe and Michelangelo as frauds. To the artists of the fin de siècle, the goal was not art but truth which has no end except the refusal to abide by the bad, the lopsided, the untrue. They wanted to say it as it really was, and the "it" is always the experience that aims at the whole and can claim no legitimacy before the forum of public knowledge. Religions also go back to experience, they have become gigantic, ossified pieces of machinery that still function in part, Christianity and Islam. But the precise expression in which experience attained self-awareness, first became what it is, was art. It is from there, and by the round-about ways of social life, that the finer forms of sociability, all the good things, come. Today, art is so totally assimilated that together with countless other forms of perception of reality, it causes the disappearance of the capacity for experience, of what remains of naiveté and belief. When people speak of higher things, they nod knowingly when they do not open their eyes wide with enthusiasm as they start getting ready to use violence. Both mean that they no longer believe. The good things should disappear, talk about them should stop, and the world appear as cold as it is. The consequence of culture is to do away with itself so that the lie is not all that remains.

Marx and Liberalism: Karl Marx spoke of "the" capitalist society which would have to become "the" communist society through the action of the proletariat. But what is at stake is not "the" society but individual states and blocs of states. To the extent that the state is part of the superstructure, there is a very concrete reciprocal relation between it and the base. During the period following liberalism, interest in the elimination of class barriers became subordinate to the interest in a higher living standard. But that standard is tied to the power and prestige of the nation, indeed it reveals itself increasingly as the nation's real meaning. Those human energies which most often seem to create proletarian solidarity, suffering attendant upon social stratification, the will toward a better, more just life, toward *liberté, egalité, fraternité,* do not issue in the right kind of society but in the people's community, and this results from the economic and political situation and the deliberate manipulation of those in control. Precisely because states exist, "Proletarians of all countries, unite," elicits no enthusiasm, but the call "allons enfants de la patrie" and the fanfare of our Kaiser Wilhelm: "parties no longer exist for me. We are all Germans now," do. We take each other by the arm and march. The National Socialism of the Führer, the "socialism in a free country" of Marshal Stalin define the bad identity which had already been anticipated in the dance around the guillotine. Fulfillment as regression, not as the preservation of what had been positive once before. Marx's theory was meant as a critique of liberalism. But it was itself a liberal critique and falls prey to the authoritarian force of history.

Prayer and Romantic Love: Prayer arose from ritual, it is a connecting thread between the Middle Ages and modern times. Ecclesiastical, political and mystical tendencies as they expressed themselves in Savonarola and especially the Reformation made the individual's prayer an essential element of religion. The historical function of cultural phenomena reveals itself retrospectively. As a psychological force, prayer contributed to the development of bourgeois consciousness, and the historical powers to whom bourgeois society owes its existence made it an element of religion. What is not yet, what is still to come, is transfigured into something eternal. The prayer in which someone no longer asks God for rain or power for his people but the furtherance of his own goals makes him the end of the infinite, an infinite end. This becomes especially apparent when others, his wife, his children, pray for him. What once held only for the all-powerful secular or spiritual ruler became the rule for the bourgeois. He is provider and master. Prayer and romantic love have a similar past. Today, they are in decline, and nothing heralds this more clearly than the propaganda made on their behalf, the praise and the inducement, the sanctions against the skeptic. If he remains merely negative, he really contributes to regression. To devote oneself to another as once one meant to in prayer, though the impotence of prayer and the nullity of man have become trivial knowledge; to become wholly absorbed in love when its social and psychological conditions have been uncovered and understood and while remaining fully conscious of them; to set aside skepticism—an impossibility before love's transfiguration in the bourgeois world—without yet forgetting what gave rise to those doubts, is the only resistance against false progress the subject can still offer. It will not delay the decline, but it testifies to what is right in a time of eclipse.

The State of Israel: Through millenia of persecution, the Jews held together for the sake of justice. Their rituals, marriage and circumcision, dietary laws and holy days were moments of cohesion, of continuity. Jewry was not a powerful state but the hope for justice at the end of the world. They were a people and its opposite, a rebuke to all peoples. Now, a state claims to be speaking for Jewry, to be Jewry. The Jewish people in whom the injustice of all peoples has become an accusation, the individuals in whose words and gestures the negative of what is reflected itself, have now become positive themselves. A nation among nations, soldiers, leaders, money-raisers for themselves. Like Christianity once in the Catholic church, but with smaller chances for success, Jewry is now to see the goal in the state of Israel. How profound a resignation in the very triumph of its temporal success. It purchases its survival by paying tribute to the law of the world as it is. Hebrew may be its language, but it is the language of success, not that of the prophets. It has adapted to the state of the world. Let him who is free of guilt cast the first stone. Except . . . it is a pity, for what was meant to be preserved through such renunciation disappears from the world as a result of it, as in the victory of Christianity. The good is good, not because it is victorious but because it resists victory. It must be hoped that the national subjection to the law of this world not meet as drastic an end as that of the individuals did in the Europe of Hitler, Stalin and Franco, and as it may under their overdue successors.

The Self as Function: The non-empirical self is a transcendental and logical presupposition or, rather, a hypothesis. The empirical self is socially conditioned. In the struggle for survival, it must constantly be reproduced by every individual, and is a constantly endangered achievement. Its sole function is to place at man's disposal the experiences of his civilization and those of his own life which have not yet become the possession of the species, and inheritable. Otherwise, man would be reduced to instinct and momentary impressions, like other animals. It is a kind of psychological digestive organ. Self-preservation in nature is its immediate, the institutionalization of social cooperation for that purpose its mediate function. The tendency toward organization, the necessity for integration also give rise to the so-called higher goals, morality and utopia. Nuances of degeneration, the independent functioning of such elements in individuals is analogous to diseases of other organs. Saintliness is an aberration.

Forms of Suffering: Only in its extreme form is the suffering of every individual the same. Otherwise it differs, depending on his nature. Compassion must discover this. Where it is of the right kind, it is as differentiated as suffering itself. There is an affinity between the quality of a person's pain, and the quality of his love and his longing. Mr. Franco does not suffer like a decent human being.

Theory of Conscience: The theory of conscience developed by Freud is correct only in pathological cases. It explains actions or the impulses to act where they derive from internalized rules. Kant's moral law is different. Here, the moral impulse is the same in every person and requires no reflection. Philosophy is needed to formulate it ex post facto, as rule or prescription, ex post facto, because the fact has existed since there have been human beings. But neither Kant nor Freud defined the origin of moral action in the individual. It is a result of mimesis. Especially during childhood, but sometimes also during later phases of development, the gestures of generosity, of love, of freedom, especially of freedom from revenge, are experienced so deeply that they become a permanent aspect of behavior. It is true that the conditions for this do not wholly lie in the specific situation but also in the biography of the experiencing subject, that interaction occurs, in other words. Indeed, one might say that experience already presupposes the quality it supposedly creates. Who could love love so deeply that it becomes his, unless he already had it. These are the kinds of speculation theology entertained in the concept of grace. Ultimately, they are besides the point. Being positivist and mythical at one and the same time, they will not admit the new, the other that may spring from a given historical situation without yet being derivable from it. And yet it corresponds quite closely to the meaning of the New Testament when one explains conscience as moral authority by the capacity for mimesis. The imitation which is to distinguish the life of the Christian, the worship of the divine founder from which imitation arises, is clearly a mimetic process. It constitutes the core of Christian teaching. Rules, laws, dogma are secondary. And although he occasionally expressed himself in imperatives, they are not really in keeping with the spirit of the Messiah. To the extent that conscience and moral action go together, rules are excessively explicit commentaries, not motives. Where they become that, jurisprudence and philosophy begin.

A Suggestion for Sociological Research: There should be a study on terror but not to denounce its frightfulness, for that has been done enough with both a good and a bad conscience. Rather, its usefulness in certain social situations should be explained. Only when it is shown how appropriate terror is to governments and populations when, for economic or foreign policy reasons or because a new regime has to establish itself, a fresh and special stimulus is called for, only then will the true spiritual state of the society become apparent. The small minority that is sacrificed, the alleged conspirators, the traitor, the kulaks, the Jews, the foreigners, the communists, the liberals—how little they count, how much fun the masses get out of it, how readily they put up with the horror, how they enjoy it, and how significant the savings in the budget! I am not thinking of civil war as in Algeria, or of conquered countries where terror is a direct necessity, unavoidable, a kind of self defense, but of the terror people are talked into, terror as a practice of governments. Such a study is needed.

Truth in Speech: When two discuss something and a third person listens and wants to take sides, he can trust the facts and the simple logic only where facts and conclusions are concerned. If something even a little more complex is involved, a knowledge of the whole mentality and its relation to the subject at issue are necessary if one wishes to judge which of the disputants is right. Indeed, what is propounded by the person with the more honest, more profound view is truer even when it appears less correct in light of the facts. Truth in speech does not accrue to the isolated, naked judgment as if it were printed on a piece of paper, but to the speaker's relationships to the world as it expresses itself in the judgment that bears on a specific topic at this particular moment. The modes in which he can be present here are infinitely various, the degrees of his involvement infinitely nuanced. This is something leaders make use of when they demand that society abstain from pedantic judiciousness, that it accept their judgment, that all those that listen act, in short, as they would toward a person that enjoys their trust. It is the caricature, the mockery of love which does not make blind but gives sight, it is its substitute. Those who run after the leaders only seem to be enthusiastic. Actually, they are perfectly aware of the naked facts, the mendacity, the pathetic character of the alleged hero. Their psychic economy welcomes the deception; they ask for nothing more than to be freed from the burden of civilization in spite of and even because they do not doubt that he is a fiend. The followers pretend to themselves and to others that they believe but actually they have no beliefs whatever. To be a follower is the opposite, the bad contradiction of an understanding that presupposes belief and makes for unconditional loyalty. The degree to which such unconditionality induces the readiness to die reveals it as the appearance it is when the leader falls, as true reason when the beloved dies.

Against the Repression of Death: I suspect that if mankind were more as it should be, it would live with a much greater awareness of death. Everything would be seen in its light, yet without tasting bitter because of it. It would be a relativizing moment that would give things the place they deserve. The repression which characterizes the present phase makes for an incorrect appraisal of goods, a foolish contentedness, a showing off with bloated trivia. This does not mean that pleasure should be renounced. On the contrary. Just as romantic love only acquires its sweetness because of its link to death, so life becomes the experience of life through the awareness of death. Ephemeral contents are not to be absolutized in an act of despair, far from it, for that is precisely the result of repression. Because such contents must persist, transitory though they be, the sorrow that surrender to them endows with truth invades them. Most of what seems good, beautiful or even amusing to industrially manufactured needs would be seen for the trash it is or which it becomes in consumption. Without pomp and advertising, much that is insignificant would continue to serve habits. But the insane greed through which power and violence take on the terror they have would lose the ground the blind will in spite of and according to Schopenhauer now has, the illusion that there is an unchangeable, binding reality and an order that prevails in it. It is conceivable, of course, that the awareness of impermanence would lend the domination, the disposition over men a special magic, as it did to romantic love, as it does to freedom or the familiar. But I do not believe so. What the monks felt when they slept in their coffins, what the Jews feel as they put on their kittel on the Day of Atonement, is not resentment's gnawing urge to be appeased but the opposite, the identity of what lives. But on a higher level, a true mankind would repeat the rite which tells it that life that seeks to forget death will fall all the more certainly under its scourge.

Normality, a Borderline Case: There is no clearer experience of the relativity of the phenomenal world and of one's own perceiving, palpable self than the radical change in subject and object, reality and one's own person as one slides into misery, becomes ill, or suffers physical or psychological pain. What is all too loosely suggested by referring to drunkenness, madness or differing dispositions as if it were an established fact that these are fluctuations of non-essential moments or borderline cases turns out to be the central thing in one's own history: it is normality that is the borderline case. It is true that it is of longer duration—or so it seems. It constitutes the medium of communication and whatever else may confirm that reality and the emotions that go along with it are what is true and appropriate. What confirms it? Its duration? Doesn't the misery that comes at the end count for more—or the night that succeeds it? The answer is a matter of chance.

Bread and Butter Scholarship: The Jews say, "You must not use the Torah as a plow," which means that you must not earn your bread through teaching. And it is true that this has not been the rule in modern times. Descartes and Spinoza did not philosophize for money. During the French Enlightenment, one became a writer, during the time of German Idealism, a professor. The effect on what was produced is apparent. The intellectuals of the eighteenth century served the emancipation of the bourgeoisie, the German philosophers its installation in the world as it was. Both were socially necessary processes and that is the reason their teaching was progressive and retained its validity. It adquately formulated a historical constellation. The theoretical achievements which are being rewarded by society today have the exclusive function of serving the domination over men and nature. The consumption of culture, even on the highest level, is part of this. For a short time, everything can still be bought, even truth. But truth only exists when it is thought for its own sake. Because it discloses itself only when history needs it, i.e., when it serves some purpose, it transforms itself into its opposite in the condemned society. Even decent plays, not to mention philosophical protests, analyses, diagnoses, interpretations, have taken on the character of merchandise whose consumption is based on industrially produced needs. And what is written about this in grief does not escape that condition. Just as the aura of the store for which it was meant still clings to the sample of a product the manufacturer gives to his family as a present, so the sphere of the lovers—however true it may be—is partly determined by the total meaninglessness that is all a commercialized language can still express. To plow with the Torah was a contradiction once. Today, even the difference has disappeared.

The Curse Is the Truth: If it were possible to recover the self and memory ten, a hundred, a million years after one's death, at any moment a person became dust, a worm, nothingness, if it were possible to again see the day of love he experiences today and to compare it to the nothingness he will be then, he will feel the longing for the paradise he will never enter. What he would experience is true of life's every evening, every end, every vanishing moment of happiness. Knowing this, he makes that experience part of the expectation of awakening, of duration which life, in contrast to nothingness, permits while it lasts. A shadow, the curse that nothing endures, the curse of expulsion falls on a future love. The love that becomes paler because of it does not deserve its name, and the love that rebels against it is vain. The curse is the truth.

The Consumers of Culture: There is not only debased art, art that has become provincial, there are also forms of conduct which are debased, half-educated. To call them kitsch would be flattering them. One is staring at paintings with celebrated names on them, listening to so-called good music, collecting of reading material, in short, the acquisitive reception of half-understood cultural products because they have prestige. Part of this is the belief, or rather the illusion, that one enjoys them. More often than not, it probably comes from the narcissist satisfaction of having contact with something so famous and exquisite, though skilful patchwork with the same signature would do as well. The mechanism here is similar to the enthusiasm provoked by the witty remark of a genius when the addressee cannot distinguish it from a triviality or, conversely, to the inability to tell the difference between the truth of the genius and the triviality of the philistine when the words they use are the same. The reception of cultural products as the collection of education, profitable leisure time activity, is so much more shallow than the unabashed use the feudality made of them. Most of them came into existence under its rule, they were instruments of prestige, pompous decoration, or the pride of merchants who wanted to emulate the feudal lords and rapidly overtook them. But to run after the so-called treasures of the past at a time when culture has long been liquidating itself is merely the other side or, rather, the systematic coarsening, rustification which is the fate of Europe, a kind of pathetic fetishization, reification of the mind and its works which, when harnessed to ends in view, once proved their independence but die the moment they are degraded into an end. Mass visits to museums and theaters are part of the innocuous preliminary exercises that lead to mass worship of another sort.

Grand Guignol: The public at the Grand Guignol around the turn of the century probably did credit to civilization. A great part of it had not repressed its cruelty but overcome it sufficiently to allow reflection about it. There was peace, and thought had no need to associate itself with the prevailing order. A distance separated sensation from reality. The less civilized an audience, the more realistic the emotion by which it reacts to cruelty on the stage. The excessive abhorrence of merely enacted, portrayed or voluntarily endured pain, as at a boxing match for example, allows one to infer that there is a great deal of cruelty in the psyche that has not been dealt with. The spectators are afraid of permitting themselves the forbidden pleasure and are waiting for a suitable pretext to yield to it. But secretly they are always lying in wait. There are those who will already make the transition to reality when they see a chiller. "Yes," they say, "there's a lot of truth in that. There must be any number of fiends that cut up their victims without aenesthetizing them." That part of the audience that tends toward such emotions compensates for the loss of pleasure that results from the failure to avow it by intensifying its thrill. There are not only the tortures the victim suffers but the delight in seeing the murderer identified as the devil in whose place one will oneself torture some day, in the real world. The secret relish is accompanied by anticipatory pleasure: the exaggerated anger about the enacted murder derives its force from the desire to commit it in fact. It seems likely that the enjoyment the generation after the Second World War derived from a strong literary diet has more to do with such simple-minded ambiguity than it does with the pleasure of the habitués of the Grand Guignol during the days when the First had not yet erupted.

Small Ethics: Virtues were for the little people, I mean the small virtues like friendliness, modesty, honesty, but not knightliness, an enterprising spirit, bravery. They belonged to the knights and the merchants. One learns what one needs, and the little people needed the small virtues. But little people are passé. They were big people without much capital, petits bourgeois, that somehow took care of themselves, and while they didn't do it as well as the big ones, they managed. They are being replaced by members of the collective, usable for a function. Everyone represents the collective but the collective never represents him. However weak the self was, it once had virtues. The only thing that counts these days is the margin between extremely rare borderline cases of usefulness for a better function, and failure. Everything has been standardized. The more abundant the variety of leisure time activities, museum, football, trips to the Adriatic, the more standardized the participants. Virtues are no longer needed. Just don't attract attention, be a cog in the wheel. C'est tout.

On Education: The difference between a good and a bad education can sometimes be discussed in such a fashion that where the decisive conditions for a good one are given, certain corollaries are also present. The decisive element is the sense of security in the home of one's parents, the love and intelligence of the mother, the sincere, traditional yet also independent mentality of the father and therefore the concepts for which he stands. However important the subjective makeup of the educator may be, the objective teaching which interacts with it and which he espouses determines the mentality of the child through the most delicate nuances it happens to have taken on during his time, in his social environment, his individual understanding. The kind of person that grows up where German patriotism is the highest article of faith will be different from one raised to believe in the establishment of justice in the world as a truly desired goal. And this not only because the content is different or gives every word, every gesture a different quality. Conditions for a good education are not independent of this. To what one declares one's allegiance is also important. The Jews in the diaspora had professed justice, God the Just as the Highest, and been persecuted. Then they had to flee to Israel to escape that injustice, and founded a state there. Who can blame them for something that was a necessary consequence of universal nationalism, the uniformization of competing states. Just as the individual once had to become a citizen if he wished to participate in the affairs of his country, it is now necessary to become a nation if one is to exist in the world. Except that Israel the fatherland now supplants justice, and a specific patriotism the hazy expectation for mankind. If he were a good Hegelian, an Israeli might point out to me that his brave soldiers, kibbutzim and pioneers are the determinate negation of the ghetto without which that hope is abstract talk, and the waiting for the Messiah the spurious infinite. I cannot deny this. But neither can I ward off the sadness that a repetition of the exodus into the Holy Land was necessary though the right day had not dawned. And I cannot overcome the fear that the allure of the contradiction will prove as hollow as it did in the Prussian model by which Hegel demonstrated it.

On Theory and Practice: Marx's teaching concerning the unity of practice and theory is already present in Kantian philosophy. There, cognition is understood as the product of the activity of the subject, the world as the result of the subject's constitution, and the mind that transcendentally determines and empirically reflects the world also sees to its practical improvement. The same ideas which regulate

cognition also show practical reason, action, how to proceed. Both
stand under the same sign, are effects of an identical power. The
view, the insight which hypostatizes itself or, even worse, the world
it produces, falls victim to the necessary appearance of its own result,
the general ideology of experience. It is like the subject which views
history, which is made by men, as fate, and therefore abides in
alienation. Marx's indebtedness to Kant is even greater than Max
Adler once thought.

The Politics of Health: Generally speaking, the physician today
has an interest in seeing the sick get well, but none that people be
healthy and not become ill. So-called professional ethics can at best
obfuscate but not change this state of affairs, for it is rooted in the
socio-economic position of most physicians. The psychological exception confirms the rule. The socio-economic position also governs the
relationship between physicians and drugs. Their interests determine
the kinds of medical chemicals that will be manufactured, and those
which are available and might serve the preservation of good health
are used only in modest quantities. In the higher interest of its
cooperation with physicians, the pharmaceutical industry must sacrifice certain advantages. And although its advertising brings it a great
deal of money, the press prefers to side with the doctors. The publicity the shortcomings of antidotes to cholesterol or the overrating of
synthetic vitamins, not to mention a non-prescription, harmful sleeping pill have received is immeasurably more comprehensive than
information about the unnecessary suffering of uncounted thousands
of insomniacs who become depressed, prone to illness and incapable
of work because they do not use barbituric acid. The not unfounded
reservations about cardiac medicines which can prevent heart attack
if taken in time seem infinitely more weighty than the number of
harried individuals whom they might protect from catastrophe. That
such examples are arbitrary and weighted proves what they stand for,
i.e., that physicians have little interest in substantive, detailed information about means for maintaining good health and would rather
give up and talk about diet than about the pills which make it
unnecessary. Vis-à-vis the patient, they act the great expert, the
modern magician whom a gulf separates from the layman. Pitiable

high school students who have no contact whatever with physics are plagued by algebra, analytic geometry and even calculus, but they hear not an iota about the methods and function of medicine. It is not up to the physician's customer to ask questions and to make demands; it is his role to suffer, he is the patient. The physician does not look for clients as the manufacturer does for customers, he is searched out, and the more society progresses, the more insistent the regressive claim to privilege becomes. The more the role of the practical physician becomes identical with that of a test mechanic or agent of specialized surgeons, the more exclusively he becomes someone that places orders with and represents the pharmaceutical industry. Vis-à-vis the public, he is omnipotent. Society hands him his monopolistic position on a platter. Billions are spent for bombs and rockets, but hospitals and schools remain too small. The men in charge can therefore do as they please, and without incurring the hazards of free competition. There is so much work that imagination becomes unnecessary. The only reason to keep people in good health would be that the mere abundance of the ill becomes burdensome. But their number keeps the physicians so busy that they don't have the time to worry about the healthy. Besides, the mass of those waiting in their offices also has its advantages. The Chinese custom that one pays one's doctor as long as one is healthy and stops when one becomes ill was the feudal dream of the burgher which he has to forget about nowadays.

Academic Philosophy and Its Representatives: Teaching posts in the liberal arts, and especially in philosophy, still afford a possibility for pursuing nuanced, critical truth and enlightenment with relative freedom, without regard for the public, publishers, career or authorities, and with a chance for far-reaching effects. Concerned thought, the longing for what is different, are part of critical truth, indeed, they are identical with it. But because truth and love have been unsettling and therefore dangerous since Christ and long before him, since there has been a society, access to teaching posts in philosophy, particularly at times such as the present, during periods of decline and a regression of the productive imagination, must be reserved for those who are harmless, authoritarian, cold, pedantic and reliable. In

Europe, there are two factors that bring about this result: bad pay—
only limited intellects take up such careers—and the vigilance of the
departments. They admit no one that refuses to shut up and be quiet.
There is such a thing as a pre-established harmony between the fate
of universities and the course of history.

Necessary Vanity: It is true that a single individual cannot change
the course of the world. But if he does not feel throughout his life
the wild despair that rebels against this, he will not even accomplish
the infinitely small, insignificant, vain, pointless little bit of good he,
the individual, is capable of.

Schopenhauer as Optimist: Where it really counted, Schopenhauer was still an optimist. Even the official optimists up to Leibniz
and Hegel did not deny the suffering in the world, they just embroidered it with the calming fairy tale of dogmatic metaphysics. Only
Kant presented the summum bonum as mere hope. Because Schopenhauer admits the denial of the will to live, the end of suffering,
in certain cases; because he closes his system, in other words, by the
conception of something like an original sin, i.e., the separation of
the individual will from all-encompassing unity and, conversely, the
return of that will into the One, reconciliation, and thus arrives at
a quietism based on insight, he relapses into optimistic dogmatism.
At bottom, he believes that greed and boredom appertain to the
individual will, not the Will itself. But in that case, what does it mean
that the thing in itself can be inferred from my nature? It is true that
his positive metaphysics does not identify salvation with his own
teaching. Nor is salvation played off argumentatively against the
reality of misery, as is done by the other philosophers. But the application of categorical structures such as "my" and "your" noumenal
character, beginning and end, guilt and unity, to the Beyond to which
categories have no relevance, is a dream, even though the interpretation of the inner nature of all beings by analogy to the experience of
his own is a truly illuminating thought. In his concept of appetition,
the *appétit*, which together with perception governs the monad,
Leibniz already made use of this idea, and even Bergson still availed
himself of it with his *élan vital* and the *évolution créatrice*. Schopen-

hauer's metaphysical optimism becomes most apparent when he takes over the myth of reincarnation where not only the transcendent fate of individual souls may vary, but even the real possibility of salvation for some among them is maintained. The separation from the One, he writes, comes to an end. A strong belief is needed to view the category of unity as less illusory than that of multiplicity, the projection of the sole ruler as more real than that of the aristocracy or liberalism. If individuation results from subjective capacities, unity is no less its product than is multiplicity, and historical conditions decide which of the two will be predominantly hypostasized, which considered mere appearance at a given time. According to critical philosophy, both are necessary appearance, and belief in the end of separation derives from the practical interest of the reason of the tormented subjects who cannot grasp that salvation from unending misery is ungraspable. Whatever a human being may dream of as the end of suffering—be it death or resurrection—whatever it may posit as absolute—heavenly or earthly love—is a moment of the bad infinite. The good infinite is a dubious consolation. Thus Schopenhauer proves right in the end in spite of himself. The fourth book of his most important work is a faux pas, a lapsus which the other three can refute. That the experience of the essence of the world becomes a quietive is a psychological, not a metaphysical process. Suffering is eternal.

A Weakness of Theology: The attempts of Tillich and so many others to save a fragment of theology by talking about the deeper significance, the meaning, the values which allegedly underlie the empirical world and particularly human acts, are praised in progressive countries, though not in France or Germany. At a time when it is really too late for this, they are recognized as attempts to use the Beyond to glorify things as they are. But the weakness of theology ultimately reveals itself in them. To the extent that something other than what is can be expressed, it appears in its true negation. Nothing is except what exists, and precisely that becomes nothingness a moment later. No act has a meaning other than its intent and effect, and in infinity, both are a nullity, just as the earth is in the universe. Atrocities and martyrdom disappear with the ephemeral memory that still distinguishes between them. They vanish into nothingness, like any such distinction, like everything else. What is true is fear and the pain fear dreads while both exist, and then it is as if they had never been.

Socially Necessary Optimism: Judging by the meaning of Christianity and the rules of a few monastic orders, things as they are afford no reason for joy. They are marked by injustice and terrible suffering. To be conscious of this day and night was a matter of course, and the sleeping in coffins a symbol, similar to the Jewish custom of wearing the shroud on the highest holy day. The thought of happiness was identical with that of eternal salvation, it referred to something other than the world as it is. National customs have always been the opposite of such belief. In the late Rome, the circenses served pleasure as the goal of life, and the peoples of modern history have always put a premium on healthy good spirits. In a different form, those decent folk that are celebrated in the paintings of the peasant Brueghel are still the goal and purpose of today's mass media. To put people into a positive frame of mind, to perk them up, to induce an affirmative spirit is the task of culture, however horrible its fundament, the arrangement of the world, the hopeless chain of history and death in pain, fear and misery may be. Without the optimism of the governed, governments have too difficult a task. But the affirmative spirit in which the horror of reality is not sublated will only serve to eternize it.

Suum Esse Conservare: "In itself," nothing is good or even better than something else, not even so-called neighborly love, let alone justice. But in certain situations decency, generosity, devotion, indeed something like correct conduct do exist, although it normally goes counter to what is called the norm. Of course, the sole criterion of such rightness is the ephemeral subject which is all the more ephemeral as it is capable of reacting as it should when the chips are down. The Stoic maxim 'suum esse conservare' is a direct call for its opposite, the surrender of the self, at least when suum esse means true reason, which tells us not to go along with the world.

The Power of Interest: What is decisive today is the alignment of interests, i.e., the constantly changing constellation of prospects for power and advancement. The difference from other historical situations lies in the conceptual clarity one has about motives, the perfect awareness that they are unalloyed. Relationships between individuals, friendliness, indifference and hatred are precisely tuned to the constellation, and impulses to resist, let alone convictions, no longer arise. What is not intended instrumentally seems necessarily the outgrowth of superstition, weakness, a parochial frame of mind. The necessary result is the marked attenuation of every other quality in social intercourse. Dialectic of Enlightenment. The eternal values are idle delusion, yet life without loyalty that is not purposive becomes as vapid as that delusion. The mediation of interests makes the difference, but not just the merely conceptual mediation but the not wholly transparent connection between human relationships and interest. Where the latter is not conscious, it may be more than mere interest.

End of the Dream: The dream of the Messiah, the dawning of justice on earth which holds together the Jews in the diaspora, is over and done with. It created no end of martyrs, caused untold suffering, and gave hope. Now the persecuted have gone to Zion without a Messiah, have established their nation and their nationalism like other peoples, and Jewry has become a religion. Those remaining in the diaspora can decide either for Israel, for absorption in the nation into which fate has cast them and their ancestors, or they must become provincial as Jews, romantic sectarians without historical substance. The diaspora is the backwoods. The Jews are remnants. Their situation is not dissimilar to that of communism and socialism. The Social Democrats have long since made their truce with unjust nationalist society, and the patriotic hierarchies of the communist countries are more rigid than the form of society which was once to have been supplanted by the realm of freedom. Those who adhere to critical theory can choose one of the two forms of nationalism, so-called communist nationalism, or the social democratic variety and its alliance with those that rule. They may also become provincial, romantic sectarians. The realm of freedom is the backwoods. Those who remain loyal to theory are remnants, like those that cling to the Talmud and messianic hope.

The Church Is the Measure: Through the centuries, the Catholic and the Protestant churches compensated the harm Christ and the prophets might have caused society, had they become models, by usurping their more dangerous doctrine, and thus kept men from imitating it, from discontinuing the worship of idols, from freeing the prisoners, from loving men. The church decorated halls of justice and torture chambers with the image of the man that was hanged as the leader, and gave its blessings to that barbarism Christ and the prophets longed not to be part of, indeed to end, to flee and to redeem. The church is the measure by which mankind undertook to overcompensate for the experience of the hopeless misery of its existence, misery as a means of blessedness. That attempt has come to an end. Those who run the churches today recognize the bad contradiction, they are actually ready to make symbols of eternal salvation, and even of the God above the stars. The society which once was called Christian has become so obtuse that the experience of the prophets no longer moves it.

With Open Eyes: To be conscious of the untold, horrible physical and psychological pain, and particularly physical torture which is suffered at every moment in penitentiaries, hospitals, slaughterhouses, behind walls and in full view the world over, to see all this means to live with open eyes. Without such awareness, every decision is blind, every sure step a misstep, every happiness untrue. But happiness and truth, like truth and grief, are one. This is what Christianity means where it is not betrayed by its mindless adherents.

Liquidations: Now that science and technology have destroyed belief and paradise, not much remains of earthly paradise either. Along with hunger and work, love has also been retrenched. Intercourse is easier to come by, but that does no more for it than Horn and Hardarts does for gourmandise. The churches attempt to adapt to a disillusioned world, however, they are indulgent with skeptics, do not insist on the super-natural, abandon heaven to the sputniks, turn God into a symbol, hope into a principle, and paradise into a legend. But they do wish to continue as an auxiliary to the law, they want to carry on the work of religion as an aid to order in society. But as the intent becomes apparent, belief has already faded. The state itself must regulate views and attitudes, must become totalitarian, for religion is finished. I mourn the loss of the superstitious belief in a Beyond. For the society that gets along without it, every step that brings it closer to paradise on earth will take it further from the dream which makes earth bearable. In pleasure in the comprehensive sense of that term, the memory of paradise was still present.

Pointless Negation: A person who denounces the catholic cult as crude superstition will usually decline to join others as they cross themselves during public or private ceremonies—for reasons of belief. He thus ritualizes the omission, the omitted gesture as much as the believers. When the stakes were still smouldering, it was different. Resistance addressed itself to the reign of terror. Refusal then, like the refusal to give the Hitler salute in the Third Reich, was a signal for everyone who wanted something better. The smaller the number of sanctions that enforce a belief, the more pointless its negation becomes.

Ideologies After Marx: The critique of society denounced as ideology those ideas and cultural forms which seemed absolute and universally valid when it was actually the process of the production and reproduction of social life that determined and made sense of their specific form at a given historical moment. To show their function in the individual was justification and criticism at one and the same time. They had contributed toward the realization of something new when it was in progress and helped to keep it in motion when it was already preventing something better. According to Marxist theory, justification applies to the individual alone, but criticism addresses itself to those moments of society which impede his development. The individual and his freedom are bourgeois ideology only to the extent that the bourgeoisie contravenes its own official myth and restricts them. But in political and economic analysis, the idea of the autonomous subject dissolves no less than the center of the universe which the earth was once believed to be. The proof of its social and psychic determinants makes the illusion of a center transparent, as it does the illusion of the subject as substance. Fetishized self-consciousness is dominant during one phase of the history of the species after which it will ossify and pass away. To prove such determinacy is criticism, as is the analysis of ideological categories generally. At the same time, it is dynamic criticism for it aims at an element which underlies Marxist doctrine everywhere and secretly gives it direction. It is no longer those that rule but society itself, mankind in past and future, all that exists, that is being accused because those ideas by reference to which alone things might some day turn to the good are ideologies themselves. What remains is ephemeral memory, ephemeral grief.

War and Perversion: In the perverse pornography of Sade and Masoch, cruelty can consciously run riot as imagination, and attain to satisfaction. Real villainy employs rationalization. In times of war, which furnishes it, and in dictatorships, the perversion which can hold itself in leash subsides. Cruelty against the enemy as against the self can run riot, although it usually does not find fulfillment. Unconscious of its sexual nature, it becomes boundless as it were, insatiable. Enthusiasts for war and tyranny do not usually experience pleasure. The more they get their fill, the greedier they become. Teaching people the capacity for pleasure constitutes a decisive moment in the hopeless struggle against the dawning totalitarian epoch of the world.

Utopia as Absurdity: Helvetius and Schopenhauer taught that life's pendulum swings back and forth between pain and boredom. If the mind of the individual can still break away from this alternative, the significant connection underlying it applies to the whole no less than to the individual. Without need no pleasure, without grief no happiness, without death no meaning. The less renunciation, the more desolate reality. Precisely because of this, utopia is an absurdity, and pious self-deception the idea of a realm of freedom that sought to overcome it. And yet we have no choice but the attempt to perpetrate that absurdity. Freedom will ultimately capitulate.

Society in Transition: When the great philosophers, principally Kant, spoke of freedom, they meant primarily self-discipline, the practical recognition of what is socially necessary at a given moment, and not really action as personal need or pleasure dictated. But the more society becomes administered and finally prescribes all life within it down to its most minute detail, the more philosophical freedom, Kant's autonomy, can be dispensed with. More and more, it turns out to be a transitional phase, like bourgeois autonomy in general. The form of action that once went with it and was based on material interests either comes to coincide with what is prescribed, or loses the last semblance of rationality. It turns into unrestraint which furnishes the impetus for the further expansion of administration, a more effective substitution of standardized leisure time for freedom. The erosion of sexual taboos by technical and economic progress, the increasing birthrate which not only brings further compulsory measures but promotes administration itself, are a symbol of the process. Freedom as arbitrariness stimulates a historical development which deprives freedom as autonomy of all meaning. The subject becomes a romantic concept.

Les extrêmes se touchent: The blasphemy that "les extrêmes se touchent" goes to the very core of the world. A Jewish intellectual of impeccable credentials wrote en passant, long after her return from America, that the Mayo clinic had reminded her of Auschwitz. In reality, the antithesis between salvation and damnation is not absolute. The most modern hospitals, tests, operations, obedient, object-like patients cannot be divorced from their earlier historical stages, from a time we have left behind, the period predating anaesthesia or, even worse, the violence of medieval faith healers. Through animal experiment and vivisection, they remain objectively linked to the most modern places of torture. To what degree technical progress which necessarily entails the integration of the individual in the collective, and the road toward a nationalist and totalitarian society are one and the same, the extent to which such progress makes the autonomous individual unthinkable and turns states into hordes, would still have to be shown. It would mean that the Mayo clinic is one of the conditions that made Auschwitz possible. Les extrêmes se touchent.

Historicity of Morality: What was called moral during the past century were forms of conduct which had once been guaranteed by religion and were socially desirable and indeed essential in the enlightened, liberalist era but not enforced by law. Important among these were good faith in business and private matters, and faithfulness in marriage, love, friendship, and even toward strangers. Even in those days, they lacked a logical ground in the subject, a plausible motive. Regarding honesty from simple morality, Helvetius—or a kindred spirit—once said that the person that did not steal from an enormously rich individual when there was no chance of discovery had to be mad. Now that liberalism is declining and social reasons for moral behavior become less compelling in an increasingly administered world, and conformist reactions, what is still necessary today, function automatically so that criminality begins where they end, morality has become historical and faithfulness a romantic category. Given the encompassing transitoriness of all things, the wholehearted devotion to another, happiness that conflicts with personal material interests, is a delusion that derives from the residue of earlier social forms. The psychoanalyst has the last word. Morality stands in need of therapy. And despair and bliss need it even more.

The end of Practical Philosophy: As religious belief declines, it becomes the task of philosophy to reflect how life should be lived. But it is actually characteristic of our time that practical philosophy is continually losing its importance and interest, indeed it is becoming increasingly difficult to establish any connection between theoretical, philosophical ideas, and practice. NeoKantianism, not to mention the Vienna Circle, Husserl's phenomenology and fundamental ontology are neutral. They are so-called first philosophies which do not necessarily lead to specific forms of conduct. Of existentialism, which claims ontology as its source, the same may be said, however useful the services certain of its philosophers render Hitler and Castro may be. Max Scheler, who refused go give up, is not unjustly judged second or third rate, and of Hartman this is even more true. The official positions, phenomenology in Scheler's case, make it impossible to establish the kind of connection referred to, and that impossibility has its social reasons. The law of the epoch is the affirmation of the nation in both East and West, and that means either the affirmation of the already existing totalitarianism or the affirmation of what is tending in that direction. Practical philosophy not only presupposes the autonomous subject but gave it the ultimate decision. Today, that decision is so narrowly prescribed that speculative thought is no longer required. The most the subject can do is switch sides or sympathize with the opposite camp. The decision to do so requires politicizing, not philosophy, which has attained to a new, ultimate degree of abstractness. Instead of taking the place of theology, philosophy follows its course.

On the Concept of the Individual: The more the individual is to be preserved, developed, cultivated, the more insistently his freedom is to be maintained in opposition to the nation, the collective generally and the drift of the times, the less the individual, the striving for his material satisfaction, for power for his sake, mean. To the extent that he is wholly concerned with himself, he is an element in the mass, and conformism and submission are the acceptable behavior. Even in the brutal leader who orders murder they recognize themselves, however harsh this rule may be. He is one of them. With his constant talk about the many, his nation, he really means his own position. Everyone senses this and goes along, he is their symbol. But the true individual is not so much at one with others in the pursuit of his own immediate interests as he is with the misery of the outsiders, the sick, the persecuted, the condemned, the proscribed, each of whom is an individual in a painful, desperate sense. As he feels and acts, he is mindful of them, and this ultimately because of his own fear. But that fear can become so powerful that he gives his life and shares their fate. Fear is not a noble striving for a good life and power, and can certainly also lead to conformism. But if it becomes conscious, it can break through conformism and establish the solidarity without which the individual is not conceivable.

The Beatles Phenomenon: The wildly desperate enthusiasm for the Beatles is no more offensive than the pseudo-cultured contempt for it. But the seemingly cultured condemnation can certainly be analyzed more easily than the enthusiasm. Much that has been written about the latter is accurate but little has been said, as far as I know, about the abandonment to the phenomenon of the four musicians themselves. That they are carefully directed by one or more experienced producers is of no great importance. What is at issue is the structure in its various elements and down to those details which normally none of the fans can formulate. Among many other things, they seem to me to express the complex attitude of the young toward things as they are, the attempt to live with them without becoming wholly their slaves, as hardly any other ensemble does. This expresses itself in their "Yeah, Yeah" and their faces. Although the wild, if already ebbing mass reaction reminds one of the effect of demagogues, I doubt that those intensely involved or the nature of the involvement are the same here and there. Which is not to say that only good things can be expected from such preparatory exercises.

We Nazis: It bears repeating time and again that the confession of guilt on the part of the Germans after the defeat of National Socialism in 1945 was really an attempt to keep the sense of national solidarity alive in the post-war period. The main thing was to preserve the "we." But it wasn't even said that "we" should have rebelled or at least have allied ourselves with those who did not go along, who helped the persecuted, but of course we were afraid. The others are not the Nazis but the Americans and the resistance. What enormous coldness and detachment characterized the pitiful 20 July ceremonies. What the confession of guilt really means is this: "we" and the Nazis belong together, the war is lost, "we" have to say we are sorry, otherwise it will take too long to get back on our feet. Only when the victors wanted to draw their conclusions did those people start in with their insolent lies and maintained the opposite of guilt. "We" didn't know anything about what was going on, instead of "we" don't want to know. Even the "I" stood for the "we." "I" was no Nazi, none of us really were. The "we" is the bridge, the evil which made Nazism possible. The difference between individual and collective is abolished. The person that maintains it stands outside, he's not one of "us," but probably a communist. As if things weren't at least as bad in that camp. The individual that talks about himself when he dis-

cusses politics or any number of other things and refers to his country-
men as "they" seems a traitor to his audience, even if they don't
realize it, and a decent human being only when chance will have it.

1966–1969

Neighborly Love: In Christianity, the individual was to overcome
and sublate himself by devoting and surrendering himself to the
neighbor and the lowliest out of love for the Highest. To save egoism
by pointing to the "as thyself" at the end of the commandment is
merely a trick of sophistical theologians to ingratiate themselves with
the existing order of things. The autonomy of the subject as the
gospel understands it is the same as its negation.

The Subject in Industrial Society: In industrial society, indeed
with the beginning of modern science, the meaning of the dialectic
of the subject changes. The more thinking seeks to grasp nature, the
more it has to trace, reflect on, its workings. From clouding the sky
by naive projection, it has to come down to earth. Every forward step
of science, and especially of technology, is also an act of adaptation,
of integration. As men control nature, the individual differences of
their thought are being disavowed by exact knowledge, which is the
same for everyone. Collectives may conflict because their power
interests diverge, but to the extent that they think scientifically and
practice technology, those that constitute them are interchangeable.
The unfolding of subjects in a variety of directions, the autonomy of
many individuals, their competition from which autonomy derived its
justification, was beneficial to society in unharnessing science and
technology. With the victory of technology, indeed with its progress,
with men's control over nature, with their independence, their autonomy, autonomy regresses, negates itself. What is under way in the
bourgeois era will be completed in the automatized world. As the
subject is being realized, it vanishes.

The True Conservative: The gulf that separates the true conservative from Nazi and neo-Nazi is no narrower than that between the
true communist and the party which calls itself by that name. He is

not unlike the Christian in his relation to the Church during the Reformation and Counter-Reformation. Nazis and party communists are the servants of vile cliques which want nothing but power and its endless extension. Their true enemies, the object of their hatred, are not the totalitarians in the opposite camp, as they claim, but those who are serious about the better, the right society. The line of demarcation runs between respect and contempt for life, not between the so-called left and the so-called right, which is an already outdated bourgeois antithesis. Cliques may fight each other where their interests demand it. Their true enemies are individuals that are conscious of themselves.

For America: It is permissible to condemn the Vietnam War. But anyone in the West, and especially in the United States, that portrays the States as worse than other nations because of it or other painful, cruel events such as racial unrest, contradicts himself. That he is free to express himself without wasting away in a penitentiary, without being tortured to death, he owes to their existence, to the fact that they stood their ground. Without them, the world would long since have been divided up between eastern and western Hitlers. Such a person may want the better, the right society, but his criticism of the existing one requires devotion to freedom as a necessary ingredient. Freedom must be preserved and developed lest the violence he accuses become the unintended meaning of his talk.

On Euthanasia: In highly industrialized states—and I am confining my remarks to them—we have a proliferating bureaucracy and many people dying miserably and painfully of incurable diseases. There are drugs, enormously beneficial drugs, which would assure that people die in blissful ecstasy or harmoniously, peacefully, instead of in excrutiating agony. Why is there no agency to which the incurably ill, the doomed, could turn to empower a physician to make use of them at their discretion. The customary objection that relatives or physicians might make the wrong use of such authorization has no force. They could violate existing laws in any event. Indeed, this would be much easier if their motives were selfish but is much more difficult when they are humanitarian. The real reason nothing is done is the regressive social meaning of the autonomy of the subject, and especially the lack of interest of the medical and other rackets.

On the Critique of Political Economy: Marx's and Engel's teaching that the struggle for higher wages and shorter hours of work would finally put an end to the pre-history of mankind is a pathetically secularized Messianism, infinitely inferior to the authentic one. But the critique of political economy is a perfectly rational basis for an understanding of social development. Because liberalism led to economic crises which it could not deal with, the centralization and concentration of capital was intensified to such a degree that the rackets control everything more or less according to plan, the capitalists through conflicts among each other and with the unions, those that have coalesced into nations by conflicts with other nations. Precisely for this reason, western and eastern society are becoming increasingly alike, although the rackets in control in the East are less developed and enjoy a much smaller measure of security than those in the capitalist West which can therefore preserve a disintegrating culture for a time. An interpretation of economic, political and cultural phenomena without the precise categories of criticism remains superficial. So-called economics has nothing to compare with them.

Keep Smiling: An enormous number of symptoms testifies to the regression of what was once called civilization. Not a few have to do with socially respected conduct which imbues the psychic substance. The individual's friendliness not just toward members of his own class but toward others generally would be an example. Already at the beginning of the bourgeois era, the demand exceeded people's capacities. Within certain limits, the not just superficially intended but genuinely felt closeness of the noble for his like had become second nature. Among the bourgeois, it came close to being a mere gesture, and thus merely the appearance of cultivation. In a period where classes, age groups and sexes allegedly enjoy equal rights, the feeling becomes shallow. In the United States, the process is not the same as in Europe. There, closeness, at least among all whites, has a long tradition, ultimately an unconscious, Christian one which has its basis in the early stages of immigration. It never went very deep, but survived in a certain sense. In Europe, especially on the continent, friendliness toward others had not become engrained until late. Today, a general coldness and unresponsiveness are already spreading to an astonishing extent. Civilization is being replaced by utilitarian reactions which are unhampered by emotion, as is appropriate to present social dynamics.

Philosophy as Entertainment: If Kant is right in saying that the world, being constituted by the powers of the subject, is mere appearance, the same applies to the difference between appearance and thing-in-itself, to their relationship to each other, to noumenal and empirical qualities, to his entire philosophy. It is self-invalidating, and Positivism is right. Philosophy is entertainment, like music, and more serious than science for that very reason.

A Glance at the Encyclopedia: The encyclopedia is typical of the intellectual situation today. For the last fifty years, so many data, concepts, achievements, particularly in technical fields, have been entered that theoretically significant categories can be presented only in drastically abbreviated form. Recently added titles are only accompanied by sparse sketches as it is. More detailed information is of interest only to the expert. Technology affects the intellectual domain. If one wants to inform oneself in somewhat greater detail about historical, religious or philosophical topics, one has to use the relevant reference works or a specific monograph. Of course, the same applies here as in the case of encyclopedias. When one compares a modern reference work on zoology and Brehm's *Tierleben,* one discovers that as knowledge becomes more precise, the laymen is increasingly excluded. As scientifically certified material swells, it loses its relevance to cultivation. The more painstakingly belabored, the narrower the perspective of the expert to which his education progressively reduces itself. Mind is dissolving.

The True Critique of Practical Reason: In order to create the impression that morality is innate, Immanuel Kant calls the superego practical reason. But his theory is not a whit more plausible than the bad belief in God's commandment. From the point of view of so-called pure, i.e., theoretical reason and the associated capacity of understanding, both seem merely highly questionable suppositions, and both the small- and the large-scale murderer, the leader, are as rational as the saint when they are successful. That is the true critique of practical reason.

Against the Radicalism of the Left: In our time, the attack against capitalism must incorporate reflection about the danger of totalitarianism in a two-fold sense. It must be just as conscious of a sudden turn of left-radical opposition into terrorist totalitarianism as of the tendency toward fascism in capitalist states. This was not a relevant consideration in Marx's and Engel's day. Serious resistance against social injustice nowadays necessarily includes the preservation of the liberal traits of the bourgeois order. They must not disappear but be extended to all. Otherwise, transition to so-called communism is no better than fascism but its version in industrially backward nations, the rapid catching up with automatized conditions.

Religion and Society: In the Torah, the Eternal addresses the people and the individual by the same word. "Love your neighbor for he is like you" refers both to the collective and the individual. In ascribing an individual soul to every person and thus differentiating it from animals, Christianity made the individual the being that counted. Present Judaeo-Christian civilization would have had the task of bringing the two, people and individual, together, whoever and wherever they might be, to love the other nations and individuals, and to order the world according to the commandments. Instead, a society that is automatizing itself integrates the individuals as autonomous subjects and makes the collective, the nation first of all, into an idol. The Eternal and His commandments disintegrate.

The Priority of Foreign Policy: That foreign policy is coming to play a role of ever increasing importance in man's consciousness is a further moment in the reduction of the individual subject. Nations are essential, one concerns oneself with them before one goes to sleep. One worries less about the relations between individuals whom one has the power to serve or to harm. Becoming less and less of a person, the individual participates in what the media discuss as the citizen of a country. That is one of the negative aspects of publicity which intends to serve the person. Death on the battlefield symbolizes what occurs in every home without bloodshed, in war and in peace, the disappearance of the subject. As it experiences itself as totally conditioned, it becomes aware of itself as the impotence which characterizes it in society.

Democracy as Its Own Enemy: The more democratic a democracy, the more certainly it negates itself. Whenever serious, critical periods set in, the right- and the left-wing radical forces will avail themselves of their democratic rights to introduce the rule of specific groups or, rather, totalitarian rule. Democracy is government by the will of the people. But to the extent that there is such a will, it has little to do with reason and tends much more toward obedience than autonomy, and this quite apart from political mechanisms, election tactics and manipulation. Those that support democracy should mistrust it. Like man's freedom of which it is a part, it has always been its own enemy.

On the Student Movement: Unless I am mistaken, the purely psychoanalytical explanation of puberty refers to the complete internalization of paternal demands by the psychic substance of the adolescent. He now judges the father by his own morality, and rebels against him. Unless Freud already said so, I think it should be added that once the physical and reasoning powers of the young have developed to a certain point, they result in the negation of dependence, in the detachment from older persons, as is also true among many animal species. The more the traditional ties in the family, and therefore conscience, recede, the more decisive this moment becomes.

Belief and Knowledge: Any person that clings to the theological tradition in however tenuous a manner should also be sincere enough to admit that there is a contradiction between such loyalty and not just science but any form of thought that sees reality for what it is. Any assertion that something is this way or that, here or there, now, in the past or the future, means that I or others can ascertain, or, if necessary, correct such a statement by using dependable sources, calculation, or our own eyes. Theology is the opposite of knowledge, it derives from levels of consciousness where perception was complemented by instincts, impulses and emotions which are no longer appropriate to contemporary experience, which is served by machines. Knowledge is ultimately governed by purposes. Theology wants to be free of earthly ends. It is both lower and higher than any form of knowledge.

The Course of Philosophy: From the comprehensive theoretical and practical doctrine about the world down to the paltry specialized discipline, the course of philosophy is the repetition of the course of religion and theology. In both processes the same thing happens, the disappearance of a conscious relationship between man and totality, indeed of serious concern about life and the world. Everything dissolves in partial knowledge and partial reactions, without any reflection about a possible relation between the parts, and what they are part of, unless it be of "science" as a profession. The road into nothingness—probably because nothing else remains. Man is really becoming an animal, perhaps a complex, more highly skilled animal. Perhaps.

Without Illusion: An understanding of reality by reason also includes the judgment about the human species. The difference between it and the animals is wholly biological. In relation to the universe, it is decidedly irrelevant, i.e., it equals zero. A human genius has special talents, achieves extraordinary things, like an ant which first scents something digestible and then finds a way which will play a role in the ascent toward well-being, survival, progress of the species, the tribe or the swarm. From the nearest planet, the Milky Way, or even after a few millenia, not to mention the infinite, provided that concept still has a meaning, the difference between individual representatives as among species is irrelevant. Such knowledge is the beginning of self-consciousness if it renounces illusions.

A Horrible End: To the extent that someone can take wholly seriously the finiteness of every living being, he discovers the relativity of his own life, the ultimately insurmountable nullity of the difference between himself and any sentient being. Such a person will be content—and justifiably so—that his own fate spared him any experience of the horrible. But his awareness of his finitude will limit his gratitude because he knows what was, is now, and will be fearsome in the living and dying of others. The difference derives simply from the hypostatization of the ultimately merely apparent self, from the absolutizing of appearance which is negated even among herd animals, beehives and ant colonies. It is this insight which might compensate for the fear over the trend of human society toward automatization and finally toward the smoothly functioning overall structure of the species. Rationalization means both the end of delusion and the end of mind.

Without Love: Erotic love is paling, and with it all positive ties among human beings and to everything that is not means to an end. Erotic love was the basis of art, of the ideas of something other than empirical reality, of the imagination. In the family anchored in love, the child experienced that happiness and that grief, that longing which—though always rare—is now fading into nothingness. Material needs and pragmatic collaboration can be no substitute for it. Without love which ultimately owes its existence to the erotic, community engenders the collective creed which tends toward fanaticism.

On Critical Theory: The Jewish prohibition against portraying God, or Kant's against straying into the noumenal world both recognize the absolute whose determination is impossible. This also applies to Critical Theory when it states that evil, primarily in the social sphere, but also in individuals, can be identified, but that the good can not. The concept of the negative—be it that of the relative or of evil—contains the positive as its opposite. Practically speaking, the denunciation of an act as evil at least suggests the direction a better one would take. The insistence on the difference in the truth of the two judgments rests on many elements. One of the most important of these lies in the relation to history, to time generally. Evil largely refers to the present; the good has to prove itself as such. To take confirmation for granted exceeds the capacities of the person making the judgment, represents the absolutization of a hypothesis—and this quite apart from the metaphysical impossibility which such absolutization involves. The critical analysis of society points to the prevailing injustice. The attempt to overcome it has repeatedly led to greater injustice. To torture a person to death is purely and simply an outrage; to save him, if possible, a human duty. If one wishes to define the good as the attempt to abolish evil, it can be determined. And this is the teaching of Critical Theory. But the opposite—to define evil by the good—would be an impossibility, even in morality.

On Pessimism: The immanent logic of social development points to a totally technicized life as its final stage. Man's domination of nature reaches such proportions that scarcity, and thus the necessity of man's dominion over man, disappears. But at the same time, the end is total disillusionment, the extinction of mind insofar as it differs from the tool that is reason. Material want was the condition of injustice, of suppression, as it was the condition of longing and imagination. The human species fulfilled its destiny by attaining to the condition of an especially skilled, sophisticated animal species. By way of science, it reached technology, automation, and finally the appropriation of precise procedures by the psychic substance, as inheritable instincts and skills. The process may be interrupted by incidents. To reject it, to fail to participate in it instead of promoting it ultimately becomes romantic foolishness, tantamount to superstition, the aberration of individual representatives of the species. All this is part of the dialectic of the Enlightenment, the change from truth into unconditional conformity with meaninglessness, with reality generally.

The End of an Illusion: Freud teaches that culture is the result of sublimation. If he is right, then the current negation of the figleaf in the mass media, in public entertainments, and indeed in much of fashion, is simultaneously the liquidation of culture. Sexual renunciation is becoming a thing of the past, it no longer requires the transforming work of the imagination to overcome it. With the suspension of the taboo, longing also ceases, and with it the idea/of all that is other than present reality. Love itself will finally come to an end. Not only religion, spirit also falls victim to instrumentalism. The end of an illusion extends to everything beyond naked reality.

Kant's Error: According to Kant's transcendental theory, the world known to man where he believes all life goes on, is one of appearance, i.e., an order creating product of human, intellectual functions. To this extent, he is at one with Hume, and that means ultimately with Positivism. But he thought—and this is decisive in his philosophy—that he would overcome Hume by declaring appearance to be the appearance of the true, the noumenal, something relative which testified to the Absolute. He did not consider that such an assertion is itself merely an idea, that it derives from the same categories as all appearance, or that empirical statements fulfill biological and pragmatic functions whereas speculative ones—and the relation of the relative to the Absolute is already speculative—reveal themselves as inadequate, unreal, a game within reality when one looks at them more closely. Kant himself stated that thought had to renounce straying into the realm of the noumenal. His philosophy ignores that prohibition, becomes uncritical whenever it believes that it is going beyond mere appearance, indeed when it wants to present appearance no longer as immanent in all that appears, i.e., as dependent on anthropological processes and therefore pragmatic, but in its relation to something that differs from appearance, as something beyond it, and thus metaphysically. The longing for what eludes the instrumental reason of science cannot be overcome by science, even when it claims to be metascience.

Antinomies of Critical Theory: Today, Critical Theory must deal at least as much with what is justifiably called progress, i.e., technical progress, and with its effect on man and society. Critical Theory denounces the dissolution of spirit and soul, the victory of rationality, without simply negating it. It recognizes that injustice is identical with barbarism, but that justice is inseparable from that technological process which causes mankind's development into a sophisticated animal species that degrades spirit to the level it had attained in its childhood. Imagination, longing, love, artistic expression are becoming moments of infantilism. Not only the natural sciences but even psychoanalysis already testify to this today.

The Difference Between Critical Theory and the Idea of Faith: Faced with the sciences and the entire present situation, my idea of expressing the concept of an omnipotent and benevolent Being no longer as dogma but as a longing that unites all men so that the horrible events, the injustice of history so far would not be permitted to be the final, ultimate fate of the victims, seems to come close to the solution of the problem: the role of faith becomes central. The essential difference is that faith is burdened with too many ideas, such as that of the Trinity, that are difficult to accept; that a compulsion that can hardly be submitted to any longer attaches to it, and that it nonetheless became dogma once again. That explains a tendency toward aggression that sees itself as religious.

Beyond Ideology: Prepared for by Hegel and others, a new epoch of philosophical thought begins with Marx. It is no longer the life of the individual, of every individual, his relations to empirical and transcendental reality, his duty, his meaning, that are at stake, but a changing collective, the community, a particular society, one or several collectives, their past, present and future, what they want and should or ought to do. The thinking and action of the subject relate to a majority, and ultimately to politics. I do not wish to deny the importance of this, but it is my view that even today, true thinking must adopt a critical attitude toward such a restriction and not surrender the impulse of great philosophy. However socially conditioned the individual's thinking may be, however necessarily it may relate to social questions, to political action, it remains the thought of the individual which is not just the effect of collective processes but can also take them as its object. Consciousness of this is no less part of an admittedly limited freedom, part of spirit, than its social determination, its degradation to ideology, the name which even today serves so-called Marxists as the designation of their own belief.

For Non-Conformism: That society is moving from liberalism which was characterized by the competition of individual entre-preneurs toward the competition among collectives, corporations, commercial and political alliances and blocs is an insight that need not lead to conformism. The importance of the individual is waning but in theory and practice, he may critically intervene in this develop-ment. Using up-to-date methods, he can contribute to the creation of collectives that are out-of-season, which can preserve the individual in genuine solidarity. The critical analysis of demagogues would be a theoretical, the union of men who psychologically, sociologically and technologically see through them, a practical element of noncon-formism in the present.

Afterword

When Max Horkheimer died in 1973, an era came to an end. Yet, of all the names associated with the Frankfurt School, that of the long-time director and propelling spirit of the now legendary Institute for Social Research is least known in the United States. Theodor Adorno, Erich Fromm, Leo Lowenthal and Herbert Marcuse have all left their mark on American social thought; even Walter Benjamin is a common reference nowadays. But it was Horkheimer who laid the groundwork for (and whose intellectual biography most closely coincides with) that approach which, under the name of "Critical Theory" of society, was to become one of the most influential social philosophies of this century.

One of the most fundamental tenets of Critical Theory was that the function of a theory is very much part of its substance—a "revisionist" position that generated considerable animosity from both left and right. Theories do not enshrine timeless truths; the very self-evident truths and "facts" of one period are the problems of another. The aphorisms, notes and mini-essays in this book span the very beginning and the late phase of Critical Theory, and in their juxtaposition, without the history of their development, they sometimes seem plainly contradictory—just as the present often "contradicts" the past of thirty or fourty years ago. As dialecticians, Critical Theorists knew that empirical/historical and logical contradictions are not identical and, as Adorno once remarked, it is not the task of consciousness to remove contradictions which do not have their base in consciousness but in reality.

When Horkheimer assumed the directorship of the Institute in 1930, the historical situation seemed to justify hope: developments in the Soviet Union were perceived as delicate experiments—which should not be disturbed or discouraged by open criticism. Although, in the late twenties, another member of the Institute, Friedrich Pollock, had returned from the Soviet Union with mixed feelings and reports, no official criticism was brought forth until, in the wake of Stalin's show trials, there was no denying that the "experiment" had failed. By 1940, in an essay entitled "The Authoritarian State," Horkheimer openly compared the Soviet Union to other authoritarian states. Only in the anonymously published *Dawn* can we discern early doubts, not only about the doctrinaire self-righteousness of the Communist orthodoxy; Horkheimer also challenged such central Marxist tenets as the eschatological role of the proletariat (Horkheimer diagnosed decisive shifts in its composition and "interests"), or "the necessary coming of the socialist order," a belief which Horkheimer feared might jeopardize correct action under changed conditions. Stunned, no doubt, by the experience of Lukacs's (et al.) surrender of independent judgment to the self-styled vanguard of history (the Party), he violently chastised those "Marxists who, in view of suffering, quickly proceed to reduce" Marxism to a theory in which such suffering made sense—for instance as a temporary necessity in the "inevitable" evolution toward socialism. That inhuman conditions today have human (not natural) causes, is a charge Horkheimer was able to direct to both camps. "As long as history follows its logical course [instead of being consciously "made"], it does not fulfill its human destiny," he charged.

Of course, Marx had never suggested the necessity of one party. Moreover, to assume that the same groups would always and inevitably be the—quasi-predestined—agents of revolutionary change, seemed tantamount to saying that the historical situation had not changed, and could not change in this respect. Given obvious shifts in the makeup of the working class, given the split between subjective and objective class interest (evident, for instance, in the widespread proletarian support of fascist movements, as one of the first empirical studies of the Institute discovered), perhaps for the time being different groups had to become guardians of Marx's legacy. Who and what were to be counted as contributions to the revolution is not decided by an a priori principle but by the future, Horkheimer insisted. Because of the growing pacification of the proletariat, he had even counted on a temporary victory of fascism. Yet, to Horkheimer and

his friends, fascism was but the climax in the development of capitalism. The working class (if anyone), still in a strategic position in the
production process, might play a crucial role in its downfall and in
a new order. And in view of the escalating crises in capitalist states,
and of the development of the forces of production, socialism still
seemed, by and large, a concrete possibility in Western Europe.

There is hardly a trace of such confidence in the later notes *(Decline)*, and it is here that the changes in Horkheimer's position are
most incisive. Explicit references to Marx and Marxism had always
been rare in the *Zeitschrift für Sozialforschung*, the official organ of
the Institute; the salient topics and concerns, however, were dis-
tinctly Marxian. Among the handful of unorthodox Marxists who
tried to redeem the "true" Marx from the mechanistic distortions of
the "official" doctrine of the Second International, Horkheimer
staunchly defended the humanist dimension, the emphasis on emancipation in Marx's work. Issues which Marx himself had failed to
elaborate (such as the relation or mediations between base and superstructure) or whose relevance he had not anticipated (such as the
tendential reduction of the working class from the subject to the
object of history) became focal points of Critical Theory to the extent
that they assumed contemporary urgency. If, toward the end of his
life, Horkheimer was much more concerned with preserving the
residues of liberalism, the reasons were hardly a matter of private
preference but of objective changes. (The shift cost him and other
members of the Institute the support of the very student revolutionaries whose theoretical tools they had, in part, provided in the first
place.) After the formative experiences of fascism and Stalinism, of
mass culture and of the disappearance of the revolutionary subject,
no collectivity seemed capable of conscious emancipatory action.
Revolution no longer seemed a viable or reasonable goal under conditions of new and infinitely more insidious forms of control. With
consciousness itself in bondage (older forms of oppression had at least
allowed for opposition in thought), with no social base for the revolution and no one even aware of the need for revolutionary change,
Horkheimer feared a revolution would merely revert into new tyranny
and terror. Yet, without a "subject," what was the (changed) meaning of revolutionary "praxis"?

Neither Horkheimer nor most of the Institute's central circle had much faith in the mechanistic notion of an "applied" theory. Marx's famous dictum, that theory would become praxis upon grasping the masses, had been fatally misunderstood, Horkheimer felt. That very demand presupposed that a certain (emancipatory) theory had become the correct or natural form of consciousness for the masses—not that they would blindly follow an allegedly vicarious consciousness regardless of their understanding. An "applied" theory short-circuits the dialectic between theory and praxis: any praxis is theoretically mediated—we always deal with a conceptually appropriated reality, never with reality per se, as Marx kept insisting. The dialectic between theory and praxis is that between two levels of theory, so to speak: a preconscious, "naive" one informing our everyday behavior and orientation and containing the "self-evident" and "natural" assumptions about the way things are. In that sense, an ideology is simply the common sense of a given reference group. On the other hand, an avant-gardistic theory and consciousness, as forces of production, transcend assumptions about what is or appears natural about the way things are (the quasi-ontological "facts" of everyday life), and reveal why people did, and *had to* think a certain way. (Marx had spoken of "necessary illusions.") In other words, such a theory exposes the social contingency of forms of thought and behavior. To expose these forms means to have already transcended them; the new perspective literally constitutes new objects, and thus practical orientations.

The ideological, "naive" consciousness indeed merely—though often accurately—"reflects" the base, and is nothing but "conscious being." In this sense, it is both a truth and a lie—a lie about the fact that the objects of experience, no matter how reified and seemingly natural, had been "constituted" by human beings, and thus could be changed by them. A merely reflective consciousness however, could never find a perspective beyond the given (from which to legitimate or criticize it), and thus would have to leave change to the immanent dynamism of history for which humans can, at best, act as "midwives"—a common argument during the Second International (e.g. Bebel). Intervention would be "bad subjectivism." But as long as history blindly follows its natural course (its prehistory, Marx would have said), it does not fulfill its *human* destiny, Horkheimer had countered; it cannot be consciously "made" by a consciousness which merely reflects what it should change. If the revolution was to be more than a change of guard, subjective emancipation was its precondition. If theory—as the correct consciousness—is a force of production (and Horkheimer insisted that it can be, just as insights into the historical contingency of one's position), its functions grow to the precise extent that the arena for direct political action contracts. And to the same extent, subjective arenas of experimentation, possibility of radical ruptures and leaps grow in importance in such situations. Marx, in the *Critique of Political Economy*, had tied the revolution to certain "inevitable" developments. But Marx had been wrong, Horkheimer explained in the sixties; to remain faithful to Marx might mean discarding some of his own "contingent" assumptions.

Over the years, defending these arenas for the conception of alternatives became a central concern for Horkheimer. Although he never focused at length on any particular, concrete area (in contrast to Marcuse and Adorno, for instance), this concern is a crucial component of his never-ending preoccupation with the fate and concept of the bourgeois individual (and its "agent": goal-setting reason). When Horkheimer retrieved the epistemological dimension in Marx, it was for eminently "practical" reasons. What was at stake for Horkheimer was the constitution of objects of experience (and thus of action); the concepts which human beings form in confrontation with specific historical tasks and conditions are not distortions of an "actual" way things are, but were the respective working truths of those situations, so to speak—Marx's "necessary illusions"; analogously, the early Horkheimer had praised Vico for his discovery of the truths of myths. Myths were the first attempts on the part of humans to confront themselves in object form. Their typologies and exemplary dramatic designs are the only categories available: through them, experience is screened and mediated. Such mediated consciousness is not bad consciousness, it is the only consciousness we have, and the nomenclature "critical theory" testifies to the centrality of this Kantian problem. According to Habermas, Kant had been the first "critical" philosopher, for he had inquired into the very *conditions of the possibility* of knowledge—in other words, its "constitution." We never perceive objects in themselves, Kant had argued, but only what the categories of our understanding coordinate, from raw sense data, into objects or events. Kant had still considered these categories universal, timeless, and fixed in number, but it was only a small, though decisive step from here to point to the historical contingency of these categories of perception and knowledge. After Hegel had taken this step, Marx underscored their material (rather than Hegel's spiritual) roots—and the "critical" outlook had acquired a historical-materialist base.

The official and simplistic "copy theory" of perception bypassed these questions despite their obvious practical implications. For Horkheimer, critique of ideologies would have to specify *all* the mechanisms mediating between base and superstructure including, for instance, the crucial but neglected social-psychological dimension. From the beginning, therefore, Horkheimer had made it a principal project of the Institute to investigate the "psychic links" between "mind and reality." Why, for instance, would people act, and even think and feel, in opposition to what appeared to be their own objective interests? Why, Marxists wondered, would workers support movements which perpetuated their lot? What needs found expression in such support, and what forms of social organization and pressure produced such needs? With such questions becoming politically relevant and even urgent, Horkheimer demanded the incorporation of a systematic social psychology into historical and political analyses, and from the first pages of the *Zeitschrift* on, this symbiosis —required by the subject matter itself, as Horkheimer saw it—was never dissolved. As a theoretical bridge between base and superstructure, psychoanalysis offered to explain their mediation in terms of an acquired psycho-structure. Drives and needs, in their specific forms, could be seen as reactions or adaptations to the pressures and possibilities of socio-economic settings—which in turn, were reproduced through functional character types, drives, needs, etc. Whereas these programmatic formulations of a "psychoanalytic social psychology" came mostly from the early Fromm (who had joined the Institute in 1932), Horkheimer's sharp eye for the contingency on specific settings of behavioral forms, psychic barriers, moral imperatives and certain goals often finds striking illustrations of such "mediators" in everyday affairs—and not infrequently rivals Benjamin's intuition of significant details.

Horkheimer's strong methodological concerns and polemics against positivism must be seen from this perspective as well. No perception without perspective, and Horkheimer never left any doubt about the cognitive interest of Critical Theory. Throughout, the "constitution problem" (what factors "constitute" objects of experience and action) remained a central methodological focus, and it provides the link to many of his later positions. Certainly the progress of science is not identical with the progress of humanity, Horkheimer argued against both positivists and vulgar Marxists; it is obvious that people can physically and materially impoverish inspite of it. But more importantly, Horkheimer insisted, forms of knowledge are never neutral but are perceptual screens and orientational guides, i.e. forms of praxis.

Scientism, which was fast turning into an entire world view, a total approach and life form, seemed to carry with it a rather specific ontology under the guise of a pure, universal and neutral methodology. Comte's famous designation of the task of science—*savoir pour prévoir*— had revealed scientific knowledge to be knowledge for purposes of control—a value and attitude built into the very "approach" of science. With the exclusive ascent of (this) one orientation at the expense of others, and with the acceptance of this one dimension of rationality as rationality per se, alternatives were beginning to appear increasingly "irrational." To be sure, domination—control over the vicissitudes of (external and internal) nature—has been the precondition of human autonomy; however, in a reversal of means into ends, Horkheimer suggested, control/domination was becoming just another—exclusive and heteronomous—ideal, preventing liberation just like any other monism.

This totalizing tendency, for Critical Theorists, smoothly translated into totalitarian tendency—because it aimed at the suspension of autonomous judgment and decision. In this respect, it was closely tied to the ever more pervasive "exchange rationality" which also defined the identity of things and people in terms of something other than themselves. Qualities were reduced to functions, and this trend toward total absorption seemed universal indeed: it was apparent in the development of an all-integrating mass culture, for instance, or in the tendency toward comprehensive bureaucratization; it was likewise manifest in authoritarian states, in the all-encompassing commodification of human relations, in the fashionable fundamental ontologies, and even in the contemporary program of a "unified science." Insofar as it was legitimate to speak of a crisis in science, therefore, it was because of its part in a general crisis, Horkheimer suggested in response to Husserl. Among the most obvious symptoms were the revival of first, final and absolute principles and values, be they substantive, teleological, or methodological—i.e. the fetishization of "actual" truths and irreducible bases, passively to be accepted as premises rather than as objects of thought and action.

Such developments could no longer be explained in terms of economic or political pressures alone—especially as they were equally evident in both political camps. A more comprehensive theory was needed, and from the late thirties on, its tentative articulation determines the development of Critical Theory. The categories of the *Critique of Political Economy* no longer satisfactorily explained recent history. Marx had based his analysis of exchange rationality on the labor theory of value, and on the overall commodification of human relations. Horkheimer and Adorno saw its universality as based on instrumentalization (even thinking in terms of "unity" tends toward exchange rationality, they suggested in the *Dialectic of Enlightenment*), i.e. the fetishization of something with supposedly overriding validity which reduces everything else to a derivative and instrumental status, and claims to be exempt from historical contingency and thus from rational challenge. Official dialectical materialism itself was a case in point. Critical Theorists, by contrast, quite naturally assumed that their theory would be the truth of only *this* stage of history, and would be invalidated (hopefully) at a later, better stage—by being realized. Their focus, therefore, was not only on what there is (a preliminary necessity) but on what there could be, and this task-concept of truth entailed praxis as a built-in dimension, in terms of a *break* with the given (certainly not a "revisionist" position). The difference between "traditional and critical theory" was their concern for correctness and truth respectively. Truth was a critical concept, dating back to the idea of a reasonable order of which any given reality always falls short. The true is the whole, Hegel had asserted, and this truth included the suppressed and unrealized potential. "Identity," correspondence between reason and reality, was an ideal and task, and we may fulfill it not just by adapting our ideas to a given reality (which we thereby affirm), or by exorcising those ideas that do not already correspond (as did the ideal of scientism). Truth (the whole) is not the opposite of illusion but of reality (as is).

"Non-identity" in this sense is the starting point for a critical theory—and an index of oppression, of reason chained as a force of production. Any idea overshoots reality, and instead of reducing consciousness to a mere reflection or correspondence, we should favor those cognitive faculties which do not share "the mythic scientific respect for the given." For Horkheimer, as for Adorno and Marcuse, true science and cognition were distinguished from ritualistic procedures by its anticipatory aspect, and those human faculties that shared it had a clearly cognitive function. Rather than silence them, they should be considered integral parts of human reason, Horkheimer argued. Yet, the idea of reason itself had undergone this reduction. Once a corrective and critical standard, reason seemed to be moving more and more into a servile position; today, it is to implement goals and values which themselves are neither products of reason nor, therefore, subject to rational discussion or challenge. The idea of a reasonable goal is inconceivable to the current idea of rationality, Horkheimer complained; even the faculty with which this could be conceptualized as a loss becomes atrophied. The "rationalization" Weber had spoken of was hardly the triumph of reason; to them it was the abdication of autonomous reason, its reduction to its instrumental dimension. Horkheimer left no doubt that he considered this development a regress, and an index of historical immaturity.

Instrumentalized, reduced to questions of inferential procedure (so that it could not address itself to substantive questions any longer) or of end-means strategies, reason had finally abdicated as an active guide for formulating goals in view of concrete possibilities. Yet, this abdication was not entirely due to external cause alone, Horkheimer and Adorno argue in the *Dialectic of Enlightenment*. Reason, which once had challenged any authority, finally had to turn that challenge against itself. Its own authority was arbitrary—unless it, of course, could be tied to a congenial telos such as human autonomy, human self-determination. For Critical Theorists, reason was not a timeless human faculty hovering over the vicissitudes of history and the object world; it was a historically evolving human capacity for self-transcendence. Reason and freedom are nonsense without each other, Adorno used to assert.

If reason was thus the "agent" of the free individual (as Horkheimer put it), it made sense that the autonomous individual and autonomous reason were jointly eclipsing. The employee, taking his directives from sources other than himself, was becoming the dominant character type, slowly supplanting the independent, decision-making, self-accountable bourgeois individual whose "moral substance" Kant had still tied to the freedom of choice. Despite his vision of socialism in terms of a thoroughly planned and administered society, Marx had upheld the ideal of the self-realization of the sovereign and substantive subject—based on the premise of the *Critique of Political Economy* that the progress of the forces of production unchained would also mean the progress of freedom. Originally a rational goal amidst unchecked laissez-faire capitalism, Marx's vision had become dismayingly true, Horkheimer noted—without the consequence of freedom. Under the imperatives of technological rationality, the superstructure tends to collapse into the base, and replace human interests with alleged "objective" ones—with no superstructural correctives (such as reason or morality), with humans fungible, with alternatives appearing irrational by definition. Progress had produced its own gravediggers, so to speak, rendering obsolete the very subject it was meant for. The theme of the time is still self-preservation while there is no self to preserve any longer, Horkheimer diagnosed drily.

As the substantive individual seemed to be disappearing as a historical phenomenon, the task became to preserve, extend or construct enclaves in which the desire and capacity to transcend the merely given could thrive. Horkheimer's late plea for such spheres as religion and the family must be seen under this perspective—as pleas for the maintenance of oases in which "the yearning for the totally different" would not be coopted and neutralized, but could be translated into concrete images and anticipations. Anachronistic as they may appear, they represent Horkheimer's equivalent of Adorno's and Marcuse's preoccupation with the subjective margins in which alternatives might emerge (such as the aesthetic mode, new sensibilities, even systematic irresponsibility and focus on the useless). In the face of the universal regress toward heteronomy, toward vicarious reason, Critical Theory tried to redeem the humane dimension of classical individualism, while replacing its original metaphysical justification (the assumption of a unique soul or self) with pragmatic, i.e. in the last analysis eudemonistic considerations. Despite his lifelong empathy with Schopenhauer, Horkheimer at no point espoused any form of determinism or fatalism, as some biographers have claimed. For the logic of history is "not final," Horkheimer and Adorno knew even in their darkest phase. "The instruments of manipulation," for instance, "which are to manipulate everyone—language, weapons, and finally machines—can also be manipulated by everyone. Thus even amidst domination, the aspect of rationality prevails as something transcending mere domination." Perhaps, the late Horkheimer mused, the very leveling tendency will turn out to be an equalizing tendency as well, and if hierarchies grow irrelevant and unfunctional, perhaps so will domination—and thus heteronomy. Horkheimer's trust in "rationality" is a trust in dialectical reversals, not as a "cunning of reason" but precisely because of its essential negativity, its overshooting quality, the dialectic of limits. One of the last entries in *Decline* reaffirms this faith, that the thought of individuals is not just the product of collective processes, but can reflect on these processes as objects.

Amidst his retreat from direct political issues, Horkheimer may have preserved a pivotal truth of the revolutionary phase of bourgeois thought: the very abstractness (and negativity) of the bourgeois individual had been its chance. Its essential solipsism had entailed its ideal freedom from a particular ideology—and in this sense, as a capacity, a historical possibility, it was just that: free and universal, no matter how contingent this possibility was on particular social relations. "That humans can change and yet remain identical with themselves" (in this capacity) seemed an inaccessible truth to traditional logic, Horkheimer once observed. The historical precedent had been set, and the idea would be irreversible, Horkheimer hoped. Given material conditions today, the once utopian possibility had become a concrete one. Horkheimer clung to it till the end of his life: "What we do not want to lose," he emphasized, "is the autonomy of the individual." As critical reason comes increasingly to bear the stigma of arbitrariness and subjectivity, the thoughts in this volume bear out Horkheimer's trust in the untamed mind, the tenacity of autonomous reason.

EIKE GEBHARDT

New York
June, 1977